Back to the Front

50 years on: The Battlefields of Europe Revisited & Remembered

First published January 1998
by Forces & Corporate Publishing Ltd,
Hamblin House, Hamblin Court, 92-94 High Street,
Rushden, Northamptonshire NN10 0PQ, England.
Telephone: 01933 419994

ISBN 0 9529597 2 0

Typesetting and design by Forces & Corporate Publishing Ltd.
Printed by GreenShires Print Group, Kettering, Northamptonshire, England.

Foreword

This is a heartfelt, personal account of a soldier's return to the World War Two battlefields, fifty years on.

Howard Hollingshead attended the 50th anniversary commemorations of most of the major conflicts of the Second World War, in many of which he had participated. We had the pleasure of accompanying Howard on several of these occasions. The anniversaries triggered moving memories of a boy living in innocent, but more disciplined pre-war days when everything had its correct place, and the life of a serving war-time soldier in the proud regiment, the 5th Royal Inniskilling Dragoon Guards.

Howard's reeaction to the ceremonies and his wise comments will be of value and interest to students, to military historians, members of the general public and, of course, to fellow veterans who wish to perpetuate the memory of those stirring days. It is a labour of love and we are delighted to herald its introduction to a wider audience with this foreword.

Tonie and Valmai Holt
Founders of Major and Mrs Holt's Battlefield Tours
Authors Major and Mrs Holt's Battlefield Guides

Preface

This is a unique, fascinating collection of memories, stories and facts about the momentous historical events of the late 1930s and the first half of the 1940s. Put together by an appropriately unique and fascinating septuagenarian - Howard Hollingshead. Howard was born in 1923 in the Shropshire town of Oakengates and after what many will regard as an idyllic childhood went to work with a local accountant before obtaining employment in a junior administrative capacity with Shropshire County Council. In mid 1942 he was called up for the forces and following initial training joined the 5th Royal Inniskilling Dragoon Guards.

The Regiment went to France shortly after the outbreak of war in September 1939 and was evacuated from Dunkirk in the early days of June 1940. Later it took part in the Normandy landings in 1944 and saw action in France and Germany, gaining various battle honours. After VE-Day the Regiment was quartered in northern Germany - Schleswig-Holstein - and he returned to civilian life from there in 1947 and subsequently enjoyed a distinguished career in administration in the Home Civil Service.

Since retirement Howard has travelled extensively throughout the past 12 years with Holts Battlefield Tours and also more recently with his Regimental Association. In addition to these interests he is a member of the Western Front Association, he supports the Royal British Legion, and he is a Friend of the Imperial War Museum. He has been in demand as an extra curricular school speaker on the subject of life in Britain in the 1930s and on his experiences as a civilian turned soldier in World War Two.

The contents of his book are intended to give just a little bit of modern history about the greatest war of all time. While it is hoped that readers over a wide audience will find an interest in the short Anniversary stories which may whet their appetites for additional reading, it is further thought that the book may be of very real educational value for young people. Since the book covers a very wide spectrum, inevitably not all interests are covered and oft-times it has only been possible to scratch the surface of events.

Frank Day
August 1997

Appreciation

I wish to acknowledge, with grateful thanks, the invaluable contributions from the following friends:
Maj Tonie and Mrs Valmai Holt; Lt Col Mike Martin; and Holts' Battlefields and History Tours.
Capt CJ (Jim) Boardman and 5th Royal Inniskilling Dragoon Guards;
Maj Pat Whitmore MBE;
Capt Derek A Philo;
John Rayner, Aviation Art, Victoria, Australia.
Maj Richard K Malott, Canada.
Dr Bernard Williams; Lt Col 'Tod' Sweeney; Jean-Claude Homberg;
Tiemus Deenen; Aloys Kemp; and Frank Stalpers; Frank Day;
and all the many other friends whose names are mentioned throughout the book, together with the following:
Don Atkins; Alf Jenkins; Tom Miles; and, specially, to Peter Simkins IWM, for his advice on compilation and aspects of presentation which were priceless to me. 'A friend in need is a friend indeed' and finally I wish to record my appreciation to Ron Impey for his generous support throughout the period of production of this book.

H Hollingshead, August 1997

Photographs

Where a photograph is denoted IWM these are used by kind permission of the Imperial War Musuem, Lambeth Road, London SE1 6HZ.

Contents

Mr Winston Churchill photographed leaving No 10 Downing Street after attending the War Council Meeting. ***(IWM HU 73115)***

1

'If you want peace, prepare for war'

Having had a career as a public servant - mostly associated with admin work - I suppose that it is no surprise that I was required to handle a fair amount of paper during that time, some of it quite important, much of it not so. However, I can well remember one of the most significant pieces of paper in my lifetime ever handled by anyone - and that was the one held high by a former Prime Minister, Neville Chamberlain, on his return to the United Kingdom from Germany following his *tete-a-tete* with Adolph Hitler in September 1938 which promised 'peace in our time' between our two countries. Alas, war came a year later on 3 September 1939. On that Sunday morning the Prime Minister in the House of Commons declared: 'This country is now at war with Germany' and said: 'You can imagine what a bitter blow it is to me that all my long struggle to win peace has failed. Yet I cannot believe that there is anything more or anything different that I could have done and that would have been more successful'. Winston Churchill, later to become Prime Minister, reminded the nation that 'Outside, the storms of war may blow and the land may be lashed with the fury of its gale, but in our own hearts there is peace. Our hands may be active but our consciences are at rest'.

The previous decade had consisted of my school days, mostly at the local village Church of England school where it was customary to be reminded of the various challenges and disciplines of our daily life. In the yearly calendar were some lighter occasions to be kept such as Shrove Tuesday (pancake day); Good Friday (hot cross buns); 1 May (Maypole day); Whitsuntide (Whit-Monday carnival with jazz bands, displays, and a variety of entertainment). Mid summer sports day and the long summer holiday; and 5 November (Guy Fawkes day with its bonfires and fireworks).

Some more thoughtful days were included in the religious calendar which were closely observed - Ascension Day; Easter-time; Whitsuntide and, of course, Christmastime, all of these at times requiring our attendance at the nearby parish church. In addition, there was recognition of certain national days, particularly St George's Day on 23 April; Empire Day on 24

May and Armistice Day on 11 November. Each year Armistice Day was a most sombre occasion, a day which was sincerely observed by the whole nation, indeed many people had special thoughts of the loss or disablement of their loved ones resulting from over four years of war from 1914 to 1918. During the 21 years which followed this was probably the most memorable time in every year - at 11 o'clock, on the 11th day of the 11th month, November. Throughout the length and breadth of the United Kingdom at this time Remembrance parades and ceremonies would be held - nationally and locally - attended by the Royal Family; by crowds of people led by those in government; many dignitaries with wide representation and, proudly wearing their war medals, many ex-servicemen. On these occasions a bugler would play the *Last Post* after which there would be a strict two minutes' silence - you could have heard a pin drop - followed by *Reveille*. For this very short period of time at least, there was complete silence - everything stopped; everybody stood to remember that some three quarters of a million British servicemen had given their lives for King and Country during four years of war. In my locality during this short period of remembrance, work came to a standstill at the steelworks, in the foundries, on the farms, indeed everyone going about their daily business would remain silent as a mark of respect.

And as these respects were paid to the fallen there was a lesson to be remembered - that diplomatic mistakes in the Versailles Treaty failed to effectively curb the aggressive nature of Nazi Germany which led to WW2.

The nation held its first Armistice Day ceremony at the Cenotaph in Whitehall on Tuesday 11 November 1919 when HM King George V laid the first wreath bearing the inscription *In memory of the Glorious Dead from their King and Queen*. Some of the deep thoughtfulness of the occasion faded however when this precious tradition of Remembrance was changed shortly after the second world war when such ceremonies have been held in Great Britain on the Sunday nearest to 11 November rather than on the well established day. It was felt that the change to a Sunday would not affect the normal activities of a working day and consequently would be more beneficial for the nation's economy.

Nevertheless a feeling long existed that a ceremony on Armistice Day itself should be revived. After nearly half a century arrangements were made by the Western Front Association to gather for a short ceremony at the Cenotaph at the 11th hour of the 11th day of the 11th month of 1994, a Friday. The Metropolitan Police gave permission for all traffic to be stopped for such time as to allow a bugler to sound *Last Post*, followed by the silence, for *Reveille*, for the laying of wreaths by association representatives, and for a blessing by a padre.

This first revived ceremony was attended by several hundred association members and their friends who were joined by many members of the public who were in Whitehall at the time. Afterwards a special memorial service of Remembrance and thanksgiving was held in the nearby Guards Chapel by kind permission of the General Officer Commanding Household Division. Among those present on that morning there was a strong feeling that 11 November had once again been reclaimed as a 'special day' - *a Day to Remember* - in the calendar of our nation. And again the day was 'Remembered' on 11 November 1995, a Saturday. In the media, particularly some daily newspapers, there had been much speculation at both VE (Victory in Europe) Day and VJ (Victory in Japan) Day in the commemorations of May and August earlier in the year, about the return of this day - 11 November - as the nation's Day of Remembrance instead of, or possibly in addition to, Remembrance Sunday. In the event 11 November 1995 was only partially observed.

As it happened the Western Front Association had already made arrangements for the second year running to hold a special Remembrance Service at the Cenotaph on 'the day' as in 1994. On this occasion the ceremony was well attended, not only by WFA members but also a sizeable crowd of members of the public who were in close proximity at the time. The arrangements were similar to the original ceremony and ended with a lament played by a Scots Guards piper encircling the Cenotaph.

It was not surprising therefore that for the third year running arrangements were made by the WFA for 'the day' to be remembered at the Cenotaph on 11 November 1996, a Monday. On this occasion, however, there was support from the Royal British Legion which had campaigned strongly nationwide to restore the two minute silence on Armistice Day. The political parties and the media also strongly supported the idea, the Prime Minister saying that the country should pause to remember on 11 November in addition to Remembrance Sunday and he continued: 'It is fitting that each of us should also have the opportunity for reflection. With many others, I shall be pausing for two minutes at 11 that morning to remember and to resolve anew that the sacrifice of those who gave their lives shall not be in vain'. As previously, a special memorial service was held at the Guards Chapel where an address was given by a WFA vice-president, Maj The Earl Haig OBE DL who referred to the close association between the Western Front Association and the Royal British Legion and to his life as a child and as a young man at the time when his father helped set up the Legion shortly after the Great War to assist and support ex-servicemen at their time of need.

For the fourth year running, the re-established 'Remembrance' Ceremony was held on Tuesday 11 November 1997 at the Cenotaph in Whitehall, attended by a large crowd.

At the stroke of 11am by Big Ben everyone present observed silence of two minutes during the short ceremony when Whitehall came to a standstill with the permission of the Metropolitan Police. At the Special Service of Remembrance which followed in the Guards' Chapel at Wellington Barracks, the Director General of the Imperial War Museum, Mr Robert Crawford, gave the address during which he indicated that with the assistance of the Western Front Association and others, it was hoped to compile a record of some 54,000 war memorials throughout our country bearing the names of those who made the supreme sacrifice in time of war.

No Remembrance ceremony would be held without the *Last Post* and *Reveille* played by a bugler. As every soldier is well aware the *Last Post* and *Reveille* are two of the principal calls used every day in the Army. The *Last Post* to denote the end of the day's labour and the Army at rest, *Reveille* the call signifying the dawn of another day.

From time immemorial it has been the custom of the Army, when her sons are laid to rest, to pay as a tribute the greatest honour the Army can bestow, the Presenting of Arms and the sounding of the *Last Post*, and from the highest to the lowest as the body is laid to rest, this great and last tribute is paid.

The *Last Post* signifies that the warrior's labours in this earthly life are over and the mortal remains are at rest. If this were the end it would indeed of itself be a worthy tribute to the memory of one of her sons whom the Army desires to honour. But this is not the end!

Throughout the ages the church has taught the great message of the Christian faith - our Lord's assurance by his sacrifice and resurrection of the life to come - and the Army in simple ceremonial does not leave us at the end of the labours of the day and the darkness of the night, but with the stirring call of the *Reveille* bids us to take comfort and hope in that great lesson of our faith - the assurance of the resurrection.

For most people in Great Britain, Armistice Day and the Royal British Legion are more or less synonymous. In June 1921 Field Marshal Earl Haig formally established the British Legion which throughout many years has maintained its role at the forefront of Remembrance ceremonies. Moreover it has continued its invaluable support in a variety of ways in safeguarding the welfare of ex-servicemen by ensuring that millions of veterans and their wives and families who served our country in war can live out their lives in relative comfort. Its activities include the running of residential homes and convalescent homes; providing retraining to help redundant service personnel and helping widows to visit the foreign graves of their husbands. The annual Poppy Appeal, which finances much of the welfare work, remains; so too has the ceremony attended by HM The Queen and members of the Royal Family on the Saturday evening at the Albert Hall and which is shown on TV. It is a thoughtful experience to visit the poppy factory in Richmond-upon-Thames which has, mostly, a disabled staff all of whom are very anxious to explain what they do themselves and give illustrations accordingly. When I had the privilege of visiting the factory in 1991, I understood that in one year the output was 34 million poppies; 86,000 wreaths; and 500,000 crosses. Altogether a truly remarkable effort which included, in pride of place, a wreath for laying at the Cenotaph by HM The Queen.

During my visit my attention was drawn to a poem - *The Poppy* - written by an 11-year-old boy, Robert Snelgrove, who had visited the factory with his school early in 1991.

The Poppy

How beautiful the poppy as it grows amongst the corn,
reminding me of freedom and new life being born.
When I look at its red petals I think of all things good,
people free and happy living, like all humans should.
But it also reminds me of the blood that has been shed,
the men from the armed forces so needlessly dead.
Young men killed and injured so that we could be free,
who gave up their lives for you and for me.

The black of the poppy brings these dead heroes to mind,
As I think of all their suffering and their families left behind.
What's the purpose of fighting? What is it all for?
How could we be so blind as to send these men to war?
Knowing how they'll grieve and suffer awful pain,
Knowing deep inside they may never return home again,
I feel so sick and empty, but what can I say?
Is it enough to stand in silence on Remembrance Sunday?
Thinking of these men, killed for you and me
to live in peace and happiness wherever we may be.
But we haven't learnt our lesson - much to our shame,
for it looks as though before long we will be at war again.

Maybe the red of the poppy means '*stop*' and '*compromise*'
Stop this needless fighting where everybody dies.
For there is no real winner, only agony and pain,
so please politicians 'Think' before we march to war again.

Robert Snelgrove

This poem was written by Robert Snelgrove who visited the poppy factory with his school in early 1991. Robert was 11 and a half years old.

With hindsight it has to be said that there is much in the poem about war with which there was much sympathy during my school days in the late 1920s and throughout the 1930s. Significantly the last line of the poem ends with the words 'Think, before we march to war again'. Yet at that time events in Germany were rapidly progressing towards another conflict, indeed, many take the view that history suggests that WW1 and WW2 were simply one long war.

After the close of WW1, the League of Nations was formed on 10 January 1930 with the essential aim of preventing war as well as promoting other forms of international co-operation. Germany was a member of the league and accepted that it had no thought of invading any other country. However, Adolph Hitler assumed power in the spring of 1933 and by October of that year the Germans left the league as well as the Disarmament Conference when efforts were in train with the French to reconcile the difference in their ideas. And so began a whole series of hostile activities by the German nation.

Hitler's first demand was the return from the French of the valuable Saar coalfields, indicating that 'only a madman would consider the possibility of war between the two countries'. In 1934 he made a non-aggression agreement with Poland. Five years later the Germans mercilessly over-ran that country. The following year, 1935, he declined an offer from Great Britain and France to remove military restrictions imposed by the Treaty of Versailles, moreover he made it known that he already had an airforce and would be introducing conscription. At the same time he dismissed any claims to a neighbouring country, Austria.

The Germans marched into the Rhineland in 1936 and began fortifications to secure their ill-gotten gains. By 1937 Italy became an ally and, as a consequence, rearmament in both countries continued apace. And so to 1938 when in March of that year Hitler's troops marched into Austria, because, he said, German nationals in that country were affected. In September of the same year the Prime Minister of Great Britain was assured that there would be no ambitious movement against Czechoslovakia.

However, six months later - in March 1939 - the Czech State suffered a similar fate to Austria.

And again after a further period of only six months Hitler, with the aim of driving east for world domination, attacked Poland. Great Britain and France gave him an ultimatum to withdraw all attacking forces but he failed to do so.

After this long calendar of aggressive happenings, it was possibly no surprise to anyone that when Hitler refused to withdraw his troops from Poland, a declaration of war with Germany by Great Britain and France was inevitable to fulfil their obligations in going to the aid of Poland.

On 3 September 1939, after nearly 21 years of peace, Europe was again at war.

In a broadcast to the nation 15 minutes after Britain had declared war on Germany, the Prime Minister said:

'This morning the British Ambassador in Berlin handed the German government a final note stating that unless we heard from them by 11 o'clock that they were prepared at once to withdraw their troops from Poland a state of war would exist between us. I have to tell you now that no such undertaking has been received, and that consequently this country is at war with Germany.

'You can imagine what a bitter blow it is to me that all my long struggle to win peace has failed. Yet I cannot believe that there is anything more or anything different that I could have done and that would have been more successful. Up to the very last it would have been quite possible to have arranged a peaceful and honourable settlement between Germany and Poland. But Hitler would not have it. He had evidently made up his mind to attack Poland whatever happened, and although he now says he put forward reasonable proposals which were rejected by the Poles, that is not a true statement. The proposals were never shown to the Poles, nor to us, and, though they were announced in a German broadcast on Thursday night, Hitler did not wait to hear comments on them, but ordered his troops to cross the Polish frontier. His action shows convincingly that there is no chance of expecting that this man will ever give up his practice of using force to gain his will. He can only be stopped by force.

'We and France are today, in fulfilment of our obligations, going to the aid of Poland, who is so bravely resisting this wicked and unprovoked attack upon her people. We have a clear conscience. We have done all that any country could do to establish peace, but a situation in which no word given by Germany's ruler could be trusted and no people or country could feel themselves safe has become intolerable. And now that we have resolved to finish it, I know that you will all play your part with calmness and courage. At such a moment as this the assurances of support that we have received from the Empire are a source of profound encouragement to us.

'When I have finished speaking certain detailed announcements will be made on behalf of the government. Give these your closest attention.

'The government have made plans under which it will be possible to carry on the work of the nation in the days of stress and strain that may be ahead. But these plans need your help. You may be taking part in the fighting services or as a volunteer in one of the branches of civil defence. If so you will report for duty in accordance with the instructions you have received. You may be engaged in work essential to the protection of war for the maintenance of the life of the people, in factories, in transport, in public utility concerns or in the supply of other necessities of life. If so it is of vital importance that you should carry on with your jobs.

'Now may God bless you all and may He defend the right. For it is evil things that we shall be fighting against, brute force, bad faith, injustice, oppression and persecution. And against them I am certain that the right will prevail.'

The British final note

At 9am on 3 September his Majesty's Ambassador in Berlin addressed a communication to the German government in the following terms:

'In the communication which I had the honour to make to you on 1 September I informed you, on the instructions of His Majesty's Principal Secretary of State for Foreign Affairs, that, unless the German government were prepared to give His Majesty's government in the United Kingdom satisfactory assurances that the German government had suspended all aggressive action against Poland and were prepared promptly to withdraw their forces from Polish territory, His Majesty's government in the United Kingdom would, without hesitation, fulfil their obligations to Poland.

'Although this communication was made more than 24 hours ago, no reply has been received but German attacks upon Poland have been continued and intensified. I have accordingly the honour to inform you that, unless not later than 11am, British Summer Time, today 3 September, satisfactory assurances to the above effect have been given by the German government and have reached His Majesty's government in London, a state of war will exist between the two countries as from that hour.

'No such assurances having been received within the period stated, the German Charge d'Affaires in London has been formally notified that a state of war exists between the two countries as from 11am, 3 September.'

Official announcement in the London Gazette

It is notified that a state of war exists between his Majesty and Germany as from 11am today, 3 September 1939.

On the instructions of His Majesty's Principal Secretary of State for Foreign Affairs, his Majesty's Ambassador, at Berlin addressed on 1 September a communication to the German government in the following terms:

'Early this morning the German Chancellor issued a proclamation to the German army which indicated clearly that he was about to attack Poland.

'Information which has reached His Majesty's government in the United Kingdom and the French Government indicates that German troops have crossed the Polish frontier and the attacks upon Polish towns are proceeding.

'In these circumstances it appears to the governments of the United Kingdom and France that by their action the German government have created conditions (viz an aggressive act of force against Poland threatening the independence of Poland) which call for the implementation by the governments of the United Kingdom and France of the undertaking to Poland to come to her assistance.

'I am accordingly to inform your Excellency that unless the German government are prepared to give His Majesty's government satisfactory assurance that the German government has suspended all aggressive action against Poland and are prepared promptly to withdraw their forces from Polish territory, His Majesty's government in the United Kingdom will, without hesitation, fulfil their obligations to Poland.'

The German reply was immediate:

'The Reich Government and the German nation refuse to accept, or even to satisfy, demands in the form of an ultimatum from the British Government.

'On our eastern frontier there has for many months already reigned a condition of war. Since the time when the Versailles Treaty first tore Germany to pieces, all and every peaceful settlement was refused to all German governments. The National Socialist government also has since the year 1933 tried again and again to remove by peaceful negotiations the worst rapes and breaches of justice of this treaty. The British Government have been among those who, by their intransigent attitude, took the chief part in frustrating every practical revision. Without the intervention of the British Government - of this the German government and German people are fully conscious - a reasonable solution doing justice to both sides would certainly have been found between Germany and Poland. For Germany did not have the intention nor had she raised the demands of annihilating Poland. The Reich demanded only the revision of those articles of the Versailles Treaty which already at the time of the formulation of that Dictate had been described by understanding statesmen of all nations as being in the long run unbearable, and therefore impossible for a great nation and also for the entire political and economic interests of Eastern Europe. British statesmen, too, declared the solution in the East which was then forced upon Germany as containing the germ of future wars. To remove this danger was the desire of all German governments and especially the intention of the new National Socialist People's government. The blame for having prevented this peaceful revision lies with the British Cabinet policy.

'The British government have - an occurrence unique in history - given the Polish State full powers for all actions against Germany which that State might conceivably intend to undertake. The British government assured the Polish government of their military support in all circumstances, should Germany defend herself against any provocation or attack. Thereupon the Polish terror against the Germans living in the territories which had been torn from Germany immediately assumed unbearable proportions. The Free City of Danzig was, in violation of all legal provisions, first threatened with destruction economically and by measures of customs policy, and was finally subjected to a military blockade and its communications strangled. All these violations of the Danzig Statute, which were well known to the British government, were approved and covered by the blank cheque given to Poland. The German government, though moved by the suffering of the German population which was being tortured and treated in an inhuman manner, nevertheless remained a patient onlooker for five months, without undertaking even on one single occasion any similar aggressive action against Poland. They only warned Poland that these happenings would in the long run be unbearable, and that they were determined, in the event of no other kind of assistance being given to this population, to help them themselves. All these happenings were known in every detail to the British government. It would have been easy for them to use their great influence in Warsaw in order to exhort those in power there to exercise justice and humaneness and to keep to the existing obligations. The British government did not do this. On the contrary, in emphasising continually their obligation to assist Poland under all circumstances, they actually encouraged the Polish government to continue in their criminal attitude which was threatening the peace of Europe. In this spirit, the British government rejected the proposal of Signor Mussolini, which might still have been able to save the peace of Europe, in spite of the fact that the

German government had declared their willingness to agree to it. The British government, therefore, bear the responsibility for all the unhappiness and misery which have now overtaken and are about to overtake many peoples.

After all efforts at finding and concluding a peaceful solution had been rendered impossible by the intransigence of the Polish government covered as they were by England, after the conditions resembling civil war, which had existed already for months at the eastern frontier of the Reich, had gradually developed into open attacks on German territory, without the British government raising any objections, the German government determined to put an end to this continual threat, unbearable for a great Power, to the external and finally also to the internal peace of the German people, and to end it by those means which, since the Democratic Governments had in effect sabotaged all other possibilities of revision, alone remained at their disposal for the defence of the peace, security and honour of the Germans. The last attacks of the Pole threatening Reich territory they answered with similar measures. The German government do not intend, on account of any sort of British intentions or obligations in the East, to tolerate conditions which are identical with those conditions which we observe in Palestine, which is under British protection. The German people, however, above all do not intend to allow themselves to be ill-treated by Poles.

'The German government, therefore, reject the attempts to force Germany, by means of a demand having the character of an ultimatum, to recall its forces which are lined up for the defence of the Reich, and thereby to accept the old unrest and the old injustice. The threat that, failing this, they will fight Germany in the war, corresponds to the intention proclaimed for years past by numerous British politicians. The German government and the German people have assured the English people countless times how much they desire an understanding, indeed close friendship, with them. If the British government hitherto always refused these offers and now answer them with an open threat of war, it is not the fault of the German people and of their government, but exclusively the fault of the British Cabinet or of those men who for years have been preaching the destruction and extermination of the German people. The German people and their government do not, like Great Britain, intend to dominate the world, but they are determined to defend their own liberty, their independence and above all their life. The intention, communicated to us by order of the British government by Mr King-Hall, of carrying the destruction of the German people even further than was done through the Versailles Treaty is taken note of by us, and we shall therefore answer any aggressive action on the part of England with the same weapons and in the same form.'

In his message to the German nation, Hitler said:

'England has for centuries pursued the aim of rendering the peoples of Europe defenceless against the British policy of world conquest by proclaiming a balance of power, in which Great Britain claimed the right to attack on threadbare pretexts and destroy that European State which at the moment seemed most dangerous. Thus, at one time, she fought the world power of Spain, later the Dutch, then the French, and, since the year 1871, the German.

'We ourselves have been witnesses of the policy of encirclement which has been carried on by Great Britain against Germany since before the war. Just as the German nation had begun, under its National Socialist leadership, to recover from the frightful consequences of the Diktat of Versailles, and threatened to survive the crisis, the British encirclement immediately began once more.

'The British war inciters spread the lie before the war that the battle was only against the House of Hohenzollern or German militarism; that they had no designs on German colonies; that they had no intention of taking the German mercantile fleet. They then oppressed the German people under the Versailles Diktat the faithful fulfilment of which would have sooner or later exterminated 20 million Germans.

'I undertook to mobilise the resistance of the German nation against this, and to assure work and bread for them. But as the peaceful revision of the Versailles Diktat of force seemed to be succeeding, and the German people again began to live, the new British encirclement policy was resumed. The same lying inciters appeared as in 1914. I have many times offered Great Britain and the British people the understanding and friendship of the German people. My whole policy was based on the idea of this understanding. I have always been repelled. I had for years been aware that the aim of these war inciters had for long been to take Germany by surprise at a favourable opportunity.

'I am more firmly determined than ever to beat back this attack. Germany shall not again capitulate. There is no sense in sacrificing one life after another and submitting to an even worse Versailles Diktat. We have never been a nation of slaves and will not be one in the future. Whatever Germans in the past had to sacrifice for the existence of our realm, they shall not be greater than those which we are today prepared to make.

'This resolve is an inexorable one. It necessitates the most thorough measures, and imposes on us one law above all others: If the soldier is fighting at the front, no one shall profit by the war. If the soldier falls at the front no one at home shall evade his duty.

'As long as the German people was united it has never been conquered. It was the lack of unity in 1918 that led to collapse. Whoever offends against this unity need expect nothing else than annihilation as an enemy of the nation. If our people fulfils its highest duty in this sense, that God will help us who has always bestowed His mercy on him who was determined to help himself.'

In his declaration to the Nazi party Hitler repeated his threats to the disgruntled 'Whoever withdraws from his duties or makes attempts at sabotage,' he said, 'is going to be most rigorously punished. Whoever hopes to profiteer will not receive a fortune, but death.'

In Hitler's opinion, and a view held too by other misguided fellow-travellers, he had in no way been the only cause of the hostilities which began in 1939. Although in 1930 his party was less than 20 per cent, it was the largest one in a multiplicity of small parties in the Reichstag. In only three years he gained the Chancellorship of Germany by telling his countrymen what they wanted to hear, sweeping them along with his speeches and ideals and he 'put them to work' albeit towards a war footing.

Hitler's adherents point out that it was the British and the French who had decided in 1939 to go to war against his country. They had done so to support Poland who were mistreating some of his countrymen in the border area of Danzig for whom he thought that he had a responsibility.

Earlier he had taken action against Czechoslovakia and Austria for similar reasons; indeed he had been given a blank cheque more-or-less by the British for his troops to enter Czechoslovakia.

By negotiation he had recovered the Rhineland area from France which had been taken from Germany after WW1.

In the 1930s Italy had sought his friendship as a result of which they became allies. Hitler considered that he had rightly denounced the Versailles Treaty since it had enforced unreasonable reparations upon his country. From the beginning of his 'reign' his main focus had been that Germany become 'the master race'.

Helped by these many ruses he succeeded in ruthlessly taking one country after another, rather similar to the bottles in the ditty 'Ten green bottles hanging on the wall', but remarkably, and most fortunately, the bottle labelled 'GB' stood firm and survived against all his evil endeavours.

And on the evening of the outbreak of war Great Britain did stand firm behind its King on this momentous day.

His Majesty's Broadcast

The following message was broadcast by the King from Buckingham Palace throughout the Empire at 6pm on September 3, 1939.

'In this grave hour, perhaps the most fateful in our history, I send to every household of my peoples, both at home and overseas, this message, spoken with the same depth of feeling for each one of you as if I were able to cross your threshold and speak to you myself.

'For the second time in the lives of most of us we are at war. Over and over again we have tried to find a peaceful way out of the differences between ourselves and those who are now our enemies. But it has been in vain. We have been forced into a conflict. For we are called, with our Allies, to meet the challenge of a principle which, if it were to prevail, would be fatal to any civilised order in the world.

'It is the principle which permits a State, in the selfish pursuit of power, to disregard its treaties and its solemn pledges; which sanctions the use of force, or threat of force, against the Sovereignty and independence of other States. Such a principle, stripped of all disguise, is surely the mere primitive doctrine that might is right, and if this principle were established throughout the world, the freedom of our own country and of the whole British Commonwealth of nations would be in danger.

'But far more that this - the peoples of the world would be kept in the bondage of fear, and all hopes of settled peace and of the security of justice and liberty among nations would be ended.

'This is the ultimate issue which confronts us. For the sake of all that we ourselves hold dear, and of the world's order and peace, it is unthinkable that we should refuse to meet the challenge. It is to this high purpose that I now call my people at home and my peoples across the seas, who will make our cause their own. I ask them to stand calm, firm and united in this time of trial. The task will be hard. 'There may be dark days ahead, and war can no longer be confined to the battlefield. But we can only do the right as we see the right, and reverently commit our cause to God.

'If one and all we keep resolutely faithful to it, ready for whatever service or sacrifice it may demand, then, with God's help, we shall prevail.

'May He bless us and keep us all.'

Few would have thought that this message by King George VI on that Sunday evening was the beginning of a very long war, a war which brought untold suffering to millions of people whether in the service of their country or not.

2

'Peace to War'

Adolph Hitler ruled Germany for some 12 years from 1933-1945. Six of those years had been spent re-arming his country for war and simultaneously developing his country's infrastructure - roads; railways; - to pursue his evil intentions for world power.

The remaining six years were spent at war. His aim, simply, had been a '1,000-year Reich'. Throughout the inter-war years - 1918 to 1939 - Great Britain had sought peace - appeasement - so it was all too obvious that never in its long history was the country so totally unprepared for war when the government made its declaration. However, prior to the outbreak of hostilities in the year following the meeting between Neville Chamberlain and Adolph Hitler, some important steps were taken to re-arm. United Kingdom forces were increased by expanding the Territorial Army to double its strength while the Civilian Services were quickly introduced and supplemented by the formation of Air Raid Precautions (ARP) Auxiliary Fire Services; Nursing and First Aid and Local Defence Volunteers (LDV) later to become the Home Guard.

When war was declared the National Service (Armed Forces) Act was immediately passed through Parliament, providing that every male between the ages of 18 and 41 became liable for call-up for service in the armed forces of the Crown. Those who became liable for service were required to furnish particulars of themselves when notified. They were entered on the Military Service Register and any preference for naval or air service would be recorded. Later they received written notice to present themselves for a medical board and shortly afterwards a call-up notice would be issued.

The government had selected the range of ages between 18 and 41 as representing the most vigorous manhood of the nation but it did not in the least follow that the 18 group would be called up as the initial class.

On the day war was declared, a War Cabinet was established headed by the Prime Minister, Neville Chamberlain. Perhaps the most significant appointment in the Cabinet was, as First Lord of the Admiralty, Winston Churchill. He made a memorable speech in the House of Commons strongly supporting the Prime Minister, also making it plain to the nation the dreadful situation in which the whole country had found itself. At the same time, however, as only he could, he attacked the Nazis and gave much encouragement that we would come out on top in the end. How right he was.

In his speech in the House he said :

'In this solemn hour it is a consolation to recall and to dwell upon our repeated efforts for peace. All have been ill-starred, but all have been faithful and sincere.

'This is of the highest moral value. *(Hear, Hear)* and not only of moral value, but of practical value at the present time, because of the whole-hearted concurrence of scores of millions of men and women whose co-operation is indispensable, whose comradeship and brotherhood is indispensable.

'That is the only foundation upon which the trials and tribulations of modern war can be endured and surmounted. This moral conviction alone affords that ever fresh resilience which renews the strength and energy of peoples in long and doubtful and dark days.

'Outside, the storms of war may blow and the land may be lashed with the fury of its gale, but in our own hearts this Sunday morning there is peace. *(cheers)* Our hands may be active, but our consciences are at rest. *(cheers)*

'Let us not mistake the gravity of the task which lies before us: the severity of the ordeal to which we shall not be found unequal.

'We must expect many disappointments and many unpleasant surprises, but we may be sure that the task which we have really accepted is one not beyond the compass of the strength of the British Empire and the French Republic.

'The Prime Minister said it was a sad day, and that indeed is true; but it seems to me there is another note which may be present at this moment. That is a feeling of thankfulness that if these trials were to come upon our island, there is a generation of Britons here now ready to prove it is not unworthy of the days of yore, not unworthy of those great men the fathers of our land.

'This is no question of fighting for Danzig or fighting for Poland. We are fighting to save the world from the pestilence of Nazi tyranny - *(cheers)* - and in defence of all that is most sacred to man.

'This is no war for domination, for imperial aggrandisement, for material gain: no war to shut any country out of its sunlight and means of progress. It is a war pure in its inherent quality, a war to establish on unimpeachable rocks the rights of the individual, and it is a war to establish and revive the stature of Man.

'Perhaps it may seem a paradox that a war undertaken in the name of liberty and right should require a necessary part of its progress the surrender for the time being of so many dearly valued liberties and rights.

'In these last two days the House of Commons has been voting dozens of bills which hand over to the executive our most dearly valued personal liberties.

'We are sure that these liberties will be in hands, which will not abuse them, which will use them for no class or party interests *(cheers)* which will cherish and guard them; and surely and confidently we look forward to the day when our liberties and right will be restored to us, and when we shall be able to share them with peoples to whom such blessings are unknown.'

Churchill had been in the political wilderness throughout the 1930s during which he spent his spare time writing, painting and surprisingly perhaps, brick-building. At his home Chartwell in Kent which he had bought in 1922, he built, with his own hands, the brick wall round the kitchen garden, a feature which is not overlooked by the many visitors to this 80-acre estate.

Of the many important dates in the calendar of the six years of WW2, the years that changed the course of history, probably the most important of all for Britain was in May 1940 when Prime Minister Chamberlain resigned and, at a most critical time in British history, Winston Churchill became Prime Minister of a National Government. As events later clearly illustrated, some were in no doubt that without him as wartime leader, Britain would have lost the war. Certainly he inspired the whole nation and all our Allies while his salute of a 'V' for Victory was to be acclaimed everywhere. In those early weeks of his premiership Hitler had succeeded in conquering Europe and Britain found itself alone. Fortunately, a large majority of the land forces were evacuated, or should it be escaped, from Dunkirk but they were totally ill-prepared for battle had the enemy decided to proceed with an invasion at that time. It is a well-known fact that the Royal Navy and the 'little ships' came to the rescue in those dark days of summer in 1940. Shortly afterwards the third arm of the Services - the Royal Air Force - succeeded in yet another rescue operation. Before Germany could make a successful invasion of Britain, air superiority was essential.

The air battles which took place over the English Channel and southern England during several weeks in the late summer of 1940 became known as the 'Battle of Britain' - a most apt title which recognised the vital contribution made by the RAF in defence of our country. Churchill, in acknowledgement of the self-sacrifice of the fighter pilots throughout that short period, expressed the thoughts of the nation in those famous words of his - 'Never in the field of human conflict was so much owed by so many to so few'

Hitler abandoned his invasion plans and Britain escaped again. Hermann Goering, Commander of the German Air Force, afterwards saw Maj (later Gen) Adolf 'Dolfo' Galland who was in command of a group of fighters. While questioning him about the failure of the Luftwaffe, he asked Galland whether he could be of any help. Galland, it is said, replied: 'Yes, by re-equipping me with a wing of Spitfires'. He knew something!

Having lost the air battle, Hitler then decided to launch his wrath on the civilian population in the latter months of 1940.

To escape the horrors of enemy bombing of London; large cities; towns; and other vital areas such as docks and military installations, the government made plans in 1939 to evacuate children to safer areas throughout the countryside. During the war some three quarters of a million such children were evacuated from London alone. Many went to the West Country, East Anglia, and Wales. Seldom did they return until the end of the war which in some cases was nearly six years later. Leaving home - parents/relatives/friends - at such a very young age must have been a traumatic experience for most of them. However, whereas at home there were regular occurrences of living in shelters and often being surrounded by rubble, their new homes in the countryside were quiet and in beautiful scenery and more often than not they soon found some lovely friends.

And, naturally, I suppose on returning from the countryside the children often found that life at home with their own families could be shattering for them since they had grown up in a 'sunny environment' in more ways than one.

Nevertheless, not all children were evacuated from London. Ron (Impey) remained at home throughout the bombing - Hitler missed him and his folks on at least three occasions - which seemingly justified his mother's view that 'We are not moving out; if we are killed by the bombing, then as a family we shall all go (to heaven) together'.

With those sort of sentiments which prevailed during those very dark days in the 1940s it is so easy to understand why Britain was then Great Britain, determined to be 'second to no-one'.

And so clearly illustrated by the Royal Family. HM The King George VI and HM The Queen remained at Buckingham Palace despite being bombed by the enemy in September 1940. Accordingly they could relate in some appreciable way to the horrors of war when on many occasions they thoughtfully visited those areas and those people who had suffered from enemy activity. Furthermore Queen Elizabeth II - then Princess Elizabeth - served in the ATS during the wartime period.

Some words from the Winston Churchill Theme Museum give a brief description of those momentous days, 'Step into the blackout; you are inside a department store in the middle of the 'Blitz' when it's been hit by a bomb! There's smoke...smouldering rubble and the shouts of rescuers. Once in the street you witness the terrible damage - the cinema blasted open - the pub wrecked - the charred ruins of people's homes - only the fireplaces remain. Fireman fight the fire and carry a girl to safety. You are one of the lucky survivors and make your escape across the bomb crater, treading carefully past the burst water main and the 'unexploded bomb'.

In the middle of November of that year, Coventry suffered a terrifying raid which included the destruction of the cathedral. Despite these frightening experiences when Germany continued to attack 'all and sundry', the British people remained steadfast and we escaped.

At sea, however, Britain did not escape quite so easily. The Battle of the Atlantic was the longest running continuous campaign of WW2. Nowhere else were British and Allied seamen exposed to such great danger from the day that war was declared until the return of peace in Europe was imminent.

Throughout the whole period of war and despite the introduction of the convoy system, the German Navy made several significant penetrating attacks on British shipping by U-boats and surface raiders. Nevertheless one German surface raider, the pocket battleship Graf Spee, found its match as early as December 1939 when confronted by the British ships Exeter, Ajax and Achilles.

The raider was badly 'wounded' and underwent some repairs in Montevideo, a port in neutral Uraguay. It left port later to be scuttled by its captain in the River Plate estuary. Hans Langsdorf thought that there were some British 'heavies' waiting to pounce on him beyond the estuary - in fact there were none!

After nearly two years of war, and at a time when it was not easy for the British people to perceive of any way to escape eventual defeat by the Germans, two world events occurred in circumstances completely beyond our control.

Hitler attacked Russia while Japan did likewise to America. Thus within a very short period of six months two of the greatest world powers became united with Britain comprising a very formidable fighting force against

Germany, Italy, and Japan. It was now beyond question a world war.

It was mid-1941 when Hitler switched his attentions from the west to the east, making a crucial mistake by deciding to attack his Russian ally: which, he said at the time, could be overcome by the autumn. The conflict, however, continued for four years and involved three and a half million Germans against more than four and a half million Russians.

The atrocious weather that followed, particularly in the winters, severely handicapped the Germans who were totally ill-prepared for battle under such appalling conditions.

At the outset Hitler's invading troops made rapid progress but disaster overtook them eventually during the winter of 1942/3 at Stalingrad where the German Army was, more or less, defeated by the severe freezing weather conditions and the stubbornness of the Russian defenders. Later on the Russians were able to make some advances themselves. So much so that by the spring of 1945 they had not only captured Berlin but had also occupied a large part of Eastern Europe.

In December 1941 the Japanese attacked the Americans at Pearl Harbour in Hawaii which, 'at a stroke', brought the USA into World War Two on the side of the Allies. In this early December air attack the Japanese destroyed and sunk several American battleships in the harbour. Today they remain preserved as marine graves, vast memorials which contain lines of names of those American servicemen who lost their lives on such a fateful day.

The Japanese quickly overran the Philippine Islands, Malaya, Burma, Dutch East Indies and several British Islands in the early part of 1942.

More than three years elapsed before the Americans defeated Japan by dropping two atomic bombs in August 1945, one on Hiroshima, the other on Nagasaki. In the long period of struggle to overcome the Japanese the Americans suffered some dreadful losses throughout the campaign. Indeed their losses were so heavy at Okinawa in the battles for the island that a decision was made to end the war by use of the atomic bomb, so avoiding further heavy casualties in any invasion of Japan itself.

The escape for Britain and her Allies from Nazi domination came with the famous Battle of El Alamein in North Africa in late 1942, an unlikely part of the world for the 'beginning of the end' of WW2, being thousands of miles away from English shores. It was 'light at the end of the tunnel', a tunnel very long and very dark for many millions of people. Why were our troops there in such large numbers to be able to fight; and win eventually, a battle so vital not only to ourselves but to so many other countries who had fallen to the Nazi jackboot? Very simply, in the first place, the Allied

Army was there to defend Egypt and the Suez Canal, the main supply route for our shipping to the Middle and Far East.

Secondly, Hitler had succeeded in over-running so many countries. From some of those countries large numbers of Allied troops had to withdraw, from Crete, from Greece. These troops were, more or less, evacuated to North Africa not only to defend but also to attack the enemy once the opportunity presented itself and when adequate reinforcements were available. The desert troops came under command of Gen Bernard Law Montgomery - Monty - who came second only to Winston Churchill as the most well-known British personality during WW2.

After the success of the North Africa campaign, the Allies in the latter half of 1943 surprised the Italians by landing in Sicily where victory was gained by mid-August. In the meantime Mussolini, the Italian Fascist leader, was overthrown. He had tried and failed to persuade Hitler to concentrate on the Mediterranean theatre of war instead of the Russian front. An armistice with Italy was signed on 3 September, just four years after the declaration of war with Hitler. Although the German armies continued their dogged defence of Italy throughout the winter and spring of 1943/4, the Allied armies succeeded in capturing Rome on 4 June 1944, two days before the landings in Normandy.

At sea the U-boats had maintained a major threat to the Allies from the outset of war as the Germans were reading the signals going out to the convoys. However, the tables were turned against the enemy when in 1943 new radars aboard aircraft and ships, better depth charges, and the breaking of German codes, caused significant losses to the U-boat wolf packs forcing, them to abandon their attacks on the North Atlantic convoys.

In the air during the early years of the war the enemy relentlessly continued a devastating bombing offensive against the UK causing extensive damage and heavy casualties in many cities and towns throughout our country such as London, Liverpool, Coventry and Portsmouth.

The Allied air attacks on the enemy during the daylight hours were mostly carried out by the United States Army Air Force (USAAF) while the RAF bombers were responsible for the night-time raids. Inevitably casualties in these operations were often of a high level. By mid-1944, however, the Allied Air forces had almost complete control, so much so that rarely did the Luftwaffe (German Air force) venture over the landing areas of Northern France at the time of the Allied invasion.

On land the Allied successes so far - in North Africa; in the Mediterranean; in Italy - had, as it were, 'unlocked the door' and, at long last, were positioned to 'open the door' to make an escape from Hitler and his mighty Army. Although not exactly from where they had been overrun four years before, an airborne and sea landing was made by British, Canadian, French, and American forces in Northern France - Normandy.

It was an armada so great that nothing like it had ever been made by any country throughout history. Within a few weeks the Allied Armies were so successful they had the German Army in retreat from which they never recovered.

The 'door was now opened' and although an Allied airborne landing in Holland in the autumn of 1944 was a failure at Arnhem despite outstanding bravery and extreme sacrifice of the glider pilots and the paratroopers in an epic battle there, and also a last ditch offensive by the enemy in the Ardennes in Belgium in the winter, the Allied armies crossed into Germany in the early spring for the final phase of the war.

During the 11 months of the north-west Europe campaign from June 1944 to May 1945, much was happening elsewhere. The Germans had developed new weapons - the V1 and V2 - which caused widespread death and destruction in Southern England, indeed some 30,000 Londoners alone died resulting from the Blitz and these 'V' weapons.

On the other hand the Allies, in August 1944, had made a second landing in the south of France; while the Russians too had made significant progress in Eastern Europe. When the war ended in Europe it had lasted for nearly six years during which time whole families were, more or less, engaged in the war effort. In my own family, my father was employed by Great Western Railway; three boys were conscripted, two for the Army and one as a Bevin boy; while of three girls, two were conscripted for industry and one had to take 'billettees'. And mother, as with all mothers everywhere, never a dull moment!

In a small nation such as Britain women made up the loss of workers in industry and by 1943, nine out of 10 single women aged 19 to 51 were in the forces, in industry; or on the land. My wartime years were evenly divided since, as a civilian, I undertook Air Raid Precautions (ARP) duties as a messenger and as a telephone operator at the local police station which served as the district ARP control centre.

Fortunately there was no enemy activity in the vicinity of my home area during my service in the Civil Defence. However, long hours - almost nightly into the early hours - were spent on duty as the German raiders attacked the industrial/military centres in the Midlands and in the north west.

During the second half of the six war years I served in HM Forces. Under the National Service Acts I was required to register at 18 years of age; shortly followed by submitting myself for a medical examination; and subsequently receiving a call-up notice to report for service in the Army on 2 July 1942.

By this time conscripts into the Army were required initially to undergo a six-week training period at a PTW (Primary Training Wing). My training at the Duke of Cornwall Light Infantry barracks at Bodmin in Cornwall included foot drill; rifle drill; physical training; gas drill; cross-country running; shooting on ranges; and also visits for medical and dental examinations.

It was a feature of initial training that on most Sunday mornings recruits would be required to attend church parade in best battledress and highly polished boots to be marched to the local Church of England venue. As it happened I escaped these marches since at my reception at Bodmin I emphasised, indeed repeated, that I was a Methodist. At this point the NCO - a corporal - seemed to be in deep thought to find an answer to the problem. However, eventually he did accept my religious persuasion asking me to spell Methodist for him!

Actually with my schooling being Church of England I have always considered that I have been most fortunate to have, as it were, both religions. The few non Church of England recruits would invariably walk smartly to the local Methodist Church, otherwise they would enjoy doing a chore or two in the Naafi under the manageress and her young ladies!

In the short period of six weeks the PTWs sifted all recruits to decide what arm of the Army was appropriate for each of them.

Throughout the initial training period I had been fortunate in having a friend, Bertie Wood, from my days spent in the late 1930s at the Oakengates College. We had reported for Army service together from our homes in Shropshire and had been allocated to the same platoon in the PTW and billeted in the same Nissen hut. However, luck deserted us when our postings were announced and we made our way to two different RAC Training Regiments.

My posting was to the Royal Armoured Corps, 60th Training Regiment at Waitwith, Catterick Camp, Yorkshire. With many other young men of similar age I began training to become a member of a tank crew. A short period passed - some two to three weeks - when my name appeared on Orders to report for Squadron Leader's late afternoon parade. I was puzzled about this since I would have been warned by an NCO if I had been on a '252' for some misdemeanour. It so happened that my civilian qualifications and a report from my PTW about my initial training constituted potential as an officer. I found myself in front of a major who suggested to me that

I should allow my name to be put forward for a WOSB (War Office Selection Board). My immediate reaction was that I would not be in a financial position to proceed. I was questioned but at the end of the interview he reminded me that my name would be put forward if at any time in the future I changed my mind. So I continued normal training until very shortly afterwards I was again on Orders to report for Squadron Leader's office.

Naturally it seemed to me that he had decided to put my name forward for a WOSB and I resigned myself to the fact that would be it - one had to do what one was told in the Army and there was not much left to choice. However, on this occasion being aware of my civilian background in local government, he detailed me to report to the orderly room for duty the next morning.

With some trepidation I reported to the orderly room - the nerve centre of the Training Regiment - but I should not have worried - I was greeted by the sergeant with open arms.

Briefly, other than the orderly room quartermaster sergeant (ORQMS) and himself, all other personnel were absent for various reasons - leave, sick and so on. Could I type, asked the sergeant - yes, I could! So I was given a table with a typewriter and told that my primary duty was responsibility for Part 1 Orders, the daily orders of the unit. No problem for me as my education had included a two-year commercial course in which typing and shorthand (and many other subjects) were part of the curriculum. Indeed the shorthand skills very quickly came into play for the general duties and extended to others requiring work for the adjutant, which I performed with close interest for some three months. I wonder whether the adjutant later saw fit to treat the major to a whisky in the Officers' Mess for succeeding in posting to his HQ such an experienced member of staff!

Throughout the period I worked in the orderly room never a day passed when I expected to be told that I was no longer required, perhaps as suddenly as I had been posted there. I was medically A1 and was convinced that a return to tank training, with a new group of recruits, would be my lot!

The day came when the ORQMS had news for me. Unbelievably, he told me that as some recompense for some long, helpful, days I had spent on duty, I was to go on leave - which included Christmas holiday period - and that further on my return I would be posted to one of the finest regiments in the British Army. (As any other soldier is well aware he also served in the finest regiment of the Army).

And in a matter of days I became A Squadron clerk of a famous regiment - 5th Royal Inniskilling Dragoon Guards - nicknamed 'Skins'.

I had left the luxury office suite of my Training Regiment and the company of my friends in a brick built, fairly comfortable, barrack room, in the morning and by afternoon found myself all alone in a Nissen hut which, in addition to the squadron office, was also to be my own accommodation and sleeping quarters.

Fortunately on my arrival I was given a handover of a sort - my predecessor could not get on his way quickly enough. The information given in such haste about the camp, the local village, the important personalities in the squadron, and my probable duties, hit me in the face like a 'wet fish'.

I soon became aware that for me the duties themselves were far from onerous. Overall the office, as squadron headquarters and focal point, saw much activity which was confidential and therefore had to be manned at all times. My relief invariably for such as meal times, Naafi breaks and any temporary absences, was the orderly corporal for that day. There were a variety of duties, the most important being keeping up-to-date the squadron nominal roll on talc indicating the strengths of the various troops, responding to enquiries from RHQ and the completion of squadron orders for the following day. One of the more pleasant duties was to keep control of the privilege leave list and to prepare the appropriate passes and warrants for the personnel in the squadron. On these occasions the thought would pass through my mind, that's another lot gone bringing my own somewhat nearer. Naturally, 'the lads' could not get away quickly enough and the well-worn question was: 'When can I have my pass?' - the reply often was simple enough: 'When the signing officer says so'. Leave was always an enjoyable topic of conversation but, on the other hand and fortunately not too often, I found it disturbing preparing a '252', the Army form appropriately completed for anyone being on a charge for some misdemeanour such as 'not being able to return from leave on time'. There was always the thought 'there but for the grace of God, go I'.

One of the highlights of every day was the delivery of the post letters, sometimes parcels. The distribution was performed by the orderly corporal, sorting the many items into tank troops and so on, often requiring some assistance from me when exact location in the squadron could not be identified. These enquiries were of much help to me in identifying many of the personnel in the squadron - putting faces to names or, alternatively, putting names to faces because from my 'exalted' position in the office it was extremely important to remember it is not what you know, but who you know. I often needed trustworthy friends when problems arose spontaneously. It was vitally important for me to know everyone, whatever their rank - to keep my ear to the ground - and generally from an admin aspect to ensure the squadron ran smoothly.

A routine daily entry in squadron orders was a list of personnel on guard duties the following day which the troops observed carefully. Providing one could afford it, there was off duty time most evenings and guard duty could seriously affect the pleasure of friendships which many soldiers made wherever the locality - if it was there somebody would find it!

Within the squadron it was an established practice not to be detailed for guard on the night of return from an absence such as leave but where someone may unavoidably have to do so at short notice, or in an emergency, a full guard equipment would have been prepared for him within the troop for any such eventuality. Just one instance no doubt of how troops thrived - a camaraderie often initiated by NCOs.

Squadron office routines continued much the same for at least a period of 18 months during which time the Regiment had several locations throughout the UK. Sometimes the office accommodation would be in the familiar Nissen hut but maybe in a requisitioned property or quite often during the summer months under canvas.

The Regiment had done extensive training, more training, and yet more training, and had taken part in various exercises at different Army levels. In early June 1944 we received the news of the Allied landing in Normandy and after a few short weeks - mid-July - we landed there ourselves as a replacement for another regiment which had suffered severely in battle.

For me this was the end of life in a Nissen hut, thereafter a 15-cwt vehicle had been designated as the squadron office and I guarded my trunk of papers, office equipment and typewriter with my life! And to protect these valuable official belongings I had been armed, not with a rifle or a sten gun, but with a revolver with no ammunition! A welcome souvenir for any enemy.

When the Regiment was engaged in battle and the squadron tank crews were at action stations, I found myself with a group known as B Echelon (the Regimental tail). As we had only ‘soft’ vehicles it was always prudent for us to be out of the ‘range of fire’.

When in this Regimental group I found it appropriate when leaving harbour area to be towards the rear of the vehicle column - if there happened to be a withdrawal, I had decided that no way would a German filch my typewriter!

And there were occasions when I used it. Inevitably in a theatre of war there are casualties mostly as a result of enemy action but they can just as easily happen in circumstances out of battle. However, whenever there were such regrettable incidents, the squadron leader was most anxious to inform the next-of-kin before they received the official notification. At these times I would report to him for a dictated letter in which he would describe the happening in thoughtful words and in a sympathetic vein. Being able to use the office vehicle was invaluable on these occasions to maintain confidentiality. Preparation of such correspondence 'in the open' would not have been in the best interests of anyone.

During my initial training at the Primary Training Wing it was made known to all recruits that the Army was reluctant, for obvious reasons, to arrange postings to regiments to serve with relatives and/or friends. However, soon after arriving in Normandy, and the Regiment becoming part of the 7 Armoured Division, I became aware that my elder brother was also serving in the Division with a battalion of the Queen's Regiment. Although the Normandy battlefield area at the time was not very extensive, the opportunity to meander around on such an errand to find him was very risky and so many movements, albeit often only short distances, did not permit me to make such a personal foray. Surprise, surprise, when one day a very good friend in the squadron, Jack Edwards, who came from near Wolverhampton, and who was a scout car driver in HQ Troop, was full of news that he had met my brother who had apparently recognised the troops in the Fifth Dragoons and had asked him whether he knew Hollingshead in the Regiment. Of course, Jack hardly had to think because I understood that he replied, more or less: 'Yes, everybody in the squadron does, he's the squadron clerk!'

After the events in Normandy, the Allied advance moved rapidly - 'Tiffies' (RAF Typhoons) often being called in by the ground forces to deal with any stubborn defence by the enemy. Within a very short period of time we had come to a halt inside Belgium and it was there that my squadron leader pin-pointed the Queen's position for me, handed me the map, and gave me permission to go. Needless, to say a bike just happened to be nearby, so I found it to be an agreeable form of travel for the journey. In those times it was not advisable to stay around too long so in a short while I was 'on my bike' for the return journey. A little while later in a letter from home I learned that my brother was in hospital in Stratford-upon-Avon - seemingly he had sustained a leg injury caused by a vehicle which necessitated his evacuation to the UK where he continued his Army service until demob.

Fortunately, after the Normandy battles the Allied forces mostly moved forward, the Regiment doing likewise but there were two occasions - the Arnhem operation and the enemy attack in the Ardennes - where advance stumbled. If the enemy drive in the Ardennes to Antwerp had succeeded it would have cut off much of the British Army including ourselves who were then positioned on the German/Dutch border. However, weeks and months passed - autumn, winter, and spring - when there were many times I was part of B Echelon, but for much longer periods in the campaign I was with A Squadron where I was more fully occupied with normal duties. Shortly after the end of hostilities all the squadrons of the Regiment came together in barracks in Itzehoe in Schleswig Holstein. I continued as A Squadron clerk until, when the orderly room sergeant left on demobilisation, I was transferred to RHQ to replace him. I was assigned to a billet where two sergeants were already resident - APT Sgt Boyd, the Regimental physical training instructor, a Scotsman, and the Regimental interpreter, Sgt Hans de Vaal, who had joined us during the campaign in Holland. Myself being the Regimental admin sergeant, made a trio of enjoyable variety to say the least. But there were times when my two 'foreign' friends caused me to think I should have the services of a personal interpreter, the proverbial Irishman for instance. Coincidentally shortly afterwards I discovered another friend from my days at Oakengates College, Sgt Jeff Jervis, who had responsibility for HQ Squadron transport, which was perhaps not too surprising since his family had a haulage business at home.

Life in the orderly room was much more of a challenge if only because at that time there was much more activity at regimental level - officers and other ranks were leaving on demobilisation while new recruits were arriving as replacements. Demob operated on a system of age and service group numbers, which were dependent on age and length of service in the forces. Many of the senior officers and NCOs with vast experience, including an ability as instructors for tank crews, were leaving almost daily. In such fluid situations there were many questions to be answered about the regimental strength of personnel. Often to supply information required much time to do so since there were various records containing different information. I was also aware from my squadron duties that RHQ often requested returns for 'this and that'. To circumvent the many records and requests I prepared two card systems - one of all personnel in order of squadrons and one of all regimental personnel by A and S number. This was quite a mammoth task but once in operation with all essential particulars, answers were available almost immediately questions were asked and such promptness allowed me plenty of free time afterwards in what I considered to be a rather coveted post. With hindsight the two records could possibly be described as a 'manual computer'! As a regiment in the Regular British Army there was always a welcome for anyone who chose to remain for a period of service. However, having a superannuated post with my local authority I was in no doubt about my future career. I was required to make way for a 'Regular' soldier to become orderly room sergeant and I was posted to Army Records HQ in Hamburg to represent my Regiment for a very short period before resuming my civilian life. In recent years, having joined the Old Comrades Association, I have been aware that I was most fortunate in serving with genuinely friendly, often humorous, young men as we all were at the time, and in a Regiment which after nearly five years' service proved to me was 'one of the finest in the British Army'.

Out of curiosity I recently requested from Army Records Office the details of my service, to include a reference of my conduct. The details of my service were correct in every detail but I was disappointed in the reply for conduct - 'Not recorded in the file now held'. However, I was delighted to discover two letters from regimental officers - A Squadron leader in September 1945 had said: 'Some people may think that the job of squadron clerk is a cushy one but I know that is not true. It is a never ending task - there is always something to do. It is not only hard work, but it is also a responsible job and on the person who does it depends the smooth functioning of the squadron - not only from the official angle of the orderly room but also, even more importantly, from the point of view of the men in the squadron. The highest thing I can say about this is that A Squadron would be very sorry to see another chap in your place. The very best of luck to you - you may be in civvy street sooner than you now expect'.

Much of the detail for the daily squadron orders was left to me as clerk, the squadron leader often giving the brief outline only. However, there is not much that happens in life that has not been done before and that certainly happened in my office days. The content of orders was often to be found in earlier ones - but sometimes a little more lengthy. News reached me on one occasion that when the orders were received one evening by a junior officer in the Officers' Mess he decided to read them to all present, and to much amusement he interpreted the heading - A Squadron Orders for...day,...date, issued by Maj Howard Hollingshead and typed by LCpl Creagh Gibson - probably one day when I produced the orders in the absence of Maj Gibson. Not only officers but also the whole squadron, however, appreciated that 'orders were orders' and thus had to be read, understood and acted upon - in a way they were one of the highlights of each day.

And the Brigade Commander, 7th Armoured Brigade (during my time in the orderly room Colonel of the Regiment) said in February 1947: 'During my period of command of my Regiment, the 5th Royal Inniskilling Dragoon

Guards, Sgt Hollingshead served me most loyally and efficiently. Soon after taking over command my orderly room sergeant was demobilised. There appeared to be nobody to take his place who had the necessary experience. Within a short time he became a most efficient and reliable orderly room sergeant, a most likeable and pleasant character with a quick brain and conscientious in every way.

These words from those who really had been aware of the performance of my duties I consider far outweigh any 'record of conduct' not included in the official records.

And not to forget my several weeks of training, the chief instructor at RAC Training Regiment reported under Specialist Training: 'A keen, conscientious and efficient clerk. Has carried out the duties of shorthand correspondence clerk and Regimental Part 1 Order clerk'. The report further included under Gunnery Training '...taught in guns, 2-Pdr; 7.92 Besa (and fired), Bren, TSMG, 15.00 Besa, Boyes, and a 6-Pdr, which was essential basic training as a gunner/wireless operator on a range of British tanks.'

Well, after nearly five years in a tank regiment I was probably one of the very few people who could truthfully say 'I never went into a tank'. Even I could not do two things at the same time!

The 5th Royal Inniskilling Dragoon Guards had many moves during the war years, most notably serving in France from September 1939 to 2 June 1940 and again going to Normandy in France on 17 July 1944, then onwards as part of 'Monty's' Army to Belgium, Holland, and finally Germany, remaining there for several years after the end of hostilities. In the four years between their 'Continental tours' the Regiment formed part of the armoured reserve at home. An interesting article appeared in *The War Illustrated - I was there* series in January 1947 which gave the following record of the Regiment from 1939 to 1945...

5th Royal Inniskilling Dragoon Guards

This regiment was formed by the amalgamation in 1922 of the 5th Dragoon Guards and the Inniskilling Dragoons. The former were raised by James II in 1685 the latter were raised in Northern Ireland to oppose him after his dethronement. Both regiments saw their baptism of fire at the Battle of the Boyne in 1690. During Marlborough's campaigns both gained several battle honours in the Low Countries. The Inniskilling Dragoons at Waterloo in 1815 formed with the Royals and Greys the Union Brigade which played a large part in the victory. In the Crimea both regiments took part in the charge of the Heavy Brigade, and both served in France throughout the first great war.

After completing mobilisation the Regiment embarked for France and landed at St Nazaire at the end of September 1939. A few days were spent unloading the vehicles and collecting stores, then the trek to Northern France began. The first stage was a train journey to Malincourt, near St Pol, thence to the Lille area, in and around which the rest of the winter was spent training. Occasional increases in tension, which threatened the unreality of the 'phoney' war, caused swift and usually midnight moves up to the Franco-Belgian frontier in the area of Roubaix.

May 10, 1940, found the Regiment in the outskirts of the town: an overnight air raid on Lille and varying disquieting reports over the wireless suggested interesting developments. Early in the morning news was received that the German army had invaded Belgium, and the British government had pledged its support to the latter.

At 4pm the move into Belgium commenced, the Regiment being part of the 3rd Infantry Division, commanded by the then Maj Gen Montgomery. At dawn the following morning the 5th Royal Inniskilling Dragoon Guards were in the area of Louvain. The next three weeks - up to the final evacuation from Dunkirk - was one long series of rearguard actions, the Regiment, as divisional cavalry, always covering the retirement of the infantry. During this period it worked with nearly every division in the BEF, ending up with covering the retirement of the 46th Division into Dunkirk from Bergue Canal. On the night of June 3-4 squadrons embarked independently on destroyers from the mole at Dunkirk and returned to England. The Regiment reformed and mobilised shortly after, first as an anti-invasion force in lorries, and later as an armoured regiment. From 1940 until the summer of 1944 it formed part of the armoured reserve kept in England against the possibility of a German invasion and went on training steadily with various types of armoured vehicles in preparation for the invasion of Western Europe.

The Regiment went to Normandy in the middle of July 1944, and joined the 7th Armoured Division immediately after the second battle of Caen, replacing the 4th County of London Yeomanry which had suffered very heavy casualties in the fighting around Villers Bocage. Within two days of joining the division the Regiment went into action for the first time since Dunkirk. During all August it took part in continuous attempts all along the British line to engage the enemy armour and contain it while the Americans broke through on the right. The fighting, though without outstanding features, was continuous and hard, and the Regiment operated under both the Canadian 1st Army and British 2nd Army. By the end of the month the Falaise Gap had been closed and the German armies in France were on the point of retreat.

Tremendous Reception in Belgium

Next, the Regiment took a leading part in the memorable five days' pursuit through France, the 7th Armoured Division—the left hand armoured division of the British Army - being directed on Ghent. The 250 miles from the River Seine to Ghent were covered in five exciting days, a mixture of sharp rearguard encounters with the Germans in retreat and a grand triumphal procession through the heart of northern France. The Belgian frontier was crossed on September 4, late at night, amid scenes of great rejoicing from the Belgians: and Ghent, the final objective, was reached the following day. Once in position there the results of the pursuit came quickly and within 24 hours the Regiment had captured 1,500 prisoners.

It had a particularly warm reception in Belgium, as it soon became known that King Leopold was its Colonel-in-Chief; and many were the toasts drunk to the 'Regiment du Roi.' After a short rest it moved on again, and was soon in action to the west of Eindhoven at the start of the combined air and land offensive against Arnhem. The Regiment had the task of clearing the main road between Eindhoven and Nijmegen after German counter-attacks had cut it. Here it first met and worked with elements of one of the American airbourne divisions.

Great, however, as was the success gained, the final objective was never achieved. The bold plan having miscarried, it became necessary to build up the lines of communication and particularly to free Antwerp before the assault on Germany could be considered. The next major operation was the assault on S-Hertogenbosch. For this, the Regiment was placed under the command of the 53rd (Welsh) Division. The initial attack lasted for four days and was a great success. The town was captured and the major part of two German divisions was destroyed.

Then the Regiment reverted to its own Division and took part in clearing the southern bank of the River Maas as far west as the Dutch islands. After a short period of training in Belgium it again went into the line just before Christmas, north of Sittard. It was then on the extreme right of the British line with American 9th Army as neighbours. Von Rundstedt's offensive against the Americans passed to the south and the Regiment was left unmolested.

The New Year brought with it a period of great cold and snow but, in spite of the weather, in the middle of January the Regiment took part in the limited British 2nd Army attack which cleared the Germans from the triangle formed by the rivers Maas and Roer and the British front line. Here the Germans had two months in which to lay minefields and construct anti-tank obstacles and it was realised that the advance would be slow. The attack was launched, and after 15 days' fighting, with the thermometer always showing 30 degrees of frost, the Regiment found itself on the banks of the river Roer, looking at the fixed defences of the vaunted Siegfried Line - and hearing there-from at all too frequent intervals.

This was the first occasion that an armoured division had been asked to take a major part in a winter offensive, and the results had shown once more that the limitations by ground and weather are relative and not absolute in the employment of armour. The Regiment's tanks were impressive in their white paint as camouflage against the snow.

The weather broke at the end of January, and the Regiment was lucky in being able to extricate all the tanks when the order came to hand over to the Americans and go once more out of the line and into Belgium.

While the Americans and the 1st Canadian Army set out to drive the Germans from the west bank of the Rhine the Regiment had a breathing space to clean up and prepare for the last offensive which all were waiting for - the assault over the Rhine and the pursuit through Germany. After a period of tense waiting the regiment saw the Airborne Divisions fly over one sunny morning and it knew that the final round had started. The Regiment crossed the Rhine some 70 hours after the initial assault in the early morning on March 27.

The 7th Armoured Division was the first armoured division to cross the river and as leading regiment it was obvious that the 5th Royal Inniskilling Dragoon Guards were in for a busy time. With the exception of certain SS and paratroop formations it was not expected that the bulk of the German Army would be capable of any organised resistance, and a quick break-out would entirely prevent the German High Command from any effective control of the battlefield.

After passing quickly through the dropping zones of the Airborne Divisions - an area covered with coloured parachutes, gliders and all the wreckage of battle - the Regiment passed through the leading elements of the 6th Airborne Division and took the lead.

An average of 12 miles a day was kept up for four days and nights of continuous fighting. Chief causes of delay were blown bridges and various isolated self-propelled guns and AA batteries that the Germans had not been able to withdraw. After an initial advance eastwards of some 25 miles the Regiment was directed north-east to reach the Dortmund-Ems canal to the area of Rheine. The latter was reached on the fourth day after crossing the Rhine after many German self-propelled guns and more than 300 prisoners had been taken. This was the first phase of the final offensive, and the Regiment had been fighting its way forward over a distance of 80 miles continuously for four days and nights.

The general pattern of the Allied drive was now becoming clear. To the south of the British 2nd Army the Americans, after a tremendous encircling movement in the Ruhr basin, were advancing rapidly against diminishing opposition, while on the Regiment's northern flank the Canadians and XXX Corps were fighting a hard but successful battle against a German paratroop army which was withdrawing slowly. The 5th Royal Inniskilling Dragoon Guards in the middle, so far had been lucky, and though it would be incorrect to say that no opposition had been encountered, it had never been determined. The beginning of April, however, brought the Regiment two days of very heavy fighting to secure a road leading through the plateau to the north of the Dortmund-Ems canal. Fanatical resistance was met from cadets and NCOs of the Hanover Infantry School and in a fierce two-days battle the ridge was secured.

Once this nest of opposition had been crushed, resistance became less determined, and the Regiment drove on north-eastwards towards the River Weser. With the leading elements of the Division on the Weser, the Regiment was directed north towards Bremen in order to cut the escape routes of the German parachute army retreating before the Canadians. This was achieved in two days, in spite of an unexpected night attack on Regimental Headquarters - on the last night before the Regiment was relieved of its position. It then went on again, eastwards, over the rivers Weser and Aller.

The German Naval Headquarters at Buxtehude on the Elbe was captured, complete with its admiral and 400 German Wrens who were far from pleased at finding that they were no longer considered to be of the 'master race'. After much parley and discussion Hamburg surrendered and, with that surrender, to all intents and purposes, the war in the British sector was over. Hamburg presented a spectacle that will be remembered for a long time by all who drove in that first day. The BBC's familiar announcement 'Our aircraft bombed Hamburg last night' took on new significance on May 3 - the ruins of Coventry, Southampton and London paled before the enormity of the damage over so wide an area.

The following day the Regiment marched to the Kiel Canal, where the news of the end of the war was heard on the wireless. It was lucky to finish up in a district of pleasant farmland completely unspoiled by war, where, apart from one short interlude, it has since remained. It the six years of war the Regiment earned five DSOs, 11 MCs, seven DCMs, 12 MMs and two Croix-de-Guerre; and at the end of hostilities it had supplied from its pre-war officers one corps commander, three brigadiers, and seven lieutenant-colonels commanding armoured regiments. Equipment varied from bren gun carriers and light tanks, in 1939, through Stuarts, Covenanters, Crusaders, Shermans, Cromwells to Comets in 1945.

Sadly because of cuts in UK Defence expenditure, after a period of 70 years since their last amalgamation, the Regiment amalgamated yet again in August 1992, on this occasion with the 4/7th Royal Dragoon Guards, to become The Royal Dragoon Guards.

And resulting from amalgamation came the end - almost - of 'Fare Thee Well Inniskilling' with those words unforgettable to all those who have at any time served in the Regiment.

Fare thee well Inniskilling

A beautiful damsel, of fame and renown,
A gentleman's daughter near Monaghan town:
As she rode by the barracks, this beautiful maid,
She stood in her coach to see Dragoons on parade.

Chorus:
Fare thee well, Inniskilling! Fare thee well, For a While
To all you Fair waters and every green isle!
And when the war is over we'll return again soon,
And you'll all welcome home the Inniskilling Dragoon.

These Dragoons were all dressed just like gentlemen's sons.
With their bright shining swords and carabine guns:
Their brass-mounted pistols she observed them full soon
Because that she loved an Inniskilling Dragoon.

Chorus
She looked on the bright sons of Mars, on the right,
With their armour shining the stars of the night.
'O Willie! Dearest Willie! You have 'listed too soon
To serve as a brave Inniskilling Dragoon.'

Chorus
'O Flora! Dear Flora.' Your pardon I crave!
'Tis now and forever that I am your slave:
But your parents they have slighted you both morning and noon
for fear that you'd wed your Inniskilling Dragoon'.

Chorus
'O Willie! Dearest Willie! Don't mind what they say!
Sure maidens must ever their parents obey:
When the foe you are fighting they'll soon change their tune.
And cry, 'Send you safe, Inniskilling Dragoon'.

3

BEF Evacuation, Dunkirk, France

Dunkirk was probably the biggest withdrawal - retreat - escape by the British Army in the whole of its long history. How did it come about?

Great Britain and France had declared war on Germany on 3 September 1939. As in World War One (1914-1918) the British Expeditionary Force immediately went to France and took up its position on the frontline alongside the French. The RAF also moved units across the Channel to bases in Northern France. During the autumn and winter of 1939/1940 there was virtually no military action throughout the whole of the frontline, so much so that these months became known as the period of 'phoney war'. However, the spring of 1940 arrived and the situation changed dramatically. The Germans attacked and within days had over-run Denmark, Norway, Holland and Belgium, which had been unable to offer much resistance to Hitler's 'blitzkrieg', a violent campaign bringing about speedy victory.

On 10 May 1940 the BEF moved into Belgium to stem the enemy advance but when, in only a few days, the small Belgian Army was surrounded, it had to withdraw. The Germans, who in the several years prior to the outbreak of war had built an all-conquering military force, then attacked France and were able to make significant advances avoiding the much vaunted Maginot line. For the BEF it became a question of fighting a rearguard action to avoid being overwhelmed. The situation was desperate since by then the only port open to them was Dunkirk. In Great Britain it was well known that the plight of the British Army was serious. The German attack heightened - shells landing on the beaches and in the town, bombing and machine gunning. At this critical time the call went out to all those having small boats of any description along the whole of the south coast from Devon to the River Thames to proceed to the beaches of Dunkirk.

The BEF made its way to the beaches and men were ferried by the smaller boats to the bigger ships which lay off shore. Many men who had been waiting in queues decided to wade out until they were standing in water up to their chests. A figure of upwards of 350,000 Allied soldiers escaped from France between 20 May and 4 June 1940. Whether such an outstanding evacuation would have been possible at Dunkirk may have been very much in doubt but for Brig Claude Nicholson, who, with four British Regiments - the Royal Tank Regiment, the Rifle Brigade, the 60th Rifles and Queen Victoria's Rifles - refused to surrender at Calais. For their splendid actions there throughout the period 22-25 May 1940, they were awarded the battle honour *Calais 1940*.

During the several months of 'phoney war' on the French/German border which was followed by the enemy's overwhelming 'blitzkrieg' through Belgium and Northern France, the Royal Air Force was most actively deployed from French airfields.

In addition to attacking the German fleet when and where it could be found, bomber aircraft were used at the outset of the war making leaflet raids on German towns and cities. Also at that time, because of a lack of adequate official information available to them, bomber crews had to find the targets themselves when attacking military installations. Together with the French Air Forces, the RAF delayed and weakened the superior enemy mechanised forces by making low-flying attacks against their advancing columns; at road junctions; and railway marshalling yards, and thus relieved the pressure on the withdrawing Allied armies. RAF losses were inevitable. On 10 May the Advanced Striking Force had 135 serviceable bomber aircraft but in five days they had only 75 left, indeed from 10 May to 20 June when France finally asked for an armistice, Bomber Command lost 40 per cent of their first line strength.

The 5th Royal Inniskilling Dragoon Guards left England on 28 September 1939 and landed at St Nazaire in France the following day. After a short stay there the Regiment moved via St Pol, Magnicourt (near Arras) and Cambrai to the village of Verlingham, some five miles north-west of Lille where it remained for the winter months.

Early in the New Year the Regiment moved to Bethune, an unattractive industrial town, later to Mouvaux near Lille for a more comfortable stay and then to a concentration area near Amiens. Eventually the Regiment moved towards the Belgian frontier at La Croix-Roubaix.

When Germany violated Belgian neutrality on 10 May 1940, King Leopold appealed for help to France and Britain. Accordingly the Regiment, as part of 3 Division, found itself advancing to the area of Louvain, taking over defensive positions on the general line of the River Dyle.

However, by 13 May 1940 Belgian soldiers began to withdraw from the front and when the Germans broke through in the Ardennes it became prudent to withdraw from Belgium to avoid being outflanked. While the

Dunkirk evacuation. Some of the small craft that took part, sailing up the Thames, 9 June 1940. *(IWM HU 3383)*

initial withdrawals were fairly orderly, at later stages it was often necessary to retreat rapidly - causing some confusion at times with civilians - since the enemy was taking full advantage of Allied forces on the run.

By 20 May the Regiment was back in France and fortunately in one piece. But the Germans attacked relentlessly and by 24 May, when in the area of Hazebrouck, it seemed that the Regiment's fate would be encirclement.

The British front degenerated and, as there was to be no rally by the French Army as in 1914 at the Marne, orders were given on 28 May to dump all unnecessary equipment and make for the coast at Dunkirk.

Arriving at Dunkirk on 30 May the Regiment awaited evacuation but on 31 May it became mobile reserve for 46th Division which was occupying a bridgehead position.

It was 1 June when the Regiment's turn came for embarkation and RHQ left on that day, leaving the three squadrons on the beach before fortunately embarking that night for all to be back in England by 2 June.

The Regiment had not however returned to UK without a heavy casualty list - 60 men being killed, wounded, or missing. For their part in the 1939-

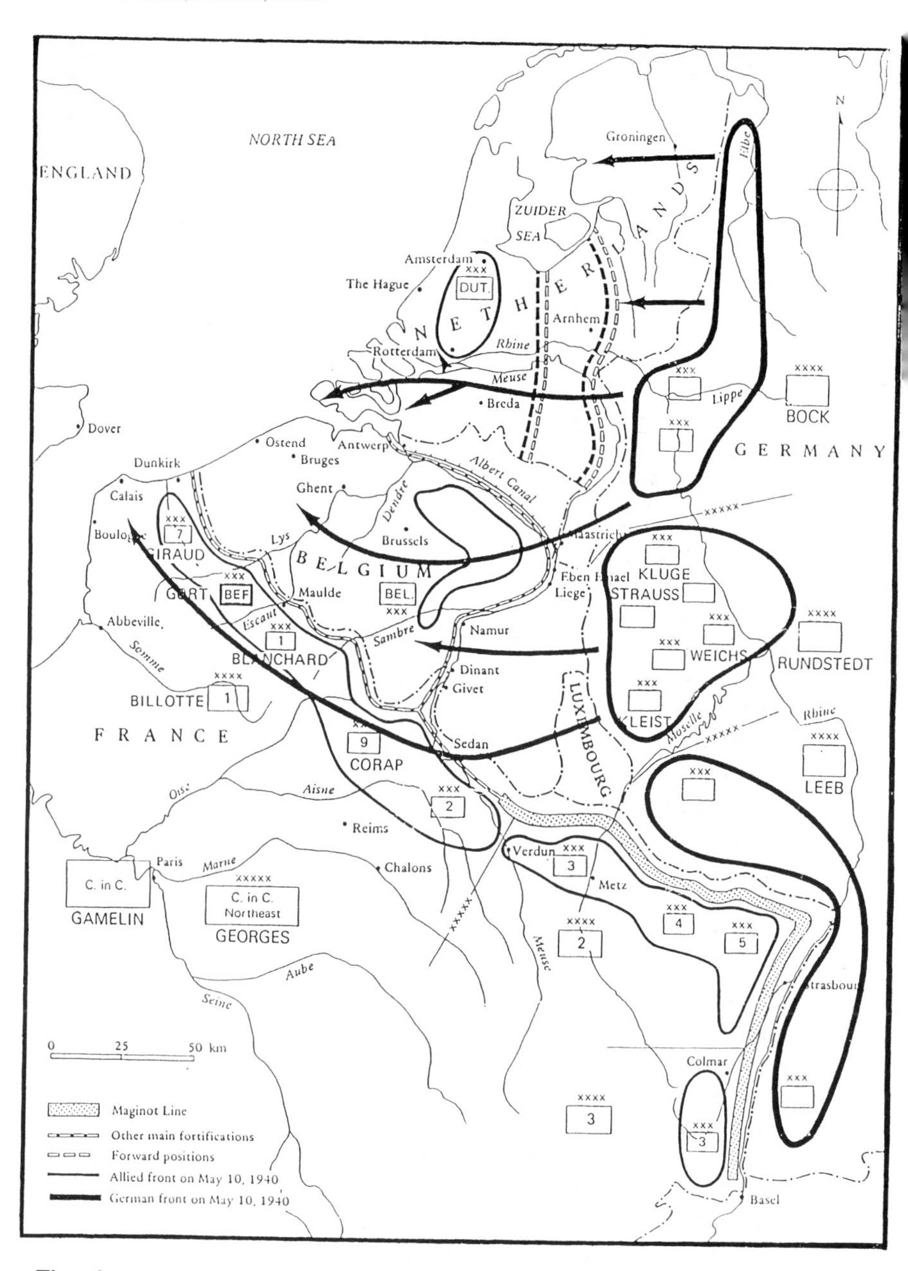

NORTH SEA
ENGLAND
Groningen
ZUIDER SEA
Amsterdam
The Hague
DUT.
NETHERLANDS
Arnhem
Rhine
Rotterdam
Meuse
Breda
Elbe
Lippe
BOCK
GERMANY
Dover
Ostend
Bruges
Antwerp
Dunkirk
Calais
Ghent
Albert Canal
Dendre
Brussels
Boulogne
GIRAUD
Lys
BELGIUM
Maastricht
Eben Emael
Liege
KLUGE
STRAUSS
GORT
BEF
Maulde
BEL.
Abbeville
Escaut
BLANCHARD
Sambre
Namur
WEICHS
RUNDSTEDT
Somme
Dinant
Givet
BILLOTTE
LUXEMBOURG
KLEIST
FRANCE
Moselle
Rhine
Sedan
CORAP
LEEB
Oise
Aisne
Reims
Verdun
Metz
Paris
Marne
Chalons
C. in C.
GAMELIN
C. in C. Northeast
GEORGES
Meuse
Strasbourg
Aube
Seine
0 25 50 km
Colmar
Maginot Line
Other main fortifications
Forward positions
Allied front on May 10, 1940
German front on May 10, 1940
Basel

The plan.

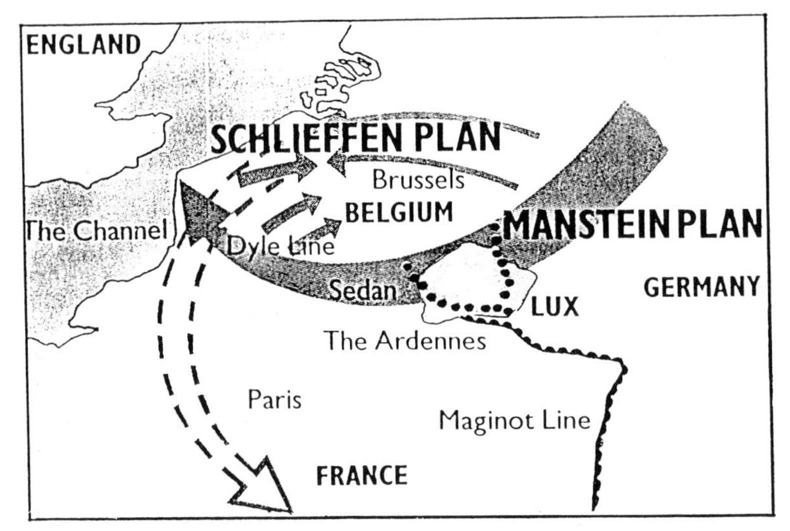

The old 'one-two'.

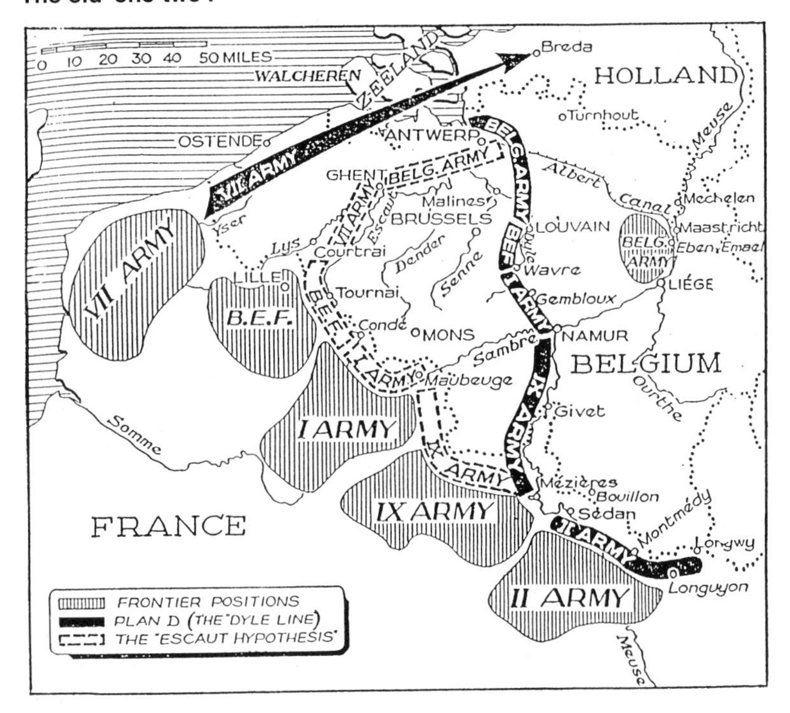

The theory.

1940 campaign the Regiment was awarded Battle Honours for *Withdrawal to the Escaut*, for *St Omer-Le-Bassee* and for *Dunkirk*.

On the Holts' 50th anniversary tour to Dunkirk from 25 May to 27 May 1990 we were reminded that at the time of the evacuation there were some 700 craft, which included yachts and cockle boats, indeed almost anything which could float, on their way from all around the coast of south east England to the beaches of Dunkirk to rescue several hundred thousands of British and Allied troops.

While we were on tour there we saw about 70 of the surviving little ships which had joined the Royal Navy to commemorate this very memorable anniversary of those tremendous nine days of the summer of 1940 and the success of the Dunkirk operation against such desperate odds.

Immediately our party got off the Dover to Calais ferry on this three-day tour we found ourselves in the battlefield area, indeed our hotel was also there.

Straightaway we proceeded to the coastal area sites at Calais where our leader, Maj Tonie Holt, described the British defence of the port by Brig Claude Nicholson and his four regiments 50 years ago against an overwhelming German attacking force. Nicholson, together with 1,000 French troops, held Calais to the end, refusing to surrender to the Germans. He was eventually taken prisoner after the last stand on 26 May from dawn until four o'clock in the afternoon.

In the Calais/Dunkirk area a propaganda leaflet was dropped on the Allied forces by the Germans with a map giving their precarious position which indicated that they were entirely surrounded and should stop fighting and put down their arms.

Tonie followed up his talk on the morning of the second day when our party had an extensive tour of Calais visiting many sites - Fort Risban, Bastion 12, Fort Lapin, Fort Nieulay, the Citadel, the Rifle Brigade Memorial where 'Tug' Wilson, one of our regular travelling friends whose regiment was there at the time was able to recall experiences of those critical days; and finally visiting the Calais South CWGC Cemetery.

In the afternoon our tour party visited the Dunkirk area and, in particular, the Perimeter, Pont-a-Mouton, Moeures CWGC, Bray Dunes, the French Memorial, De Panne, Gort's HQ, and the memorial.

Sunday 27 May 1990 was commemorated as the 50th anniversary of Operation 'Dynamo' which was the codename for the rescue operation of British and Allied soldiers from France. On this commemoration day the Holts' party made one special visit and attended two commemorative events. The special visit was to the British part of the Dunkirk Town Cemetery

Allied soldiers are evacuated from Dunkerque. Forced to retreat to the Channel coast by on-rushing German tank units, British, French and Belgian soldiers wait at the port of Dunkerque to be evacuated by boat to England. ***(IWM NYP 68075)***

which we approached through an avenue formed by the columns of the memorial to the 4,534 soldiers of the British Expeditionary Force who fell in the 1939-1940 campaign and have no known graves. In addition, in plots adjacent to the memorial rest 810 British and Allied soldiers, sailors, and airmen of the war. I found this visit most poignant since, while observing the memorial, I saw the names on Col 2 of 13 men of my Regiment who had lost their lives on various dates between 19 May and 1 June. At the same time, the Holts' party nearby had stood at the Cross of Sacrifice in silence for their usual wreath laying and the exhortation spoken by a member of the group.

Some information pages from the Commonwealth War Graves Commission at Maidenhead for the Dunkirk Town cemetery indicate that...

'There is hardly a corner of France that does not contain the grave of a soldier or airman of the Commonwealth who fell in the 1939-1945 war. Some among this host lie in small churchyards or communal cemeteries;

many are gathered together in large war cemeteries; others lie beside those of the previous generation who gave their lives in the years 1914-1918. Widely scattered as their graves are, their numbers are far fewer than those of the years 1914-1918 - approximately 45,000 as compared with 530,000 for the earlier war. Apart from that comparison, their deaths have meant that many a home has suffered bereavement for a second time within 30 years.

'Most of the graves contained in war cemeteries and the larger communal cemetery plots lie within relatively small regions: close to the beaches in Normandy, along the Channel coast, and near the Franco-Belgian frontier. It is also to be remembered that the graves scattered in small groups in hundreds of cemeteries from the Mediterranean to the Straits of Dover are often those of airmen who failed to return from raids, of men drowned at sea whose bodies were recovered on the shores of France, or of men who worked with the forces striving within France for her liberation. '

Later in the morning we attended our first commemorative event, a 'patriotic ceremony' which was held in the town centre attended by large and well represented crowds of Dunkirk veterans and local French associations displaying their banners before taking part, as the bands played, in a grand march-past attended by Mr Michel Delebarre, the French Transport Minister and also the local mayor, who described Dunkirk as 'a proud page in the history of our two nations', while Mr Cecil Parkinson, the British Transport Minister, said: 'We are not commemorating a victory - no-one would lay claim to that - but a very successful operation which prevented the defeat of the core of the British Army and preserved a basis of land forces on which the foundations of subsequent victory were built. Dunkirk was a turning point in the war, which enabled us to continue fighting. If anyone had invented such a story, you would never have believed it'.

After lunch on this very special day we assembled for our second commemorative event in the area of the beach among a huge crowd of veterans and local people for the off-shore ceremony of Remembrance. In brilliant sunshine a helicopter passed over out at sea followed by RAF planes of 1940 - the Spitfire, the Hurricane, the Lancaster - and these were followed shortly afterwards by a flypast of the famous Red Arrows aerobatic team.

Among the many boats offshore was the paddle steamer *Waverley,* packed with spectators and relatives who laid personal wreaths. *HMS Alacrity* and other Royal Navy ships took part. The two minutes silence was held - the Last Post sounded - and then Reveille - which brought the

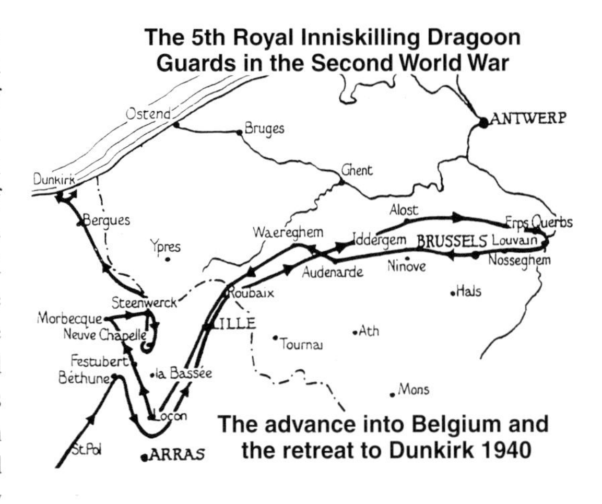

The 5th Royal Inniskilling Dragoon Guards in the Second World War

The advance into Belgium and the retreat to Dunkirk 1940

ceremony to an end. It was a mixture of commemoration and celebration for the rescue of such a huge number of Allied personnel - some seven times more than the planned number - and as the veterans with their relatives and friends slowly made their way from the crowded beach area in sombre mood, no doubt the thoughts of many of them dwelt on the dreadful days for the British forces half a century before. And while this Remembrance ceremony was taking place at Dunkirk, remember too the magnificent defence of Nicholson's men at Calais who held off German armour for three days and made possible the rescue of our expeditionary force from Dunkirk.

The withdrawal by the BEF from Dunkirk is sometimes described as a defeat for Allied forces who indeed were mostly British. In June 1940 very few doubted that was not so.

Nevertheless, as the British Army more or less successfully evacuated from France, these vitally experienced forces were able to form part of an Allied army which, inter alia, some four years later, landed in Normandy and in less than one year had defeated the Dunkirk enemy. The tables had been turned - the Nazi Germans had surrendered. Without the 'evacuation troops' the British Army may never have recovered sufficiently to attack the enemy on the continent of Europe which ultimately ended in victory - a victory which many observers consider started at Dunkirk in June 1940 with a so called 'defeat'.

By the time that the Allied Armies returned to Northern France in June 1944, the German occupation had extended to a period of four years.

Of the French Channel ports of Le Havre, Boulogne, Calais and Dunkirk, the first three fell to the attacks of the Allies in September/early October 1944 but the Germans did not surrender Dunkirk - from which the Allies withdrew in June 1940 - until the end of the war in North West Europe in May 1945.

4

Battle of Britain

The Battle of Britain was a short, sharp, fierce struggle which extended over a period of just about four months from early July to end of October 1940.

The evacuation of the BEF from France finally took place on 2 June 1940. In fairness to the French, however, their forces significantly assisted the British withdrawal since they did continue fighting the Germans until nearly three weeks later when, finally, they were forced to surrender on 22 June.

It was at about this time that Winston Churchill said: 'What Gen Weygand called the Battle of France is over. I expect the Battle of Britain is about to begin'.

In a radio broadcast on 18 June 1940 Winston Churchill addressed the nation:

'Upon this Battle depends the survival of Christian civilisation. Upon it depends our own British life and the long continuity of our institutions and our Empire. The whole fury and might of the enemy must very soon be turned on us. Hitler knows that he will have to break us in this island or lose the war. If we can stand up to him, all Europe may be free, and the life of the world may move forward into broad, sunlit uplands; but if we fail, then the whole world, including the United States, and all that we have known and cared for, will sink into the abyss of a new dark age made more sinister, and perhaps more protracted, by the lights of a perverted science.

'Let us therefore brace ourselves to our duty and so bear ourselves that if the British Empire and its Commonwealth lasts for 1,000 years men will still say: 'This was their finest hour'.'

Such was the prelude to the Battle of Britain and with this dire warning by the Prime Minister everyone throughout Britain and all her friends elsewhere needed no reminding that this was the *Darkest Hour* in our long history. And the German Luftwaffe was not long in coming either. It was during the hot summer months of 1940 that this greatest Air Battle in history took place over the southern counties of England and the English Channel, much of it over the county of Kent. German bombers, escorted by fighters, incessantly raiding throughout each day; throughout each week; and throughout each month; until finally the brave British fighters inflicted a crushing defeat on the Luftwaffe invaders.

In the diary kept by my sister of day-by-day news items, much information about aircraft losses is given, such as...

10 July:	Nine German aircraft brought down yesterday; four Italian aircraft brought down at Gibraltar, five disabled, and the rest fled behind a smoke screen. Ten enemy aircraft shot down over the Bristol Channel area.
11 July:	14 enemy planes shot down and 23 severely damaged and two British planes lost, when Spitfires and Hurricanes attacked Dorniers, Messerschmitts and Heinkels. Five Italian planes brought down over Malta. 37 enemy planes believed shot down yesterday.
12 July:	New Zealand airmen - pilots and observers - arrive in UK.
14 July:	12 enemy planes were destroyed yesterday with several more damaged over the English Channel. Two British fighters failed to return when enemy aircraft attacked shipping in the Straits of Dover.
18 July:	Four German airmen rescued off the Scottish coast.
21 July:	12 enemy planes were lost in all over our coasts yesterday; two British fighters missing, 150 planes took part in a two-hour battle.
22 July:	24 enemy planes were destroyed during the weekend.
26 July:	28 enemy bombers were brought down yesterday.
29 July:	100 enemy planes over south east coast; 15 of them shot down within half-an-hour. Two British planes lost.
31 July:	Now known that 240 enemy aircraft have been shot down in July over English coasts.
12 August:	62 enemy aircraft destroyed yesterday - 40 out of 200 were lost over Portland. Three British planes lost.
13 August:	126 planes of the enemy shot down in two days; 13 British fighters were lost.
16 August:	Now known that 169 enemy planes were shot down yesterday.
19 August:	152 enemy aircraft shot down when 600 raided. 16 British fighters lost - eight pilots safe. 70 German Heinkels and Dorniers turned back when they met anti-aircraft fire over Croydon.

1 September:	147 enemy planes brought down in two days; 22 British lost but 17 pilots safe.
7 September:	371 enemy planes shot down in seven days.
8 September:	88 enemy planes destroyed; 22 British lost, nine pilots safe.
9 September:	Longest raid of war on Britain last night. Now known that 103 enemy planes brought down on 7 September.
10 September:	52 enemy destroyed yesterday; 18 British lost.
11 September:	RAF made a heavy raid on Berlin last night. King and Queen visited area raided by enemy. 73 enemy planes destroyed; 17 British lost, three pilots safe.
12 September:	Now known that 90 German planes were destroyed yesterday.
13 September:	King and Queen unhurt when a lone raider deliberately bombed Buckingham Palace.

A newspaper seller in the street watching a 'dog-fight' in the skies above during the Battle of Britain. ***(IWM HU 810)***

Air raid damage in a London suburb where a night raiders bomb crashed into a street. It made a giant crater breaking mains, twisting tram lines and partly engulfing a bus. 14 October 1940. ***(IWM LN 13938B)***

15 September: 18 enemy planes down; nine British, six pilots safe yesterday. 165 enemy shot down today; 25 British pilots safe.
16 September: Now known 185 enemy shot down yesterday.
17 September: Weather conditions upset Hitler's planned invasion.
19 September: RAF have crushed enemy invasion plans - overwhelming defeat for the Luftwaffe; additionally damaged shipping; military stores; and airfields.

Many similar entries were included in the diaries throughout the month of September and October.

During the period of the daylight raids from 10 July to the end of September the Germans had lost 1,408 aircraft. Although 697 British fighters had been lost, many pilots, most precious for the RAF, were saved. On the night of 25 August the RAF raided Berlin to which Hitler retaliated on 7 September by launching a big raid on London. This particular raid resulted in the Home Forces going 'on guard' for an invasion - Hitler's Operation Sealion. This enemy raid and another on 15 September were repelled - the latter day having afterwards been recognised as 'Battle of Britain Day'. About mid-September the Germans changed their tactics from daylight to night-time attacks on London and other important locations in the UK. The British fighters had gained a victory by then, albeit 'by the skin of their teeth', and by 19 September Hitler had decided to disperse his invasion forces.

The German air raid of 7 September was probably the only occasion when it was thought in Britain that an enemy invasion was imminent. My regimental history records events as follows:

'On the evening of 7 September there was an alarm of invasion which reached even as far as Keele, for that night the Regiment was put at two hours' notice. At 0300hrs next day they were warned that a state of emergency had been declared and that they were to move at once to Builth Wells in Breconshire; at 0400hrs the leading squadron moved off, and six hours later the whole Regiment was concentrated at Builth, 80 miles or so away. The alarm proved to be without foundation but the squadrons stayed on in Wales (until 12 October)'.

Mrs E Colcombe, of Llandrindod Wells, Powys, says: 'I remember the Inniskilling Dragoons coming to Builth Wells. I was about 20 years old at the time and working in a private house. Their cookhouse was in a big garage almost opposite our front gates and I remember the lads marching down the street for their meals. They used to play a tune on their tin plates with the cutlery. The Sergeants' Mess was in the Church Hall and I was often offered a poached egg on toast (when the hen laid) and a cup of Rosie-Lea (tea). I'm afraid I declined the offer after catching them boiling the tea-cloths after washing their socks.

'When they first arrived my friend and I went for a walk by the river. As we went through the gate a voice said: 'Halt'. I had two brothers in the Army and one in the air force later, so I stopped as my brothers had told me.

'My friend walked on right up to a bayonet - the look on her face was a picture I will never forget. We had a lot of men from Dunkirk before them, they only had the clothes they were wearing and the local people put on concerts to help get supplies for them, that was a very sad time. Later there were two Regiments at Builth at the same time - the KRRs and the Queen Victoria Rifles, the latter consisted mostly of dispatch riders on motorbikes. One of my brothers was in the Royal Welch Fusiliers and when that was disbanded he was sent to the Border Regiment and after into the Chindits. He was behind the lines for many months and the War Office sent my mother and I a letter each every month saying he was well. When he returned he told us he had to pay for them before he went and they did not know if he was alive or dead when they sent them, it was to keep us quiet'.

Mrs Gwen Davies, of Builth Wells, Powys, recalls: 'I was a schoolgirl at the time but well remember the boys who were here in Builth Camp in 1940. My parents invited them into our home for a meal and a sit by the coal fire. They came here direct from Dunkirk as they had been kitted out with new uniforms and their 'flashes' were sewn on by the local WVS ladies.

I kept an autograph book and still have the names of two Inniskilling boys who were here - Tpr Tom Orme; and LCpl Ted Glynn DCM (he called it 'Don't come Monday') - I well remember you. They were here such a short time but I think they were the first soldiers to occupy the newly built camp and they made a pleasant impression on this small town of Builth Wells.' - Vestigia Nulla Retrorsum.

Mrs GE McDonald of Builth Wells, Powys, remembers: 'I was just 17 when the 5th Royal Inniskilling Dragoon Guards came to Builth where they were stationed in October 1940. They were the first Regiment to come here, before a permanent camp was built. Other regiments followed in quick succession, mostly artillery as the ranges extend from nearby to Brecon and Sennybridge in the south. The 'Skins', as they were called, were billeted in various empty dwelling places and hotels used for officers. They made friends with locals very quickly and one businessman was telling me he owes his life to two of the troopers who pulled him out of the river as a small child. They made themselves very popular in the short time they were here. Although an Irish Regiment there were a surprising number of Scots in it. My late father, an ex-Regular Black Watch Battalion and a Scot, became very friendly with a number who were made welcome to my home on more than one occasion.

'We had a piano which I played and most evenings had a sing-song. A young Irish boy, Paddy Clydesdale, had a very nice tenor voice and often sang Danny Boy and other Irish airs. They held a concert on a Sunday in the local cinema and my friend, who sang, and I played my accordion for that performance. It was to raise money to buy instruments for ones they had lost, whether at Dunkirk or not I am not sure. It was a great success and they had quite clever individual artistes. One I remember played a xylophone. This was only the beginning for me as I played for dances and concerts all through the war years in aid of one benefit or another. I had a very nice letter thanking me for coming especially on a Sunday from one of their officers, Lt Fleury Teulon. At the end of each dance we stood around and sang what I took to be their special song - *Fare Thee Well Inniskilling*. Every Regiment that followed had its own song but I will never forget the Inniskilling one.

'Some of the Artillery Regiments that followed the Inniskillings were to serve in north Africa and became the Desert Rats. But I never heard where the Dragoons went. I believe they went to Northampton from here.

While here their guns and equipment were parked under the main avenue of trees in our park and there were sentries on guard every day. It was quite an experience for the young people in town to walk up this path and have the sentry call out: 'Halt...who goes there?', especially as it was in blackout and to a lot of market town country people it was a very rude awakening to the 39 war. Although we had German aircraft dropping flares on their way to bomb Liverpool - one of these aircraft was brought down five miles away and as I was working as a clerk in the railway offices then, the two that were captured were brought into my office handcuffed to military policemen.

'One of the troopers wrote in my autograph book - Vestigia - Nulla Retrorsum. No Regiment that followed quite came up to the standard the 'Skins' set and I recall fondly the happy short time they were here .'

Mrs KM Robinson, of Llandovery, Carms, wrote: 'I was born and brought up in Builth Wells and well remember the Inniskilling Dragoons being there. Where they were billeted I can't remember - they might have been in the camp at 'Pendre' as this was a permanent camp right through the war. They gave a concert in the cinema there one Sunday night. As there were requests played, my sister (now deceased) and I asked for *My Hero* from *The Chocolate Soldier.* It was beautifully played as a saxaphone solo. A few weeks after that I was called away on war work. At the end of the war I married and went to live in Manchester where I stayed for 41 years. I am now living back in Wales and occasionally I do visit Builth Wells.'

Mrs G Evans, of Brecon, recalled meeting soldiers for musical occasions at a cafe, *Jane's Parlour*, and at Sunday night concerts in the local cinema which was then called The Kino.

Alan Davies, of Builth Wells, remembered the troops engaged on guard duties, on patrols, and on various checkpoints.

Charles Owens of Hereford, who was eight years old at the time, wrote about the movement of troops to Builth Wells and he remembered that with his parents he was subject to a check when proceeding on a day visit to his grandparents.

Throughout the critical four months (July to October), the Royal Navy had also played a most significant supporting role in preventing an invasion since it had commanded any enemy movement in the English Channel and any invasion fleet leaving the ports along the enemy held coast such as Ostend, Dunkirk, Calais and Boulogne.

Neither had the RAF bomber fleet been idle while the enemy had been raiding the UK. British bomber raids had systematically been made, not only on the coastal invasion ports, but also extensively on vital targets in France, Belgium, Holland and Germany.

Air Chief Marshal Sir Hugh Dowding was appointed Commander-in-Chief Fighter Command when it was founded in July 1936. Accordingly he had the unenviable responsibility of defending the UK against the German Luftwaffe during the critical period known as the Battle of Britain.

Dowding, together with Air Vice Marshal Keith Park (No 11 Group), had between them strategically and tactically won the Battle of Britain. Park's tactics directed that the enemy bombers/fighters should be met as far forward as possible by small groups of British fighters, not only to shoot them down, but to prevent the bombing of vital inland targets. However, as the battle was nearing its end, Air Vice Marshal Sholto Douglas, Deputy Chief of the Air Staff, and Air Vice Marshal Leigh-Mallory (No 12 Group) had some different ideas by introducing larger formations of fighters which would destroy more enemy whether vital targets had, or had not been, bombed.

Hardly had Dowding become the great victor of the air battle than he was replaced by Sholto Douglas and Park was replaced by Leigh-Mallory.

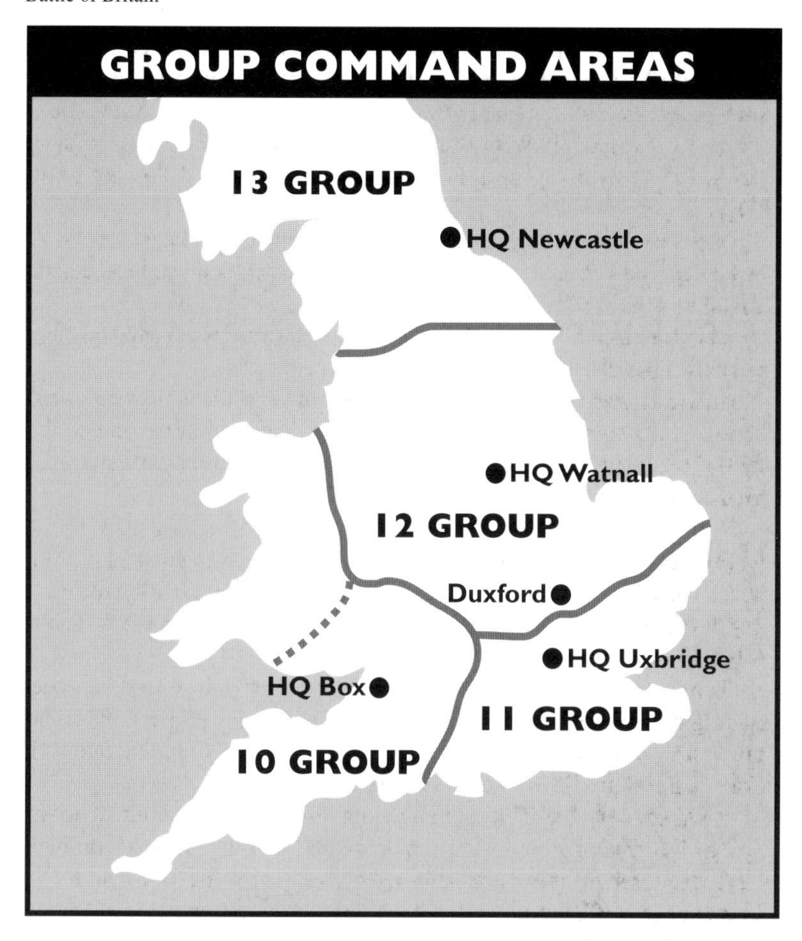

In November 1940 Sir Hugh Dowding left for the United States on a mission for the Ministry of Aircraft Production and he subsequently volunteered to retire from the RAF in 1942.

Although he lived until 1970 his great Battle of Britain victory was not recognised until many years later when, eventually, a statue was erected to his memory in London outside the memorial church of the RAF, St Clement Danes, in the Strand. Never has anyone deserved a higher inscription which reads…

'His wise and prudent judgement and leadership helped to ensure victory against overwhelming odds and thus prevented the loss of the Battle of Britain and probably the whole war'.

Portrait of Air Chief Marshal Sir Hugh Dowding C in C Fighter Command. ***(IWM D 1417)***

AVM Park lost his command shortly after the battle to AVM Leigh-Mallory, an advocate of 'Big Wings', which had by then become fashionable in the Air Ministry as a replacement for what had proved to be the very successful Dowding system.

Magnificent support had been given to Fighter Command by anti-aircraft units, the Observer Corps, balloons, radar, searchlights and radio telephony. ACM Dowding, and his brave fighters, had proved that he was one of the few Great Commanders of WW2 while later, when the bombing offensive became paramount, ACM Sir Arthur Harris also similarly proved himself.

For me there was only one county in England to visit for the 50th anniversary of this most 'exciting' battle - Kent. The tour with Holts' from 7-9 September 1990 included accommodation in a Maidstone hotel; a special visit to Hawkinge Airfield; a display in Folkestone; and two special speakers - Mr James Goodson and Herr Ulrich Steinhilper. One of many specially arranged visits was to the headquarters of the Royal Observer Corps in Folkestone where we were given a very warm welcome. During the wartime years the job of the Observer Corps was to plot the movements of all aircraft, hostile or friendly, passing through British airspace and relay this information to the area defence headquarters. They acted as the eyes and ears of the Royal Air Force, especially throughout those years when the newly-developed radar was still in its infancy and Britain lay open to attack from the German bases in the conquered countries just across the seas. It was on the information provided by these trained spotters that the national air-raid warning system depended.

As the war ended new electronic technology superseded the human eye and ear. The men and women of the Royal Observer Corps are now trained to take immediate action if any enemy were ever to launch a nuclear strike on the UK. The Corps is a unique voluntary organisation with a history of service in peace and war.

A highlight of the tour was a visit to the Kent Battle of Britain Museum at the historic airfield at Hawkinge. The history of Hawkinge as an airfield covered some 50 years from 1912 to 1961. The original wartime buildings now house the world's largest collection of relics and related memorabilia. A team of dedicated volunteers has arranged the displays of over 20 years of aircraft archeology. One of the outstanding exhibits is the Dowding Memorial Hangar, erected by the museum in tribute to ACM Sir Hugh Dowding, Commander-in-Chief RAF Fighter Command.

Together with his famous 'Few' he achieved victory in the greatest air battle in history and by so doing changed the course of WW2. The hangar contains full-sized replicas of the famous Vickers Supermarine Spitfire,

Londoners use underground railways as deep shelters. Photograph shows women and children sheltering in an underground station. 25 September 1940. ***(IWM PL 11627)***

the Hawker Hurricane and the redoubtable Messerschmitt Bf109E as well as many other exhibits such as scarce vehicles of the period. There is also a unique collection of uniforms, insignia and flying kit as worn by both sides in the conflict, together with personal items donated to the museum by pilots, both British and German, who flew in the battle.

While doing the 'rounds' of the very fascinating museum, a mum was explaining the details at the time of the battles, for example, the closeness of the English and French occupied coast, to her young son. Although only about five years old he posed the question: 'Well, who were the baddies?' - mum replied: 'They were!' Later, another boy of about similar age, about to leave the museum, raised the question: 'Well, who did win the Battle of Britain?' Those around him with one voice making sure that he got the message replied: 'We did!'

And inquisitive as these very young boys were is all the more surprising in the light of a recent RAF survey of officers which discovered that they knew little about the RAF's glorious past. The young officers had not even heard of the Battle of Britain and the daring Dambusters raid on the night of 16 May 1943.

If such news had not formed part of an official survey, it would be unbelievable. Seemingly their history knowledge amounted to no more than the recent involvement in the Gulf War. A visit to the Battle of Britain Museum at Hawkinge would unquestionably improve their basic knowledge of the RAF and its golden era.

Subsequently we visited Folkestone where we saw the special airshow for the Battle of Britain Festival to commemorate the legendary aerial conflict of 1940. It was a glorious September day, a lovely blue sky, perfect for an airshow for both those taking part and for the large crowds who were present for this major event along the seafront. As spectators we were able to view the flying from along the upper promenade known as The Leas which acted as an unusually high platform. Among the WW2 aircraft on view were the famous two British fighters - the Spitfire and the Hurricane - which were the two principal aircraft which successfully defended Britain 50 years before. The flying display ran for more than three hours during the afternoon. In addition to the two British fighters, the combat scenes included the German Messerschmitt; a P51 Mustang; and a P47 Thunderbolt.

Other well-known WW2 aircraft also took part - the Mosquito, the Gloster Gladiator and a team of Tiger Moths. The afternoon programme culminated in a massed flypast of the many WW2 fighters which had taken part in this enjoyable, exciting, and most memorable airshow.

As our special guests for the Holts tour we had the rather unusual combination of two former wartime flyers - one an American and one German.

The American officer, Lt Col James Goodson, was rescued as a teenager when sailing aboard the SS Athenia which was torpedoed by a German U-boat on the day Britain and France declared war on Hitler's Germany - 3 September 1939.

Lt Col Goodson described to our party that he was filled with 'a fury against those who use their power with such callous lack of responsibility to heap personal tragedy on the little people who only wanted to live'. The Athenia was a passenger liner bound for Canada with tourists, emigrants, and refugees aboard.

Eventually, he was accepted by the RAF and flew Spitfires over France before becoming a member of the United States air force flying Thunderbolts and Mustangs over Germany.

He was shot down - became a prisoner of war - and when the American forces advanced into Germany, he escaped and was able to rejoin his countrymen.

The German officer, Oberleutnant Ulrich Steinhilper, had seen for himself the chaotic scenes at Calais and Dunkirk following the British evacuation in the summer of 1940. While there was an abundance of all types of abandoned military equipment which they made good use of as the spoils of war, there was a very strict order issued by the German High Command which emphasised that those caught up pillaging any civilian property would be harshly punished. While in the coastal area Ulrich 'acquired' a three-axle Morris weapons carrier which served his squadron well for many years, including service on the Russian front. As a flyer during the Battle of Britain he escorted enemy bombers from attack by British fighters.

Often there were times when the bombers could not find their targets and they were forced to return home by a longer route. When this happened the escorting fighters found that their fuel reserves were insufficient to make the final crossing over the Channel, resulting in many losses by drowning since the odds against survival were very low if baling out into the high waves of a very rough sea. Although not shot down by British fighters in combat, nevertheless these enemy crashes into the sea did increase the total of their losses of aircraft during the battle. Oberleutnant Steinhilper flew throughout the Battle of Britain - was shot down on 27 October 1940 - and was a prisoner of war for six years before his repatriation to Germany.

The Cenotaph in Whitehall ***photo by Phil Mills.***

5TH
ROYAL
INNISKILLING
DRAGOON
GUARDS

This is to inform the Relatives and Friends

of

H. Hollingshead.

that he is Serving his King and Country as a

Soldier

in the

5th Royal Inniskilling Dragoon Guards

5th ROYAL INNISKILLING DRAGOON GUARDS
INNISKILLING
To COMMEMORATE
the Final Parade of the
5th ROYAL INNISKILLING DRAGOON
GUARDS at Paderborn
on the 18th July 1992

De Panne Memorial, Dunkirk - Chapter 3.

Little boats in basin at Dunkirk - Chapter 3.

Hawkinge Museum plaque - Chapter 4.

50th Anniversary flowerbed - Folkestone seafront - Chapter 4.

The famous Spitfire - Chapter 4.

The great Hurricane in desert colours - Chapter 4.

Young ladies at Canadian Cemetery, Hautot-sur-Mer, Dieppe - Chapter 5.

Ceremony at Hautot-sur-Mer - Chapter 5.

Egypt - the pyramids at Cairo - Chapter 6.

El Alamein CWGC - Chapter 6.

The author sitting at General Rommel's desk - Chapter 6.
(Photo Ron Impey)

Above and below: 'In the blue' - the desert at El Alamein - Chapter 6.

El Alamein villas - Chapter 6.

HM The Queen - Maritime Museum, Merseyside - Chapter 7.

The band of the Royal Marines - Chapter 7.

HRH Duke of Edinburgh - Maritime Museum - Chapter 7.

The Royal Yacht Britannia - Chapter 7.

Ceremony outside Amiens prison - Chapter 8. (Photo Nina Beynon)

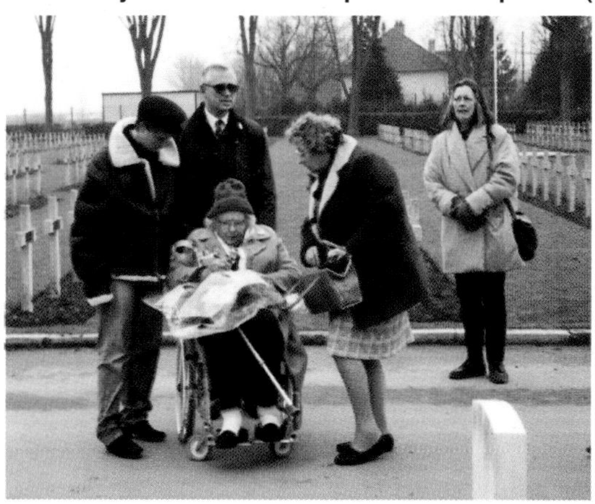

St Pierre CWGC. Mrs Dorothy Pickard with granddaughter, Nicole, Mrs Joan Lambert-Didwell and Col David Storrie - Chapter 8.

Sword beach including wellknown property on the seafront - Chapter 9.

The Queen's arrival at Gold Beach, Arromanches for the 50th anniversary celebrations. She was greeted by a 42-gun salute by the destroyer *Edinburgh* and the assault ship *Intrepid*.- Chapter 9.

At Pegasus bridge, Ron Impey, Leslie and Maisie Bryant - Chapter 9.

North-west Europe campaign - Unit forces signs - Chapter 9.

Presentation of Jubilee medal - Chapter 9.

Remembrance - Arnhem - Chapter 11.

Nijmegen bridge - Chapter 11.

50th anniversary parade and dedication of memorial, Dover seafront - Chapter 12.

RAF memorial on the cliffs at Capel-le-Ferne - Chapter 12.

Old comrades party at Uden - Chapter 13.

Above: Jim Boardman and party at St Odilienberg - Chapter 14.

Left: Anniversary medal from 's-Hertogenbosch - Chapter 13.

5

Canadian raid on Dieppe, France

During the period 1939 to 1945 when Great Britain experienced many crises there was, more often than not, some magnificent support from the many friends within the Commonwealth.

Canada would be high on any such list of countries. At all times throughout WW2 support was forthcoming from the Royal Canadian Navy whose brave men fought for six years in the Battle of the Atlantic; the Royal Canadian Air Force, which controlled the training of more than 130,000 aircrew (50,000 of them pilots) while on land Canadian troops fought many hard battles.

One Army operation by the Canadians which history will never fail to include was the raid on the port of Dieppe in occupied France on 19 August 1942. Having been on a Holts' tour with Maj Richard K Malott (Retd) he generously supplied me with a booklet *The Road to Victory - a History of Canada in the World War*, produced by the Canadian War Museum and Veterans Affairs Canada. The gallant action in the raid on Dieppe is recorded as follows…

'After the fall of France amphibious raids were conducted from Britain against German held targets at places ranging from Norway to France. Canadian troops carried out one of these successfully against coal installations at Spitsbergen, off northern Norway, in August 1941. A year later, on 19 August, the largest raid was attempted at the French port of Dieppe.

Throughout 1942 the Soviet Union, after massive German onslaughts, insisted on Allied action to ease the pressure. Though the British and Americans agreed that the European theatre was decisive, and that relieving action must be taken there, it was also agreed that no invasion of continental Europe was yet feasible. Thus, in July, they decided as an alternative to launch a joint African campaign in the autumn of 1942.

This made it desirable to foster German fears of attack in the west; it was also important to gain experience to assist in planning the great amphibious assault on North-West Europe that had to come. Such were the origins of the Dieppe raid.

The operation on 19 August 1942 was a tactical failure and the cost was high. The main body of troops taking part came from the 2nd Canadian Infantry Division. Of almost 5,000 Canadians who embarked, only 2,210 returned to England.

Close to 1,000 were killed, and 2,000 taken prisoner. Two brigades of the 2nd Canadian Infantry Division took part in the Dieppe raid, the 4th and the 6th. The 1st Army Tank Brigade provided a regiment, the 14th from Calgary, equipped with Churchill tanks.

British commandos carried out attacks on the outer flanks where coastal batteries were set on the cliffs. Landing craft carrying the group that was to operate on the left unluckily ran into a German flotilla on their way to the beach; an exchange of shots alarmed the coastal defences in that sector so that the attack miscarried. On the right, the attack was initially successful. More than half the overall land force was lost, mostly as prisoners. Evacuation ceased about mid-day.

About 70 Canadian naval officers and ratings who had trained in combined operations helped man the 179 landing craft that carried the troops ashore. Many encountered heavy fire. By the time they approached the beaches to re-embark the troops the whole area had become an inferno.

The chief task of the air force was to protect the armada of shipping off Dieppe. Of 74 Allied squadrons assigned, nine were Canadian. The Luftwaffe reacted strongly, shooting down two Allied aircraft for every one it lost. RAF losses (106 aircraft, of which 88 were fighters) were heavier than on any other day of the war; the RCAF lost 13 aircraft, 12 of them fighters.

The Holts' Special Anniversary tour to Dieppe during the period 18 to 20 August 1992 was very well supported by five coaches of travellers and was led by Lt Col Mike Martin.

Wednesday, 19 August, was Dieppe Day, or should I say Canada's Day, as 50 years had passed since the raid on that date in 1942. The highlight was the ceremony at the Canadian War Cemetery, a commemorative ceremony which included addresses by the Minister of Veterans Affairs for Canada and the French Secretary of State for Veterans. Also there was wreath laying by various organisations and finally we had the national anthems of those countries which took part in the raid. A Canadian TA Band played several well-known hymns - only two verses of each because there were quite a few - *O God our help in ages past, Eternal Father strong to save, Onward Christian soldiers, Lead kindly light, Nimrod, Abide with Me and The day thou gavest.*

After the raid on Dieppe, 19 August 1942. Dead and wounded beside a captured Churchill tank. ***(IWM HU 1903)***

The Canadian Minister of Veterans Affairs, in a speech, said: 'It was Winston Churchill who said Dieppe occupies a place of its own in the story of the war. That is certainly true in Canada. Dieppe indeed occupies a place of its own in our history and in our hearts. The raid continues to inspire hopes and research. Just a few hours of battle that led to 50 years of debate and controversy. Small wonder that all we have to do is to look at these rows of graves and realise that not a corner of Canada was spared. Dieppe touched us all and still does. We are not really sure how and why such a disaster was allowed to happen. Was Dieppe part of some great geo-political strategy? Was it necessary to gather such a payment on battles far into the future? We all have our beliefs but this is not the place for such matters. This is a time to bless the memories of those who were killed landing on these shores 50 years ago. This is the occasion to pay tribute to the unquenchable spirit of those who refused to be broken by the indignities of prisoner-of-war life.

'Canadians recently commemorated the 75th anniversary of the Battle of Vimy Ridge, a battle which inspired a nation. The soldiers of Dieppe were worthy successors of those Canadians who won on Vimy Ridge. Again in 1942 the Canadians were asked to carry the attack; once again Canadians were ordered to assault formidable enemy defences; the tragedy is that whereas our Vimy troops had unrelenting artillery support our Dieppe troops had to trust to stealth and surprise.

'Today though our thoughts are with those brave men who attempted the incomprehensive; this was a test of valour and to the horror of war.

'There are too many instances of individual courage to detail here but mention should be made of the two who won VCs. We are honoured today by the presence of Lt Col Cecil Merritt, a commander who led by himself and gave fresh meaning to the expression 'coolness under fire' as he led the South Saskatchewans ashore. Then there was the late Rev John Weir Foote, a man of the cloth, who coolly nurtured the wounded and the dying of the Royal Hamilton Light Infantry for eight hours before leaving the landing craft and possible safety to surrender and be with his troops.

Dieppe saw all our three forces in action and they all performed well under these desperate conditions. Sailors operated under a storm of fire and rescued those stranded on the beaches. In vicious air battles our pilots incurred many losses supporting the ground troops.

'67 pilots and 106 Allied aircraft were lost on that day. Let us also use this occasion, comrades to express our admiration for our Allies who are here today. They were the matchless British commandos and Royal Marines. With us, too of course, were representatives of the American Rangers who came in with 50 troops. The Royal Navy lived up to its renown, while the RAF was at its best along with the United States, New Zealand, Czechoslovakian, French, Belgian and Polish squadrons. Despite all this combined effort, 19 August 1942 was our costliest day of the war. Some 5,000 Canadians left for Normandy - only 2,200 returned to England. We had 900 fatal casualties and nearly 2,000 more were POWs - chains and death marches and loss of liberty - for nearly three years. As the years passed more and more evidence of the lessons learnt at Dieppe did indeed save many lives on D-Day almost two years later. I accept the verdict of Dwight D Eisenhower, a man with no Dieppe secrets to burden him with said: 'Except for Dieppe we would have been lacking much of the specialist equipment and much of the knowledge, much needed for the invasion'. Let us also remember the people of this area in occupied France. The raid indicated to them that they were not forgotten and that one day freedom would return to the Western Front.

And this is why long into the future Canadians will still be visiting Dieppe and coming away with an increasing pride of their own country. Today we salute their spirit and their courage on that day - 19 August 1942. Immediately after the speeches - in English and French - there were prayers, *Amazing Grace* played by the band, the exhortation, the Last Post and Reveille.

Following the ceremony at the cemetery at Hautot-sur-Mer our party returned to Dieppe for a special unveiling in Canada Square and where, in beautiful sunshine, large crowds had already gathered. This was very much a naval ceremony arranged by the Dieppe Veterans and Prisoners of War Association to commemorate the raid. The words on the plaque, in both English and French, read as follows: 'This plaque is dedicated to the proud memory of all who fought at Dieppe on 19 August 1942, and of the citizens of the town who willingly gave succour to those who came ashore. Erected by their comrades from the Naval force engaged in the Dieppe raid which suffered over 550 killed, missing or wounded.

Three VCs (Victoria Cross) were awarded for bravery at Dieppe. As previously mentioned two of them to Canadians - Lt Col Charles Cecil Ingersoll Merritt, Commander of the South Saskatchewan Regiment, Canadian Infantry Corps and The Rev John Weir Foote.

Lt Col Merritt was born in Vancouver, Canada, on 10 November 1908. The London Gazette dated 2 October 1942 gave a brief account of the deed...'On 19 August 1942 at Dieppe, France, Lt Col Merritt's unit had to advance across a bridge swept by very heavy machine gun, mortar and artillery fire. The first parties had mostly been destroyed but the colonel rushed forward and personally led the survivors of at least four parties, in turn, across the bridge, and then led them in successful attacks on German pill-boxes. Although twice wounded he continued to direct the unit's operations and having collected bren and tommy guns, prepared a defensive position to cover the withdrawal from the beach.'

As will be seen from the map of the Dieppe operation, the South Saskatchewan Regiment was involved in the landing at Pourville, Green Beach. The Rev John Weir Foote remained with the wounded and dying and became a prisoner of war with the Royal Hamilton Light Infantry. The operation map shows that his Regiment was involved in the landings in the centre of Dieppe, the White and Red beaches.

'On 19 August 1942 Capt Foote coolly and calmly during the eight hours of battle walked about collecting the wounded, saving many lives by his gallant efforts and inspiring those around him by his example. At the end of this gruelling time he climbed from the landing craft that was to have taken him to safety and deliberately walked into the German position in order to be taken prisoner so that he could be a help to those men who would be in captivity until the end of the war'.

The British officer awarded a Victoria Cross was T/Capt (later Col) Patrick Anthony Porteous of the Royal Regiment of Artillery. He was born at Abbottabad, North-West Frontier, India on 1 January 1918. The London Gazette dated 2 October 1942 gave a brief account of his deed... 'On 19

August 1942 at Dieppe in France, Capt Porteous was liaison officer between two detachments whose task was to attack the heavy coast defence guns. During the initial assault Capt Porteous, with the smaller detachment, was shot through the hand, but he nevertheless disarmed and killed his assailant, thereby also saving the life of a British sergeant. In the meantime the two officers of the other detachment had been killed and the troop sergeant major seriously wounded, so Capt Porteous, in the face of withering fire, dashed across open ground to take command and led the men in a successful charge against the enemy, when he was severely wounded for the second time. He continued to the final objective, however, but eventually collapsed after the last gun had been destroyed'.

Col Porteous was our special guest on Holts' tour and he gave a detailed description of the landing by the troops of No 4 Commando on Orange Beach in the area of Quiberville, Vasterival and Varengeville-sur-Mer, as indicated on the Operation map.

The troops involved at Dieppe were mostly Canadian but there were about 1,000 British Commandos involved in the landing whose task was to destroy coastal batteries. The operation in the west by No 4 Commando was most successful, destroying the gun battery at Varengeville and fortunately these troops made a safe withdrawal. However, the operation in the east unfortunately encountered a small German convoy - there was a sea fight which alerted the coastal defences - enabling the enemy to scatter No 3 Commando who were quickly overwhelmed. Only a small party of 20 of this attacking force succeeded in containing the defences of the gun battery at Berneval for a very vital period of time before they were evacuated.

On a glorious summer afternoon of this memorable Dieppe anniversary day, the Holts' party had free time to stroll along the sea front. Opportunities were taken for conversation with the many groups of Canadian ex-servicemen and on occasions we participated in the various commemoration ceremonies being held by several groups of veterans and their representatives. This great day came to an end with a grand firework display along the sea front. Seemingly everyone in Dieppe and the surrounding areas had decided that this was an event in their lives which should not be missed. Inclement weather spoilt our final day. A visit was made to Blue Beach at Puys where the Royal Regiment of Canada met a violent German defence and to Yellow Beach at Berneval where the British Commandos went ashore. Because of the bad weather we made an early return to the town which gave us time to visit the Hotel de Ville to collect a valuable souvenir - a special brochure of this very special anniversary.

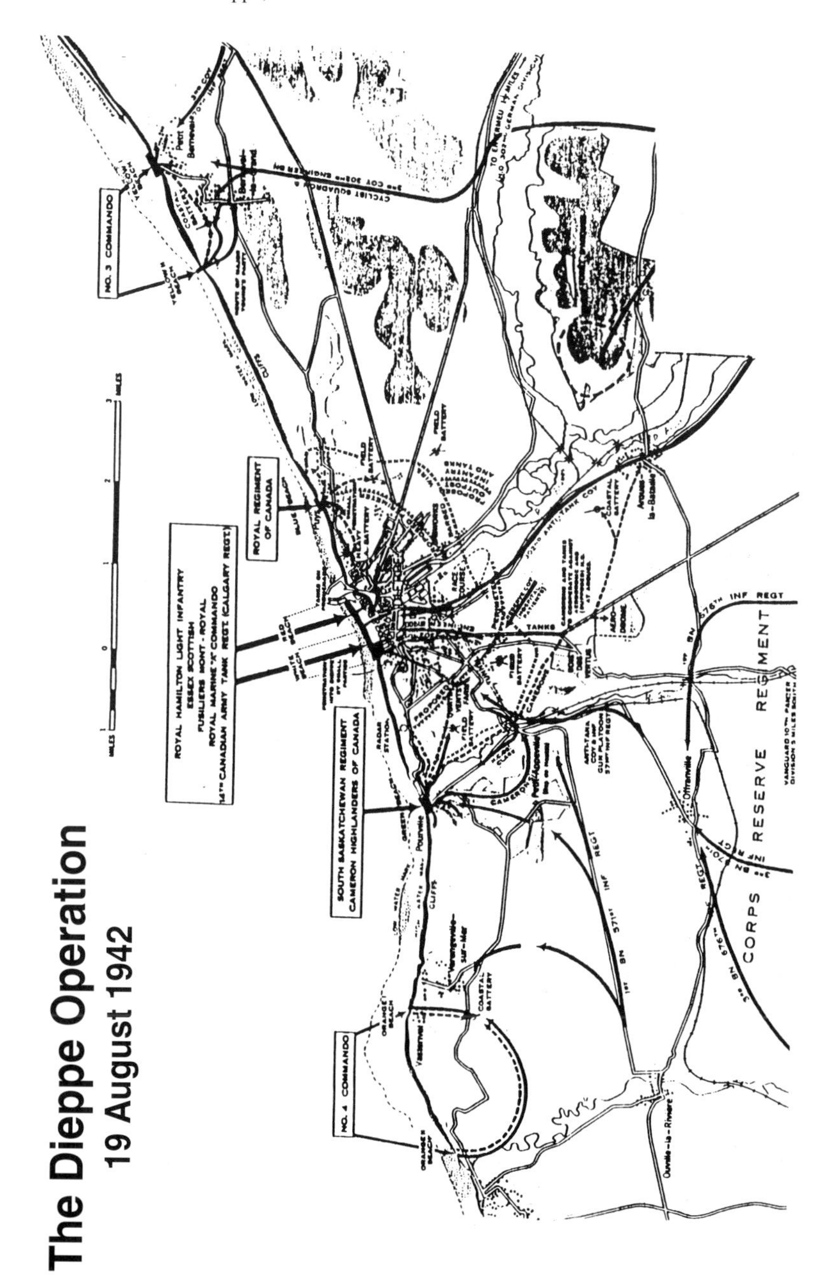
The Dieppe Operation
19 August 1942
NO. 3 COMMANDO
YELLOW I BEACH
YELLOW II BEACH
ROYAL REGIMENT OF CANADA
BLUE BEACH
ROYAL HAMILTON LIGHT INFANTRY
ESSEX SCOTTISH
FUSILIERS MONT-ROYAL
ROYAL MARINE "A" COMMANDO
14TH CANADIAN ARMY TANK REGT (CALGARY REGT)
RED BEACH
WHITE BEACH
SOUTH SASKATCHEWAN REGIMENT
CAMERON HIGHLANDERS OF CANADA
GREEN BEACH
Pourville
RADAR STATION
CLIFFS
NO. 4 COMMANDO
ORANGE I BEACH
ORANGE II BEACH
COASTAL BATTERY
Varengeville-sur-Mer
Vasterival
Ouville-la-Rivière
Offranville
Arques-la-Bataille
FIELD BATTERY
TANKS
AERODROME
RACE COURSE
CORPS RESERVE REGIMENT
VANGUARD 10TH PANZER DIVISION 5 MILES SOUTH
1ST BN 571ST INF REGT
3RD BN 676TH INF REGT
1ST BN 676TH INF REGT
Petit Berneval
Berneval-le-Grand
MILES

6

The Battle of El Alamein, North Africa

Although the UK had declared war on Germany on 3 September 1939 the North African campaign was fought initially against a large force of Italians who had declared war on the UK on 10 June 1940.

Shortly afterwards they forced our troops out of British Somaliland, they crossed into Egypt, occupied Sollum and captured Sidi Barrani. Before the end of 1940 the British had recaptured Sidi Barrani and Sollum and 36,000 Italians had become prisoners of war. In March 1941, however, the German Afrika Corps arrived in Tripoli and thereafter with their strong Panzer forces generally had the upper hand for much of the year, capturing Benghazi on 3 April. On 10 April the British Army withdrew on Tobruk but the enemy forces encircled it on 13 April 1941. Two days before, the Germans had taken prisoner 2,000 British soldiers, including three generals. Two weeks later Sollum fell to the enemy. Afterwards there was much 'to-ing and froing' in battle until mid-1942. The North African campaign had seen several changes of command in the Allied forces throughout the previous two years culminating in the appointment of Gen BL Montgomery as Commander of the Allied Eighth Army on 18 August 1942. Before Alamein he expressed the view that '...the battle which is about to begin will be one of the decisive battles of history'. The following historical note gives some of the important events at that critical time and also mentions several of the personalities who were closely associated with those events.

In early July 1942, the Eighth Army stood at bay on the Alamein Line, the last barrier to the Axis powers gaining the Suez Canal. The two exhausted armies faced each other and after some ten days of attempts by Gen Rommel to penetrate the Alamein position, a stalemate developed and the battlefield stabilised, with patrolling, reconnaissance and development of minefields the order of the day.

At this time the Eighth Army could not understand why it had been so decisively beaten at the Gazala Line in June. The long withdrawal to Alamein had been largely conducted by an amalgam of units into various columns and morale was low.

Lt Gen BL Montgomery, new commander of the Eighth Army in the Middle East, photographed in Egypt after his arrival by air. *(IWM CM 3327)*

The Prime Minister, Winston Churchill, visited Cairo in early August and very soon changes were made in the High Command. Gen Alexander assumed command of the Middle East and Gen Montgomery the Eighth Army.

Montgomery assessed the situation very quickly and made it clear that there would me no withdrawal from Alamein, at the same time ordering up the newly arrived divisions to Alamein. Overnight, morale soared and confidence was reborn throughout the Eighth Army.

At the end of August, Rommel launched his expected offensive to reach the Suez Canal. The attack came exactly as predicted by Montgomery and Rommel's Panzer divisions suffered heavy losses against prepared positions at Alam Halfa, and from heavy bombing by the Royal Air Force. After a few days, Rommel broke off the battle and his last chance of capturing the Suez Canal had gone.

Now began the preparation for the major battle ahead, the logistic build-up, training, deception measures and rehearsals were all necessary before Gen Montgomery was ready, as he said, to 'hit the Afrika Korps for six right out of North Africa.'

Montgomery predicted a dogfight of several days and this started at 2200hrs on the night of 23 October 1942, with an immense artillery barrage which could be heard as far away as Alexandria. Under cover of this barrage, sappers breached the minefields and then the infantry and armour of British, Australian, New Zealand, South African and Indian Divisions closed with the enemy.

The dogfight did indeed last for 12 days and it was 4 November before the Eighth Army finally broke through along the Sidi Abdel Rahman track south of Tel el Eisa, and began the pursuit into Libya through to Tunisia and the final surrender of the Afrika Korps.

It was not until 23 January 1943 that Tripoli was reached. The Axis forces stubbornly held the line at Mareth in Tunisia in some of the most bitter fighting in the desert campaign. They inflicted 10,000 casualties on Allied forces which had landed with Operation Torch in French North Africa on 8 November 1942. Eventually Allied troops overwhelmed the enemy who surrendered on 7 May 1943, a quarter of a million troops becoming prisoners of war. By 12 May resistance by Axis troops in North Africa had ceased.

The Holts' 50th Anniversary tour to El Alamein commenced very much like a tour with an 'ordinary' holiday group. Having assembled at London Heathrow we flew by Egyptair to Cairo where, in the late evening after a short journey, we arrived at the Mena House Hotel which is set at the base

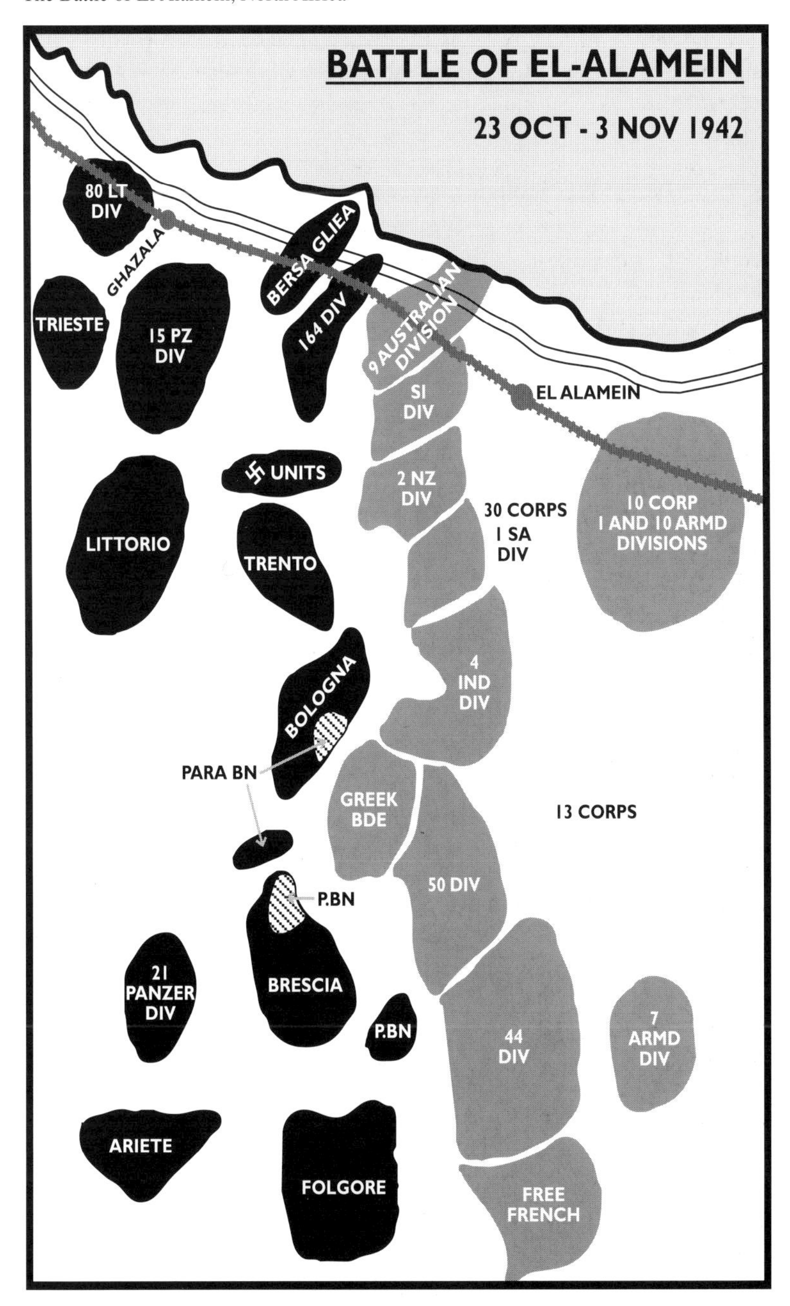
BATTLE OF EL-ALAMEIN
23 OCT - 3 NOV 1942
80 LT DIV
GHAZALA
BERSA GLIEA
164 DIV
TRIESTE
15 PZ DIV
9 AUSTRALIAN DIVISION
SI DIV
EL ALAMEIN
UNITS
2 NZ DIV
30 CORPS
1 SA DIV
10 CORP
1 AND 10 ARMD DIVISIONS
LITTORIO
TRENTO
4 IND DIV
BOLOGNA
PARA BN
GREEK BDE
13 CORPS
P.BN
50 DIV
21 PANZER DIV
BRESCIA
P.BN
44 DIV
7 ARMD DIV
ARIETE
FOLGORE
FREE FRENCH

of the Great Pyramids. During the next two days we did the usual sightseeing which included visits to the Egyptian Antiquities Museum where we saw treasures from the tomb of Tutankhamun, the Pyramids, Sphinx, Papyrus Institute, the Citadel and Mosque, Sadat's tomb, the bazaar and the Sound and Light Show.

The visit to the Antiquities Museum reminded me of a little story about an American who arrived in London some years ago when there was a Tutankhamun Exhibition in town. It must have been when things were prosperous for Americans since he immediately hailed a taxi to Tutankhamun. The driver sped away and after a short time ended his journey and requested the fare. The American alighted and being rather puzzled enquired: 'Now, where is the exhibition?' whereupon the taxi driver answered: 'I know of no exhibition on Tooting Common'. Tut! Tut!

After two delightfully interesting pre-battlefield days in Cairo, the party in 11 coaches went on its way into the desert to El Alamein - the battle area, the Mecca of the tour. The day-long journey included a mini-break at a rest house and a longer break in Alexandria for a buffet lunch. It was while making this journey that our party throughout the tour was given the protection of the police and/or the military by the Egyptian authorities, it being considered necessary following the death of a British tourist by extremists while riding in an open lorry on an overland safari trip in the south of the country. We travelled on, seemingly endlessly, only an occasional property near the roadside, sometimes a handful of brick huts, but always the desert and more desert.

Eventually as dusk fell we arrived in the El Alamein area where our party had two locations, ours was beside the azure sea, the Alamein Beach Hotel, a welcome oasis if ever there was one in this vast desert. Our villa was within a stone's throw of the Mediterranean sea - enjoyed by many - the rollers of which have long been remembered as they crept along the shore at dawn towards the villas.

The first day at El Alamein was 'battle day' the reason why we had made the long, very long, journey of a lifetime to see for ourselves the area of this battle about which Prime Minister John Major had told veterans at a reception: '…that the battle half a century ago would still be remembered 500 years from now, had it not been for the people who fought and won at Alamein, I would not be standing here tonight as Prime Minister of a free country. When you look back through the whole catalogue of battles from Agincourt and beyond, in that catalogue Alamein will be firmly placed. It deserves to be on that list and will always remain on that list. Truly it can be said to those who fought here that they will not be forgotten. They

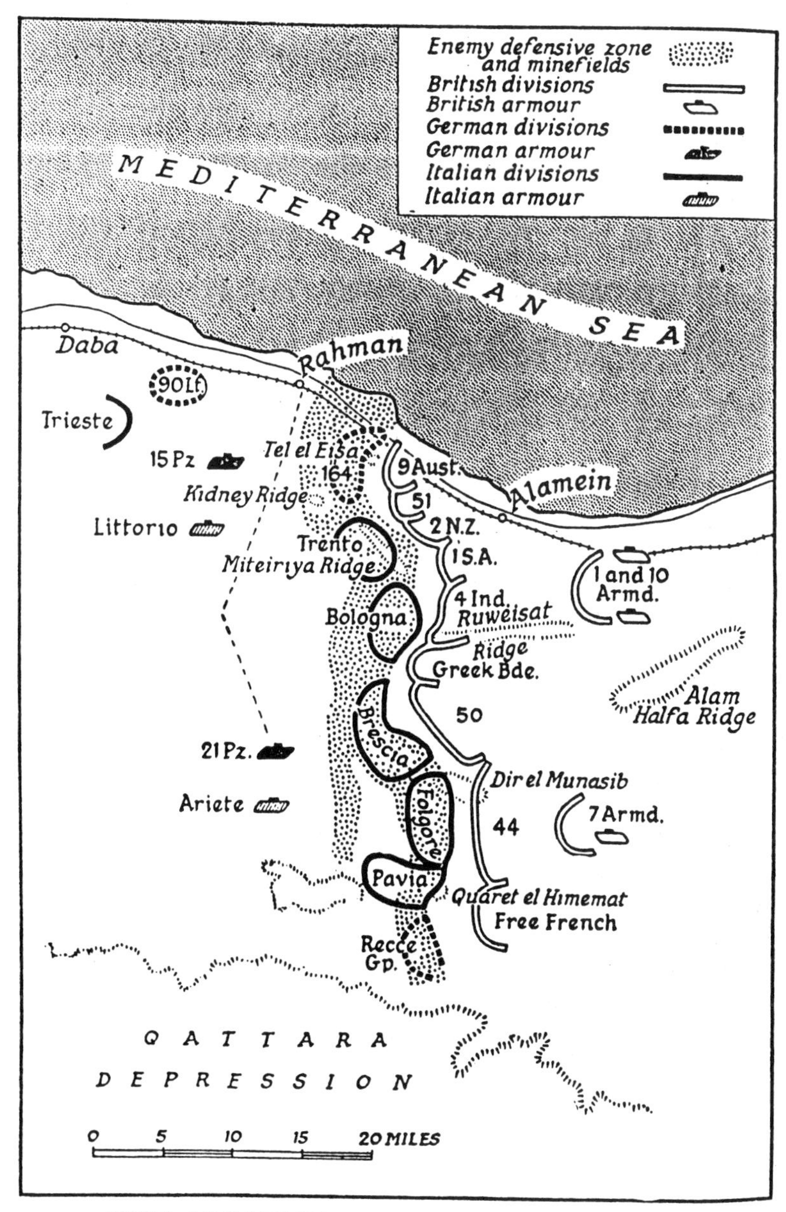

THE ALAMEIN FRONT: OCT. 23, 1942

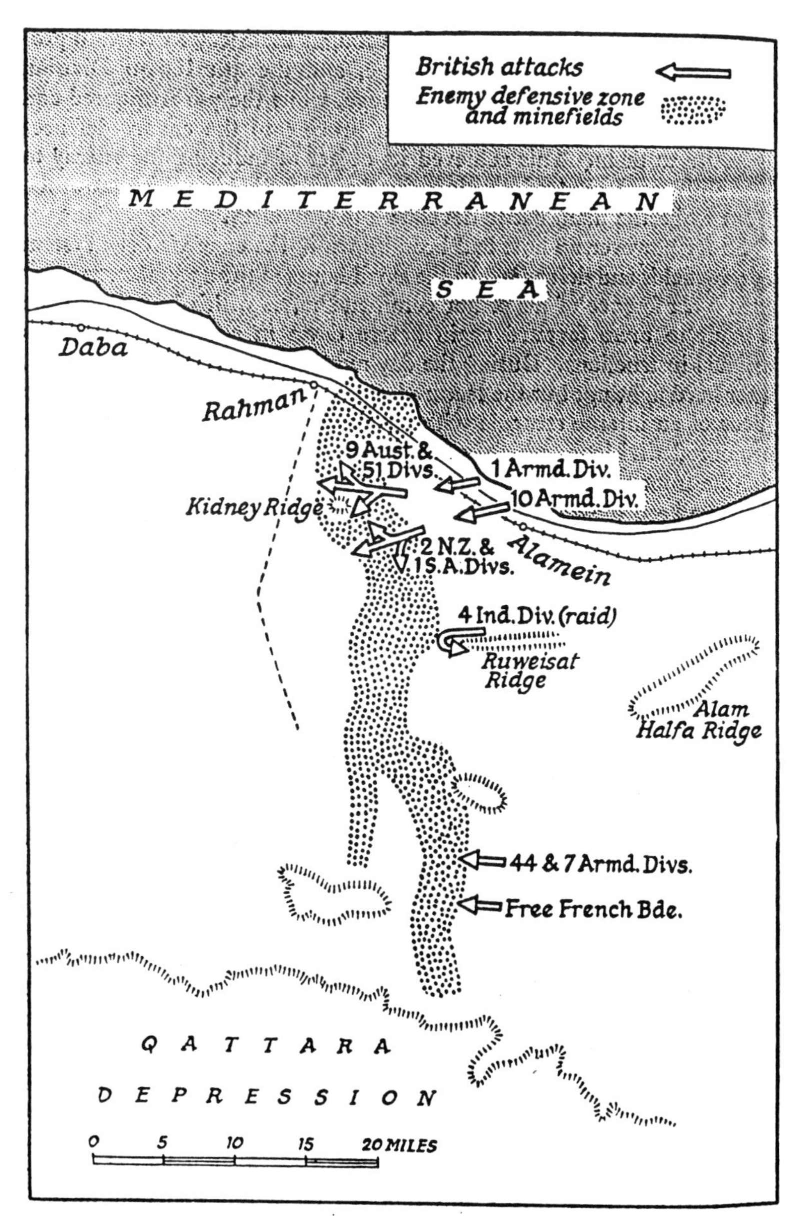

ALAMEIN: THE ATTACK

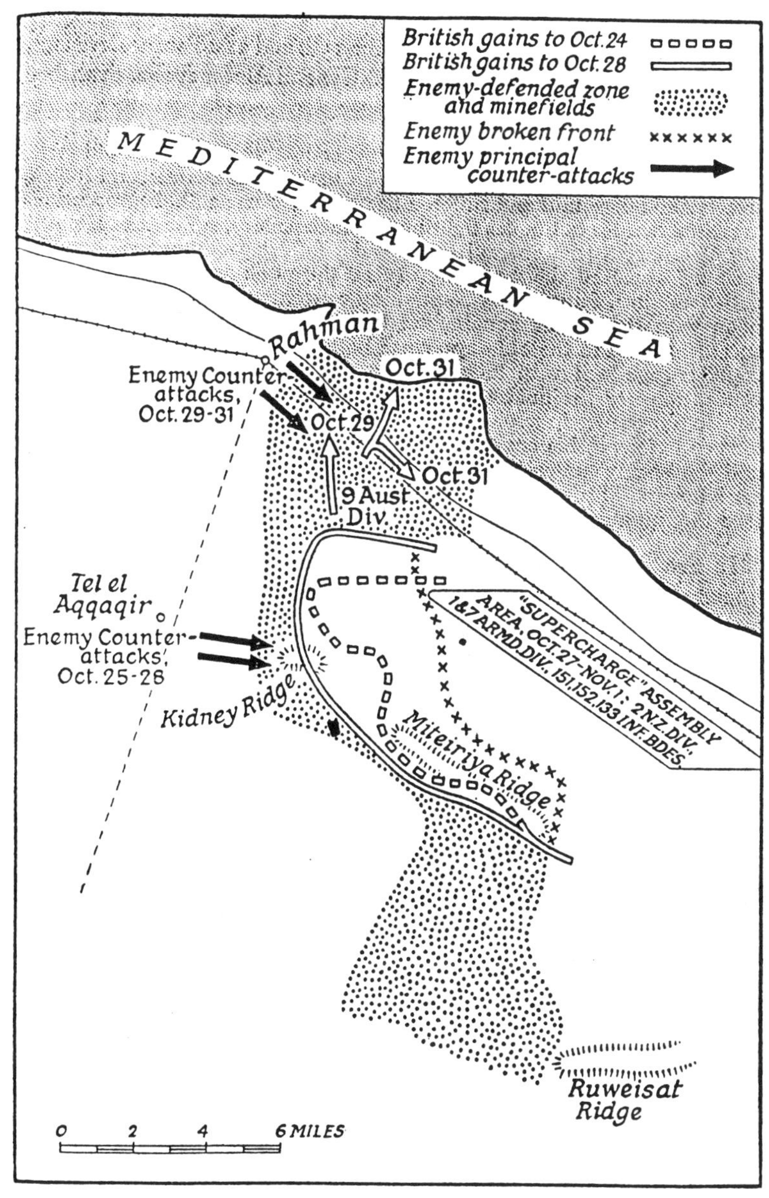

ALAMEIN: THE BREAK-IN

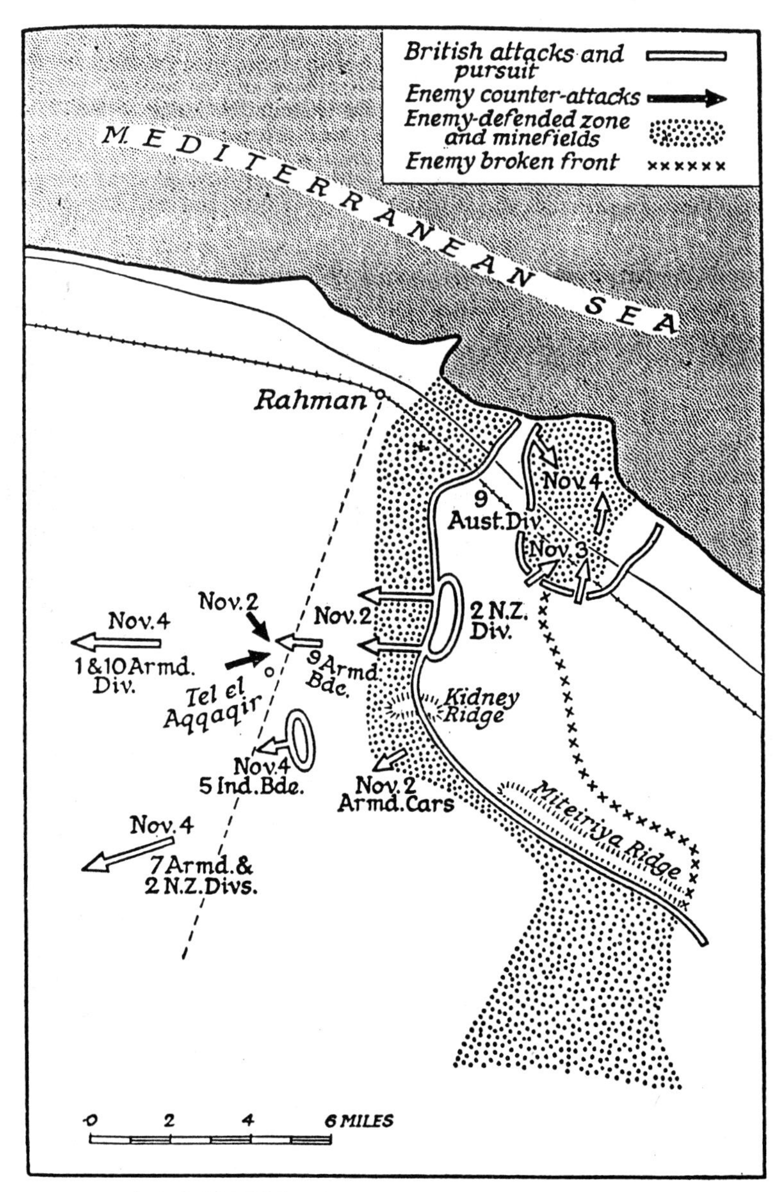

ALAMEIN : THE BREAK-THROUGH

One of Britain's surprise weapons which are taking a big part in the present battle - the Sherman tanks. They have a 75mm gun mounted in the turret and a high turn of speed. Here a number of Shermans are seen proceeding towards the battle front. *(IWM E 18971)*

deserve to be remembered and they will always be remembered.

'The victory in the desert had a place, a firm place, in our history for not only did it ensure our own freedom but also that Europe would be free.'

After an early breakfast on this day we were quickly on our way 'up the blue' for the experience of the area of battle. Our very special transport was air conditioned - appreciated by all - and we quickly found ourselves on some little-used tracks, having as our guide a local Bedouin together with our police/military escort in close attendance. As expected we were soon in 'No man's land', in the desert, and more desert, with only bits of scrub here and there. The colour of the sand was almost white and so light it almost resembled dust, nothing at all like 'the golden sands of Bognor Regis'.

At the time of our visit the weather conditions were most favourable - a bright sunny day, a clear blue sky, and very little breeze to disturb the powdery sand. To think of the conditions for the Eighth Army troops half a century before was not easy. The choking dust during the Normandy Campaign reminded some of us that the movement of tanks across this battle area, creating large clouds of sand, together with the noise of massed heavy artillery and light guns, would contribute to a deafening and uncomfortable experience for all those taking part in this epic assault on the very formidable Axis positions.

Maj Tonie Holt - our leader - had done his homework in depth and gave an absorbing description of the great battle indicating the positions of the Eighth Army and the whereabouts of the enemy at the time. A little to the north was the 'Med' - to the south was the Quattara Depression. In between, extensively defended by the enemy, was the area for the fight, the nearby Ruweisat Ridge and Miterya Ridge, where Gen Montgomery predicted a dogfight.

Gen Auchinleck, who had made the successful stand in the first battle of El Alamein, suffered from political intervention and was removed from command but, as a 'new broom', it much favoured Gen Montgomery who took over when the Eighth Army had been replenished for the vital battle. America had supplied several hundred Sherman tanks which were more powerful than the Crusaders and Matildas then in use, while the two-pounder anti-tank gun was replaced by the six-pounder, a much more effective weapon against enemy tanks.

El Alamein, although considered to be the last point of defence for Alexandria and Cairo, had become the first point of a most successful campaign which in six months removed the Axis powers from the whole of North Africa.

Gen Montgomery's initial plan was delayed until the end of October 1942 to give adequate time in the preparation for a battle he realised he must win. The plan was to attack in two sectors, in the north and in the south, with the main thrust near the coastline in the north while in the south the army formations and the 'dummies' would be part of a deception plan to prevent Axis troop movements to the area of battle. So successful were these plans that the enemy was much deceived.

In the Eighth Army's general plan of the battle 30 Corps was to open a bridgehead through the minefield and then for 10 Corps Armour to pass through this gap. On a front of nine miles there would be the fighting and administrative troops of six divisions.

The attack itself was preceded by a ferocious moving artillery barrage behind which infantry assaults were made through a mine infested area, to be closely followed by armoured formations. Although some progress was made initially, particularly by the Australians near the coastal area, the enemy's defence held enough to prevent a breakthrough. However, Monty quickly regrouped his forces and with a similar renewed attack by artillery, infantry, and armour, the enemy was overwhelmed.

The weight of this second attack was supported by the RAF who devastated the Afrika Corps not only in the desert battle area but also during the many weeks of the Allied advance along the North Africa coast. The Navy too had played an effective part in the campaign in the movement of troops and military equipment to Egypt and North Africa despite, at times, having suffered some appreciable losses.

The Axis forces never recovered from their defeat at El Alamein after a battle which subsequent events proved was the turning point in the Allied victory in WW2.

On our visit into this inhospitable area of desert we discussed with friends our thoughts of the battle during the latter days of October 1942. Those who were there had their memories, vivid memories, while most of us had deep thoughts hoping that our imagination would suffice.

The British, supported by Australian, New Zealand, South African, and Indian troops, had gained their first victory after more than three years of war; while for Germany and the Axis powers who had hitherto been all-conquering over many countries militarily and diplomatically, this was Hitler's first defeat, a defeat which stopped the enemy from capturing Egypt and the Middle East oilfields and also preserved much of our Armed forces from annihilation which enabled them to pursue the tasks of assaulting Sicily, Italy, and North West Europe.

As we left this vast desert - this historical battlefield - unlike many of the WW1 battlefields often with their trenches and perhaps 'pieces of iron', this visit to such a momentous site could well have been a visit almost anywhere inland and away from the coast.

Everything around us was most peaceful, almost silent, with very little vegetation, and no sign of animal life. Indeed we were unquestionably 'out in the blue' and it was encouraging to have our Bedouin guide to ensure our return without mishap. Tonie might not have made it!

Moving away from the battlefield area itself we were reminded of the assault support services. Since our coach party was listed as REME (Royal Electrical and Mechanical Engineers) we were fortunate in having among us some veterans of the Corps whose arrangements for the tour had been made by Brig Martyn Clark. He had told us of the formation of REME, remarkably on 1 October 1942, only a few days before the commencement of the battle, so it too was now commemorating a 50th anniversary. The very vital contribution made by the Corps in clearing the Axis forces from North Africa was recognised by Gen Montgomery who recorded that... 'it was very largely the high efficiency of the repair and recovery organisation which enabled us to retain our superiority in armour throughout the fighting'.

Just prior to the commencement of the battle Brig LH Howard-Jones (DDME) had issued some wise advice to Corps personnel: 'Keep up the discipline and training standard in your unit; keep the heaviest reserve of cigarettes and so on in your canteen during operations since men will appreciate them if supplies break down; ensure that all men know how to use a sun compass to steer clear of minefields; look after any attached personnel as your own and get the latest detail about the war to pass on to your men'. All worth remembering in a battle situation.

Not surprisingly on this tour there was time for 'remembrance'. Our first ceremony was at the German Cemetery, a fortress-like memorial built on a high hill overlooking the sea. An International Remembrance Service is held each year alternatively at the German and British cemeteries. At the time of our tour it happened to be at the German one so we attended an early morning service there.

Afterwards we attended our second Remembrance Service, a special one for the 50th Anniversary at El Alamein CWGC. The cemetery lies on the slopes of a gentle hill within sight of the sea and with views for miles across the desert, an area which cost so many Allied lives. A gravel path led to the cemetery and our first view of this oasis of Remembrance was the thousands upon thousands of rock-hewn tombstones standing in straight rows amidst a fenced garden, marking the resting place of some 7,000 men. At the centre of the cemetery is the stone of Remembrance to the 18,000 soldiers who died in the desert campaign. During the service wreaths were laid by HRH the Duke of Kent on behalf of the Queen and by the former Prime Minister, John Major, whose reading of a lesson included the words: 'Greater love hath no man than this, that he lay down his life for his friends'.

More than 13,000 Eighth Army soldiers were killed in the decisive battle which led to the rout of Gen Rommel's Axis forces and marked the turning point in the war.

Among the graves was that of Lt Gen 'Strafer' Gott who was killed in an air crash on the way to Cairo in early August 1942. At the time this fine desert soldier was to become Eighth Army Commander but fate proved otherwise.

Since those in high command may not always develop similar plans one is tempted to think that the North African campaign may not have proceeded as it did if he, rather than Gen Montgomery, had been Commander. Leaving the cemetery with our friends we had only one thought: *At the going down of the sun and in the morning we will remember them.*

Included in the tour itinerary was time for commemoration when in the presence of HRH the Duke of Kent we were invited by Her Britannic Majesty's Ambassador to attend a reception at the British Consulate in Alexandria in honour of the veterans of the Battle of Alamein.

The former Prime Minister, John Major, was also present and, inter alia, he reminded the veterans that the battle took place before he was born so his, and subsequent generations, had good cause to be grateful to them. Without the veterans he would not have been Prime Minister of a free country.

As was to be expected, the occasion permitted many old soldiers and ex-servicemen who were visiting the battlefield for the first time in 50 years, an opportunity to seek out comrades who with them had fought and defeated Rommel's Afrika Corps while in the 'bloom of youth'! There was much for the veterans to recall of that vital period in their lives, whereas for many of us it was politic to be good listeners. We had been most fortunate in commemorating with them a most famous battle and we fully appreciated we were among the most convivial of company.

But time flies at such events and our time came to leave Alexandria for our return of some 40 miles to our hotel at El Alamein.

We had a splendid evening in lovely surroundings - had a safe return journey - dinner on our late return to the hotel - and, being comfortably tired, went to our villas and bed!

An innovation on this memorable tour was a 'sandtable' exercise which was conducted by Col Mike Martin. The scene of the battle was described supported by model tanks and other markers. The support given by the RAF, by the Navy, the success of the Deception Plan and the significant contribution of ULTRA - which told us everything of the enemy - were highlighted.

There were many contributions made by fellow travellers who took part in the battle, including the experiences of a gunner, a sapper and military police. A German officer, who at the time was serving with the Panzers, had joined us for the 'exercise' and he confirmed that the Deception Plan had completely deceived them.

Dr Bernard Williams was with a field surgical unit (FSU) attached to a casualty clearing station (CCS) and he recalled his experiences of 50 years ago.

Subsequently, he sent to me a summary of his adventures, a most absorbing account, which describes more fully the events at the time.

Fifty years on: The Battle of Alamein, recollections of a surgeon

'For my six years in World War Two as a military surgeon fate was kind to me. Though I spent five and a half of them in operational areas I came through unscathed, except for a hyphaema from a tennis ball, a carbuncle on my bottom, sandfly fever, dysentery, and a black eye from a champagne cork on VE-Day. I was also lucky in that my experience of forward surgery was during advances, not retreats, when conditions were far more difficult and there was also a danger of capture. My memories of those eventful times are still vivid, and those of the desert war remain the most exciting of my life.

'Alamein marked a turning point in the war. Churchill said: 'Before Alamein we never had a victory. After Alamein we never had a defeat.' This statement was not quite accurate, as in 1940 two Italian armies had been captured, the first in Eritrea, and the second in Egypt and Libya by the Army of the Nile under Gen Wavell. In this latter campaign I was a member of a surgical team and had my first experience of forward surgery under desert conditions. Then casualties were mercifully low, as there had been early surrender after relatively little fighting.

'A new phase of desert warfare came into being at Alamein. Before it, the fighting had resembled the war at sea in that it had been between mobile units (artillery, tanks, and a variety of other armoured vehicles). The battle itself was more in the nature of a set piece in the World War One pattern, but before describing it let me recall the events leading up to it…

'Rommel had chased the Eighth Army back to a line from the Mediterranean in the north near Alamein and the Quattara Depression in the south. The depression was impassable to tanks. The front had stabilised in July 1942. Gen Montgomery had taken over command from General Auchinleck. On 30 August Rommel made an attempt to break through in the south and turn the Allied flank. This move had been foreseen and he was repulsed with considerable losses at the Battle of Alam Halfa, which was a curtain raiser.

A rough outline of the medical arrangements at Alamein was as follows. Behind the fighting formations which had their own regimental medical officers were the field ambulances, whose prime tasks were the evacuation of casualties to surgical centres, usually located in casualty clearing stations where emergency surgery to render the wounded fit for travel back to base hospitals in the Nile Delta was undertaken. Alexandria was some 40 miles away, and Cairo about 120.

The 8th Army commander watches the battle from the turret of the Grant tank in which he travelled. ***(IWM E 18980)***

'As a result of previous desert experience, field surgical units (Middle East Pattern) had been evolved. Each carried two officers (a surgeon and an anaesthetist) and seven other ranks, including a theatre assistant, a clerk and two drivers. A three-ton lorry and a staff car carried all personnel and tented theatre equipment. The units were highly mobile and designed for attachment to CCSs or FAs, larger units which provided services and beds. Mine was No 6 FSU. We joined a CCS behind the north of the line in mid-August, before Alam Halfa.

'No 10 CCS was in a group together with similar units from the New Zealand and Australian armies. They were situated not far from the desert railway between the Burg el Arab and El Alamein railway stations a mile or two from the sea. By far the largest medical group was in the south.

'At that time a certain chivalry existed in the desert war, both sides respecting each other as fighting men who were doing their duty under conditions of great natural difficulty, far from home. Both listened to 'Lilli

Marlene', a nostalgic song full of yearning for normality, and a woman's love. Both armies respected the Red Cross. To our dismay orders came through that all Red Crosses were to be removed in the build-up to the battle for security reasons. We were machine-gunned from the air a couple of times. The QM's store took a pasting but no-one was hurt.

'On the evening of 23 October a friend who commanded a field ambulance visited me. He told me the battle plan, and together we went to some high ground. There was a full moon. At 9pm the silence was shattered by the simultaneous firing of 1,000 guns. Their first targets were the enemy gun emplacements, the positions of which had been plotted during the previous weeks without returning fire. This tactic was successful and was followed by a creeping barrage.

'Before long the casualties started to arrive, and the trickle became a flood. The north bore the brunt of the fighting. The work was largely 'life and limb' surgery which meant dealing with chest and abdominal injuries, cutting off hopelessly damaged limbs and doing our best to save others. Most wounds were caused by shells, mines and machine-gun bullets. Rifle wounds were rare. Our purpose was to render the wounded fit for evacuation by ambulance to the bases in the Delta. Head and spine wounds were flown to special units in Cairo, but air ambulances were few.

'During this time we enjoyed the use of a first-class blood transfusion service. The donors were soldiers at the base who were given a pint of beer for each pint of blood. The transfusion officer worked in a pre-operation tent which had a large blackboard on which he listed the wounded in order of fitness for the theatre. The system worked remarkably smoothly and well, and the throughput of casualties was huge.

'Unfortunately the available surgical resources were not as well used as they might have been. Many units were held in reserve in the south where the front was quieter, in anticipation of a breakthrough which did not come for 12 days. In the north we were overwhelmed by the number of wounded men, and my repeated requests for help fell upon deaf ears. When finally the stream dried up, I recall falling into bed at 6pm and waking again at the same hour. I had slept the clock round, something I had never done before or have I since.

'In the preliminary battle of Alam Halfa our losses had been 110 officers and 1,640 men. Of these, 984 were British, 257 Australians, 405 New Zealanders, 65 South Africans, 39 Indians. In the main battle of Alamein we lost more than 13,000 men, the proportions regarding nationalities being much the same.

'War is a foul, dirty and dangerous business. Many of the young men of all nations concerned are trained to kill, maim and hate. They are controlled and directed by older men further back, who are in comparative safety. In a few it brings out the worst, but in many it brings out the best, and reveals hitherto unsuspected capacity for bravery and heroism. With it too comes a deep sense of lasting comradeship.

'The Army has been described as the Great University of Life. It certainly was for me.'

The tour also included a day as a 'holiday' which was indeed a rare event on a Holts' tour. We went by coach to Mersah Matruh, a most delightful journey, on a lovely day along the coastal road. There were many interesting contributions of 'battle days' by the veterans during the trip. One of them, George Wingate, of the Royal Hospital recalled a short story of that time. During the fighting many messages were received by Monty's HQ from the frontline troops. One of these stated 'Rommel captured'. Monty was immediately suspicious and before celebrating the capture of his rival decided to query the signal and understandably asked for confirmation of such breathtaking information. An amended signal was promptly returned to him duly amended - 'Camel ruptured'! Ken Bricklebank accompanied by his wife Jeannie had been prompted to return to El Alamein after 50 years which was also a pilgrimage in memory of his brother, Cecil. At 19 years of age he had been serving in the RAMC and had set sail with a medical unit in 1942 in *SS Laconia* to pick up the most severe casualties from the Middle East battle area and to get them home for specialist treatment. He was lost at sea through enemy action and his name is recorded on the Brookwood Memorial in Surrey.

Ken recalled that on no fewer than three occasions while he was in the desert he had himself been a casualty and had to receive treatment by a field ambulance team.

One of the highlights of the day was a visit to a very small museum which had been built into a cave in the cliff side. It had been the headquarters of Gen Rommel (the Desert Fox) where he had drawn up plans for operations by his troops. I was able to sit at his desk which included a detailed map of the whole desert battle area and have my photograph taken by Ron Impey. As a young trooper in the UK some 50 years earlier I could not have foreseen, not in my wildest dream, that one day in the North African desert I would sit where the German general's operational plans had been overtaken by the Eighth Army under command of Gen Montgomery. As we were leaving Mersa Matruh we witnessed a most unusual sight - a cow - making its way down the beach to the sea, presumably to have a swim!

And what of El Alamein itself? Astonishingly we found it to be a place which is almost non-existent. At the time of battle it was a Royal Army Medical Corps station of pitched tents situated where two slightly tarmaced tracks crossed by the sea. That was El Alamein then - and more or less still is!

We gathered at the adjacent railway station for a short talk by Maj Tonie Holt and this also gave us sufficient time to discover for ourselves an impression that it had been subject to the attentions of 'Lord Beeching'. There was a feeling among us, however, that if any building throughout North Africa which had regrettably become in recent years so squalid and dilapidated and would therefore qualify as a historic monument, this was surely it.

Departure day came for our party and as we travelled on the long return journey to Cairo our thoughts were of a most absorbing reminder of this important, indeed very important, 50th anniversary. Uppermost in our thoughts were the many thousands of comrades who had come from many corners of the world to help fight and win this battle and our deepest thoughts were in remembrance of those who came but never returned to their homeland. Some words never lose their significance - think of these - 'when you go home tell them of us and say - for their tomorrow, we gave our today' (These words are on the Kohima Memorial in India near the Burmese border.)

Our Holts' party arrived in Cairo in the rush-hour when traffic conditions and the standard of driving have to be seen to be believed. Eventually we arrived at the Movenpick Hotel in the vicinity of the Airport for an overnight stay. A surprise awaited us. We were taken out for the evening for dinner and a boat trip on the river Nile. Entertainment was provided throughout the evening including some belly dancing which Col Mike participated in. While making our way home to the hotel, one of the 'vets' in the coach was heard to say that he thought 'there was too much dancing and not enough belly' a thought that perhaps indicates that not all old soldiers simply fade away. Next morning we left our hotel for the nearby airport, arriving at Heathrow a few hours later, having left a temperature of 90F+ to one of approximately 50F. It was no surprise to learn later that many travellers had colds after such a temperature shock.

While our tour had dwelt, deservedly so, on the Eighth Army, success in North Africa, a most vital part in the desert victory was the successful landing in November 1942 by Anglo-American forces in Morocco and Algeria which included the British First Army led by Gen Anderson. These forces attacking from the German rear prevented the enemy from reinforcing those who were engaged in battle with the Eighth and thus helped considerably to tip the balance of success in the campaign strongly in the Allies' favour.

The Royal Navy - The Royal Air Force - the Allied Forces. Their efforts - their support - their most significant contributions to the Battle of El Alamein and indeed to the campaign in the Western Desert were invaluable. The Eighth Army, and 'Monty', completely depended upon them so much so that success in the land battle would not have been possible without them. The El Alamein battle was described as a series of 'dog fights' - 'a real rough house' - 'hard fighting' and was won by all those servicemen who participated at the time - some of the finest fighting men anywhere in WW2 in the latter part of 1942.

El Alamein

There are flowers now, they say, at Alamein;
Yes, flowers in the minefields now.
So those that come to view that vacant scene,
Where death remains and agony has been
Will find the lilies grow -
Flowers, and nothing that we know.

So they rang the bells for us and Alamein,
Bells which we could not hear:
And to those that heard the bells what could it mean,
That name of loss and pride, El Alamein?
- Not the murk and harm of war,
But their hope, their own warm prayer.

It will become a staid historic name,
That crazy sea of sand!
Like Troy or Agincourt its single fame
Will be garland for our brow, our claim,
On us a fleck of glory to the end:
And there our dead will keep their holy ground.

But this is not the place that we recall,
The crowded desert crossed with foaming tracks,
The one blotched building, lacking half a wall,
The grey-faced men, sand powdered over all;

The tanks, the guns, the trucks,
The black, dark-smoking wrecks.

So be it: none but us has known that land:
El Alamein will still be only ours
And those ten days of chaos in the sand.
Others will come who cannot understand,
Will halt beside the rusty minefield wires
And find there - flowers.

John Jarmain
Major, Royal Artillery
51st (Highland) Division
Killed in Normandy, 26 June 1944

Anniversary
(Many years later)

Sadly Alf lifted his glass,
'I don't half feel a silly arse,
What made me come? I don't know,
One more drink, then I'll go.'

'Last year, there was Harry and Fred,
Now one's in dock, the other's dead.
Neither one seemed to have ail'd,
Time's done them where Jerry failed.'

'A damned good mob in forty-two,
Of four platoon us six came through,
When it was over we made this vow,
We'd meet every year in the 'Old Dun Cow'.'

'I don't suppose I'll come here again,
The last survivor of Alamein,
Don't seem no point in it now,
Drinking alone in the 'Old Dun Cow'.'

B Cole Private
Royal Sussex Regiment

7

Battle of the Atlantic

An information broadsheet issued by the local interests in Liverpool and Merseyside for the 50th anniversary of the battle considered it appropriate that this should take place in May 1993 since it was in 1943 at this time when the 'tide turned' for the Allies.

The Battle of the Atlantic was the longest running continuous campaign of World War Two. The first encounter took place within 12 hours of the declaration of war on 3 September 1939 and the last was five years, eight months and four days later.

Nowhere else were British and Allied seamen exposed to such great danger from the onset of war until the return of peace in Europe was imminent.

Thousands of Royal Navy, Merchant Navy, Coastal Command and German U-boat personnel perished during the struggle. Over 100,000 merchant ships crossed the Atlantic to arrive safely with food and clothing for the civilian population, raw materials for industry, and weapons for the Services. Altogether during the war 4,700 Allied and neutral merchant vessels were sunk and some 700 enemy submarines destroyed. 73,000 Royal Navy personnel, 30,000 merchant seamen, 6,000 RAF Coastal Command personnel and 29,000 German U-boat men lost their lives. A high price to pay in the struggle for supremacy of the Atlantic.

However, by May 1943, after a phase of the campaign in which Allied experience and technical ingenuity had been pitted against sheer numbers of enemy submarines, the tide of the battle began to change in the Allies' favour. German U-boats were withdrawn from the main convoy routes and the Allied build-up of men, food and raw materials so essential to victory began in earnest.

It was most fitting that the 50th anniversary commemorations should be held on Merseyside since Liverpool was Britain's main convoy port throughout the six years of war, maintaining a lifeline, especially with the USA and Canada, which was crucial to Britain's survival and the Allied victory.

Over 1,000 convoys arrived in the Mersey during the war, an average of three or four each week. From 1941 the headquarters of the Western Approaches Command, the nerve centre of the planning and organisation of the battle, was based in Liverpool.

Large numbers of warships and merchant ships were built and repaired on Merseyside and thousands of Merseysiders were directly involved in the battle as Royal Navy or Merchant Navy personnel, dockworkers, port service workers or shipbuilders.

A friend, Leslie Bryant, had joined the Royal Navy in 1940. Very fortunately for him he did his initial service training in an area of outstanding natural beauty - the Malvern Hills. However, later as an engineer, he served on warships protecting convoys in the Arctic. His obvious interest in this special Holts' tour also persuaded me to accompany him to learn of some wartime experiences which, to say no more, were very much different from mine, having served in the Army.

The commemorations included many organised events throughout the period 26 to 31 May 1993. At the outset to mark this most auspicious

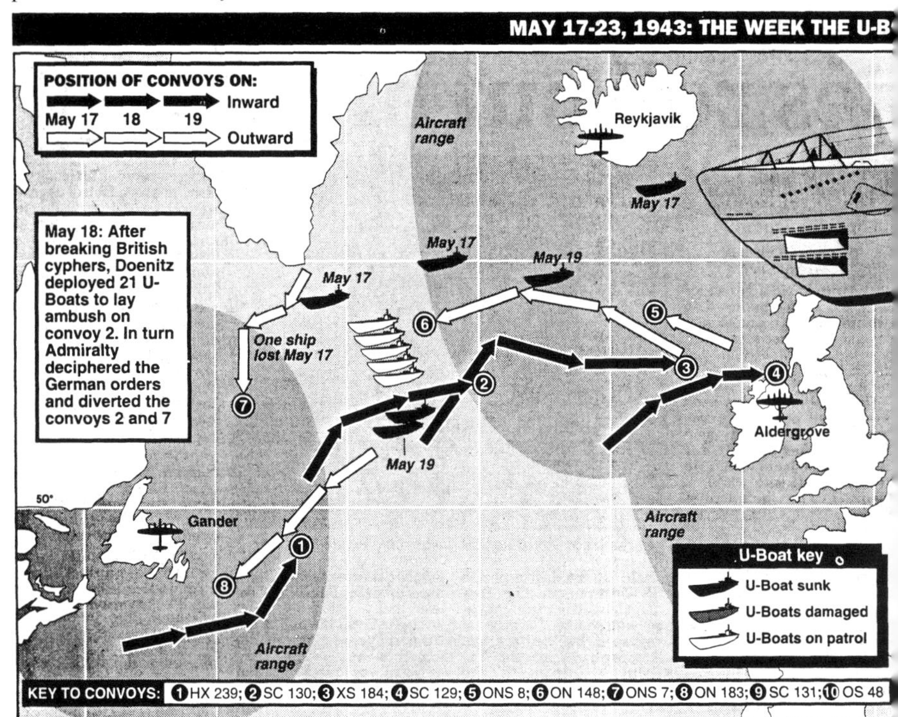

anniversary there was a Royal Review of the Fleet by HRH Duke of Edinburgh, a large gathering of warships off the coast of Anglesey in North Wales.

The party of Holts' travellers attended most of the special events. There was a Royal visit to mark the completion of the development of the Merseyside Maritime Museum at which Her Majesty the Queen and the Duke of Edinburgh were present. Crowds of people, ex-servicemen and civilians, lined the route for a grand marchpast by sailors and veterans through Liverpool city centre.

One of the highlights of the commemorations, much enjoyed by the Holts' party from the balcony of the bar-lounge of the Atlantic Tower Hotel, was a spectacular display of modern and historic aircraft over the River Mersey which included Royal Navy Sea Harriers, RAF Buccaneers, an American B17, Spitfires, Hurricanes, two Swordfish, a Firefly, a helicopter formation, a search and rescue display by a Royal Navy Lynx and a Royal Navy Sea Harrier.

At Goodison Park, Liverpool - the home of Everton Football Club - a

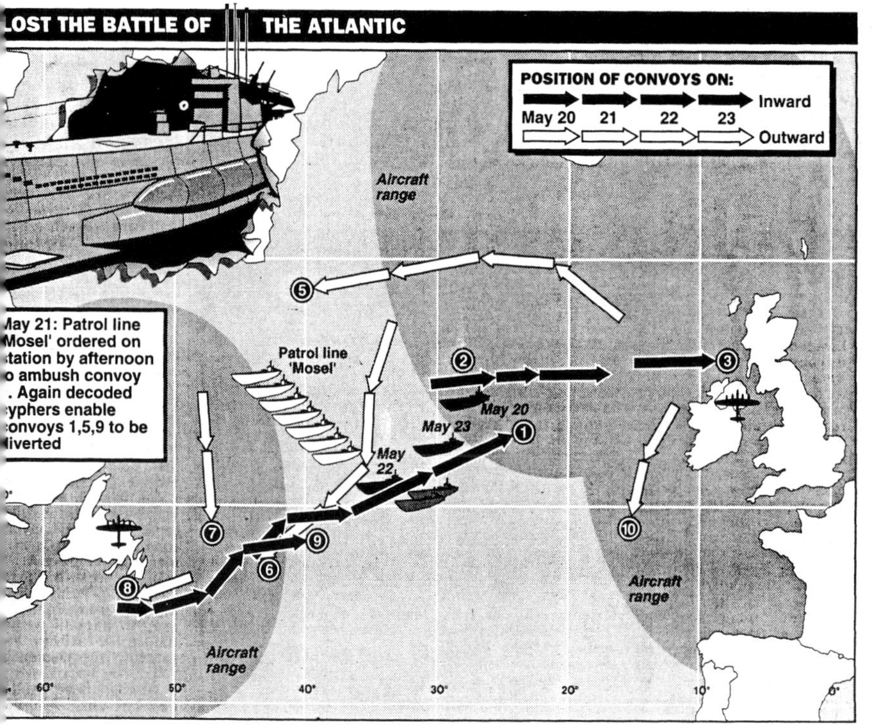

charity concert performance was given by massed bands which was attended by HRH Prince Charles. In a service of Remembrance at Liverpool Cathedral were those Royal Navy and Merchant Navy veterans who had helped bring victory in the Battle of the Atlantic. During our tour with Holts we were privileged, not only in attending the foregoing events, but also specially arranged was a visit to the Liverpool Cathedral; we went on board the Falklands War veteran *HMS Plymouth*, a restored warship frigate, in Birkenhead in whose ward room the commander of the Argentine forces in South Georgia surrendered; we went aboard *HMS Onyx*, a conventionally powered submarine, which had helped land special forces on the Falklands; and were given a most friendly welcome with food and drinks on a Greek Navy Ship, *HNS Nearchos*. The *Nearchos* is a fast, highly manoeuverable ship, carrying modern weapons for a destroyer of her class, it was built by Todd Shipyard Inc, Seattle, Washington and was launched in 1964. The Hellenic Navy flag was hoisted on 1 October 1992 in San Diego, California.

A visit by the Holts party was specially arranged to Western Approaches which had only recently been declared open to the public. The top-secret wartime headquarters, hidden underground a stone's throw from our hotel, is in the centre of Liverpool. The former war rooms had been authentically restored with original artefacts and audio-visual interpretations. It is the only permanent reminder anywhere in the UK or the western world of the Battle of the Atlantic.

To mark the 50th anniversary, arrangements were made for a battle conference at the Merseyside Maritime Museum, Albert Dock, when more than 30 speakers from seven different countries took part, covering all aspects of the battle and its bearing on the outcome of the war. Our party felt fortunate and honoured since attendance was limited to 200, most of the delegates having a depth of knowledge of naval affairs, if not expert themselves. The conference had been organised jointly by the Society for Nautical Research, the Merseyside Maritime Museum and the Naval Historical Branch (MOD). As we expected, the conference papers were wide ranging and the speakers of very high calibre.

As the first paper clearly emphasised it was 'difficult to draw a straight separating line between the control of merchant shipping and the protection thereof'. The importance of merchant shipping for the UK was of equal importance with its naval power. There were various groups of British ships - passenger liners; cargo liners; tramps; tankers; and coasters/ships on home trade. At one time British shipping was most dominant, there being over half of the world capacity, and new shipping of nearly 11 billion gross tons a year. However, World War Two was very costly for the British

Merchant Marine. It started with the sinking of the Athenia in the North Atlantic on 3 September 1939 - the day war was declared - and continued until 7 May 1945 - the day before war ended - with the sinking of the Avondale Park in the Firth of Forth. There were huge losses in both ships and seafarers - a great sacrifice made by so many in the cause of victory.

Titles of various papers included - Operational Research; Shipborne Air Anti-Submarine Warfare; Luftwaffe Support; Allied Land-based Anti-submarine warfare; Technology and Tactics; German Technical and Electronic Development; Allied Co-operation; Liverpool as HQ and Base; Atlantic Escorts 1939-45; German Submarine Bases in the Bay of Biscay; The Development of the U-boats; The Wireless War in the Battle; and many others. In all, the vast amount of written representations by the many speakers at this commemoration conference would make a good-sized book of excellent quality. Some of our party particularly found the paper on 'The Wireless War' by a German speaker very interesting. Although Poland had delivered to Britain certain information about the German cipher-machine, Enigma, it was incomplete. However, after a convoy battle on 9 May 1941 when a British force gained important cipher material from the enemy, the British Centre at Bletchley Park was able to read German traffic albeit with an average delay of a few days. This source of information became known as 'Ultra'.

From decrypted German signals, Winston Churchill learned that Hitler wanted at all costs to avoid incidents which would bring the United States into the war while he was fighting the Soviet Union. When Churchill made President Roosevelt aware of this the Americans took advantage since it allowed them a much wider area in which to chase German raiders, thus giving escort to Allied fast convoys to the mid-Atlantic ocean. It was not until March 1943 after many convoy battles that Bletchley Park succeeded in gaining the upper hand. Up to that time Ultra had been used to avoid losses by evading U-boats but when it was used to concentrate escorts and aircraft to give protection to Allied convoys, the U-boats were more easily located and sunk. Because of these heavy losses the Commander U-boats withdrew them. The breaking of the German codes together with new radars aboard Allied aircraft and ships, better depth charges, skilled destroyer commanders, and the priceless information elicited during interrogation of U-boat survivors, enabled the Allies to overwhelmingly defeat the U-boat wolfpacks. Of 146 ships in the three convoys - ONS 5, SC 130, and HX 239 - 19 ships were lost but the enemy suffered a loss of 13 submarines. Earlier in the month of May 1943, some 20 merchant ships were sunk but 23 U-boats had been lost.

While there was an 'ebb and flow' in the U-boat war the cryptanalysts at Bletchley Park achieved success at a vital time since if the change of tide in the Atlantic had come about some time later, the Allied invasion of Normandy may have been delayed and, who knows, what the grave consequences may have been to ourselves and our Allies.

The Battle of the Atlantic was described by some sources as a 'strategic victory for the Allies, to rank with Stalingrad in the east and Midway in the Pacific'. In achieving such a victory Britain should not forget, of course, the splendid contribution with signals which we were given at the outbreak of the war by friends in Poland.

Additionally, one of the little known scientists of the war was Alan Dower Blumlein, a graduate of Imperial College. He perfected an airborne radar which could see a U-boat on the surface from long range, leaving the commander unaware of danger until it was too late to do anything about it. He was killed when a Halifax bomber testing the new radar crashed over the Wye Valley on 7 June 1942 in circumstances unknown. There were many other outstanding contributions to the Allied victory including the ships of the Royal and Dominion Navies; the free navies of occupied countries and the United States and Coast Guards, air forces and their naval arms, scientists and technicians, the code-breaking and the tactical analysis scholars, the men in the shipyards producing/repairing ships, the stevedores and those in munitions. The Royal Canadian Navy made a significant contribution out of all proportion to its country's manpower which was such that a victory may not have been won without these vital resources.

Indeed throughout the war years British losses at sea regularly occurred as a result of enemy action. Without television at that time, news of the events generally emanated through the newspapers and the radio. A sister who kept a diary of events included many entries of shipping losses as the following details show -

8 September 1939:	Three British and one French ships were torpedoed in the Atlantic by U-boats.
14 February 1940:	A British tanker, 10,000 tons, sunk off the north-east coast of Scotland.
8 March 1940:	The liner, *Queen Elizabeth*, safely docked in New York harbour, alongside the *Queen Mary* and *Normandie*, however avoided disaster.
27 March 1940:	A British tanker of 6,000 tons, now overdue and believed lost.
14 June 1940:	*HMS Scotstown* sunk by U-boat. Armed merchant cruiser sunk.

24 June 1940:	British liner *Star of Wellington* torpedoed.
8 July 1940:	*Arandora Star*, another liner, sunk - torpedoed by the same enemy who sank the *Royal Oak*.
9 July 1940:	The destroyer *Whirlwind* torpedoed.
23 September 1940:	A ship, with 90 children (aged 5-15) and nine escorts, was torpedoed and sunk. 83 children and seven escorts were drowned. The ship was torpedoed by a German submarine without warning in a tempestuous sea. Some of the families had homes in London wrecked by enemy bombs. A later news item confirmed that 13 children survived.

These were a very small number of the many losses, occurring almost daily, which were announced in radio news bulletins.

In the words of Winston Churchill - 'The Battle of the Atlantic was the dominating factor all through the war. Never for one moment could we forget that everything happening elsewhere depended on its outcome'.

The sinking of a Merchant Ship

Taken from 'At the Bugle's Call'
by Alan J Colley

A moonless, starless, winters night,
the sea an inky black,
A U-boat off the starboard bow
manoeuvres to attack.

One deadly arrow pierced the waves,
her aim was swift and sure.
Ten thousand tons and a hundred sons
shall greet the land no more.

8

Allied air raid, Amiens Prison, France

Included in the brochure of Holts' Battlefield Tours for 1994 were several 50th anniversaries of that momentous, emotional, year for many of us. One of these tours was Operation Jericho, the Mosquito raid on Amiens.

On 18 February 1944 three squadrons of Mosquitos (487 New Zealand, 464 Australian and 21 British) led by Gp Capt PC Pickard, DSO and Two Bars DFC Czech Military Cross, took off in icy, wintry, conditions from Hunsdon aerodrome in Hertfordshire. Their mission was to breach the walls of Amiens Prison in a daring and dangerous precision bombing attack to release key Resistance workers held there by the Gestapo, many of whom had been betrayed by Lucien Pieri, local traitor. The prison walls did indeed come tumbling down and hundreds of prisoners escaped but many civilians were killed and 'Pick', one of WW2's most popular pilots and his navigator, Alan Broadley, were shot down by FW 190s of Adolph Galland's yellow-nosed Abbeville boys.

John Rayner, from Melbourne in Australia, a traveller in our coach party, described the Amiens Prison raid in *FlyPast* (March 1994) as follows:

And the Walls came Tumbling Down

During January 1944, information was received in London that over 100 loyal Frenchmen were being held in the jail at Amiens, France awaiting execution for their efforts towards the Allied cause. Some of these had been condemned for assisting Allied airmen to return to England after being shot down over France.

Several attempts by the Resistance had already been made to release them, but all had failed. Leader of the local Resistance, Dominique Ponchardier, requested an urgent air strike to break open the prison walls - even at the risk of killing some of the patriots - at least they would have a chance to escape rather than face certain death by firing squad.

The RAF accepted this exacting task and Mosquitos from Basil Embry's 2 Group were chosen as the aircraft most likely to achieve success. The raid, code-named Operation Jericho, was postponed several times in mid

February due to foul weather and was rescheduled for midday on February 17. Thick cloud and snowstorms again ruled out any attempt that day.

The executions were to begin two days later. The following morning produced the same atrocious weather but now it was a 'do or die' show. The aircrew from Australia, Britain, Canada, France and New Zealand met to consider the plan - everyone wanted to go!

With snow falling, 19 Mosquitos took off from Hunsdon, Herts at 1055hrs on the 18th. One by one they disappeared into the murky sky, hoping to meet up with their Typhoon escort over Littlehampton.

Once over the Channel the weather improved but conditions had by then forced two Mossies from 21 Squadron to return and two 245 Squadron Tiffies aborted due to fuel problems, while 198's Typhoons failed to make the rendezvous. The remainder of the force descended to sea level and set course for Amiens via a specially planned route.

Once over the Continent, the Mosquitos hugged the contours of the snow-covered French countryside, no higher than tree-top level. They avoided power lines, trees and known flak batteries.

Approximately 10 miles (16km) from the target, 487 Squadron's second flight leader's port engine caught fire. Flt Lt Titch Hanafin extinguished the flames. As timing over the prison was critical, he had no choice but to leave formation and turn for home on one engine. Meanwhile, the main force had swept around to the south of Albert and picked up the target marker - the long, straight road to Amiens lined with tall poplars would take them straight to the prison on the town's outskirts.

Descending to 10ft (3m) and tightening formation, the slipstream from their propellers created a snowy wake behind them. The poplars suddenly petered out, and there, a mile ahead, the great dark mass of Amiens prison stood out against the fresh snow. The Mosquitos split up and attacked in four waves from two directions, hitting the prison at 1201hrs, while the guards were in their quarters eating lunch.

First to attack were the five Mosquitos of 487 Squadron led by Wg Cdr IS Black Smith. Their task was to breach the 20ft (6m) high, 3ft (1m) thick outer wall at the east and north sides of the prison.

Following closely were the five Mosquitos of 464 Squadron and a sixth aircraft from 487 piloted by Gp Capt PC Pickard. Led by Wg Cdr Bob Iredale, they were to open the main building and destroy the guards' quarters at the east and west ends of the prison. It was intended that the cell doors would be sprung open by concussion from the bomb blasts, allowing prisoners to escape.

Escort over the target was provided by eight Typhoons of 174 Squadron,

The picture above shows the breach in the south side of the prison outer wall. ***(IWM C4740)***

while the remaining six Typhoons of 245 Squadron covered Wg Cdr IG Daddy Dale's four Mosquitos from 21 Squadron. They orbited 10 miles (16km) to the north, waiting for the signal to attack if the previous two units had failed. If so, Dale's orders were to destroy the prison entirely - the Resistance would rather die from British bombs than Nazi bullets.

One of the RAF's most celebrated airmen was overall commander of the raid, Gp Capt Pick Pickard. He was last over the prison - the exact moment captured in Gerald Coulson's remarkable painting - just seconds before the delay fuse bombs exploded. Pickard remained in the area to assess the results which were filmed by a specially equipped Film Photographic Unit Mosquito.

Flt Lt Tony Wickham and his camerman, Plt Off Lee Howard flew three passes over the prison filming the results of the attack. Prisoners could be seen making their escape through the gaping holes in the walls and running in all directions across the snow-covered fields to be spirited away by Resistance comrades. the pre-arranged success signal Red-Red-Red was transmitted to 21 Squadron, which gratefully turned for home without bombing.

By this time German air defences had reacted to the RAF's presence and FW 190s of II/JG26 intercepted the force which now had to fight its way home. A Typhoon, piloted by Fg Off Paul Renaud, was shot down, resulting in his capture. Pickard and his navigator, Flt Lt JA Bill Broadley were not so lucky.

Also lost, this time to flak, was 464 Squadron's second flight leader, Sqn Ldr Ian McRitchie. Wounded in 26 places, McRitchie crash-landed at over 200mph (321km/h) near Poix and became a PoW. His navigator, Flt Lt RW Sammy Sampson was killed outright.

Limping home on one engine, Flt Lt Hanafin was again hit by flak, paralysing one side of his body. He was met and escorted home by his leader and made a perfect landing at a forward airfield, while foul weather over the Channel claimed Flt Sgt HS Brown's Typhoon.

Dominique Ponchardier sent this message to London in March 1944. 'I thank you in the name of our comrades for the bombardment of the prison. We were not able to save all. Thanks to the admirable precision attack the first bomb blew in nearly all doors and 150 prisoners escaped with the help of the civilian population. Of these, 12 were to have been shot on February 19. In addition, 37 prisoners were killed, some of them by German machine-guns, and 50 Germans were also killed. (Later figures confirmed that 255 prisoners got away.)

Today the model used for briefing 140 Wing's crews, along with a door lock from one of the prison cells from which one prisoner escaped successfully, can be seen in the galleries of the Imperial War Museum, London. In Amiens there is a tribute at the prison entrance - and since 1946 a memorial service has been held there annually on February 18.

Holts' 50th anniversary tour of the prison air raid covered the three days from 17 to 19 February 1994.

As usual on our first day, most of the party assembled at the Victoria Coach Station but rather unusually, instead of proceeding south to Dover, we travelled north-west to London Colney where we visited the Mosquito Aircraft Museum. On arrival there we were welcomed by Ian Thirsk, of the RAF Museum, Hendon, who gave a short introductory talk. It was this site which was chosen by the de Havilland aircraft company in 1939 to develop in secret the wooden, high speed unarmed bomber, the Mosquito, the fastest aircraft in WW2 during the period September 1941 to early 1944. It was used in many operational roles which included most of the pathfinding duties during major bombing raids. A total of 7,781 Mosquitos was built in Great Britain, Australia and Canada. There was much to be seen and talked about at the museum, which had been opened by the Queen Mother some 10 years earlier. Obviously a very active restoration programme was in progress, making the viewing space for visitors almost minimal. There are plans to move to Hatfield. It was soon time to leave the museum and we proceeded to Dover for the P&O ferry via M25 and the new Dartford bridge which had been opened by HM the Queen a short while before.

For us time on the ferry was mostly taken up enjoying refreshments and generally visiting the various services and on this occasion we had ample time. Nowadays - as at Dover, departures from Calais are very smooth and in a short time our party was clear of the port area and making our way to our destination - Amiens.

During the journey the tour leader, Lt Col David Storrie, gave the usual details of the tour itinerary emphasising that it would necessarily be flexible since this was indeed a special anniversary which had attracted the attention of both the media and French representatives.

Always essential on a journey of this sort is a 'comfort' stop and there could not have been a more appropriate town for this than Abbeville where, from the nearby aerodrome, Adolph Galland's deadly Luftwaffe flew and took part in intercepting the Allied raid in 1944.

The second day of the tour - 18 February 1994 - was the 'big' day, not only for us regular travellers, but also much more so for many others who had come for this 50th anniversary from South Africa, Australia, New Zealand, Zimbabwe, Canada (ex-flyers), including those of course from the UK. A very special passenger was on our coach - Dorothy - widow of Gp Capt Pickard. She was accompanied by her granddaughter, Nicole, both of whom had made the long journey from Johannesburg to stay with friends in Leighton Buzzard.

We made our way to Amiens Prison where permission had been given for an 'inside' visit. Here the directeur welcomed us and we had an opportunity to see for ourselves where certain areas of the walls had been

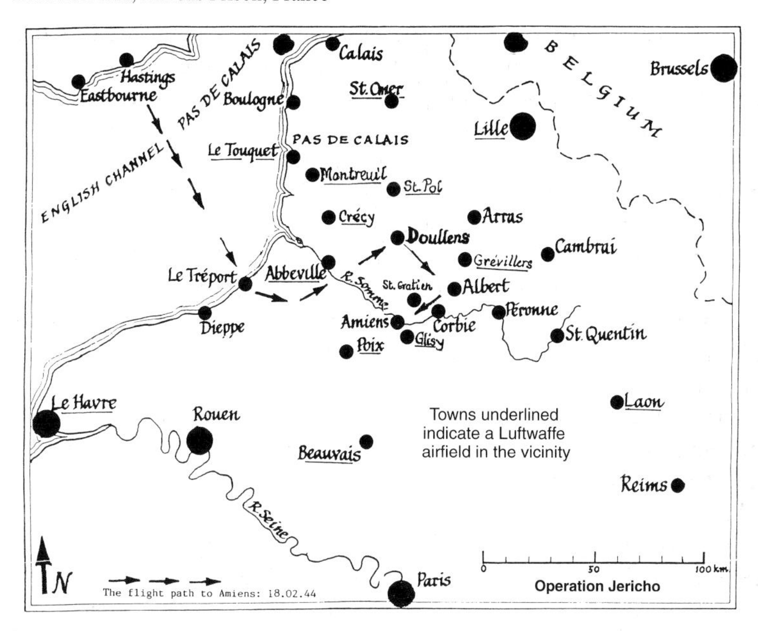

breached. However, we were soon outside again where, in front of the main gates, a wreath laying ceremony was held. The BBC, Australian and French TV, and other media were present for this, during which time the local police had seen fit to close the road to divert traffic. While there was not a large crowd present, nevertheless it was obvious that local people including one or two of the resistance fighters, had interested themselves in our visit to their town.

The short ceremony at the prison gates was indeed thoughtful but next we were to take part in a more thoughtful one. Only a short distance away from the prison was the CWGC - St Pierre - where Gp Capt Pickard, who was in command of this spectacular raid, and Flt Lt Broadley, were buried.

Our complete party of two coaches gathered at Pick's grave where we joined Dorothy, her granddaughter Nicole, her close friends, and those ex-flyers who had been with him on the raid. During the short ceremony wreaths were laid at the grave, also on Alan Broadley's grave in the row behind.

At this time the weather, while dry, was nevertheless quite chilly and we were reminded by the ex-flyers that in 1944 the weather was much more seasonal, indeed the whole area was covered in snow. It was soon time to leave St Pierre for our next stop which was the centre of Amiens near the cathedral, an ideal parking place from where it was not too difficult for us to find some lunch. It was mid-afternoon when we re-assembled with a pleasant extra item to our itinerary. The Amiens authorities, having heard of our presence in their town, had provided an English speaking representative to give an informative talk about some aspects of the cathedral, in particular the architecture at the front and some of the interesting aspects inside. The cathedral was built in the 13th century and is the largest in the world, its spire reaching up to 112 metres and 4,000 carved figures decorate its stalls.

Shortly after the Allied air raid on 18 February 1944 the Germans held an impressive memorial service at the cathedral for 87 of the victims to demonstrate how evil the Allies were by their bombing of the defenceless inmates of the prison.

After this 'special one-off', we continued with the itinerary and toured Amiens seeing places of interest from the years of the German occupation which included the Gestapo HQ in Rue Jeanne d'Arc. I suppose most of us had some absorbing thoughts as to the 'devils who had been in residence there' during the first half of the 1940s.

It was now late afternoon and most essential for us that we arrive in the village of St Gratien before dusk since it was there on the outskirts where Pick's Mosquito, 'F' for Freddie, crashed on 18 February 1944. We had a short stop in the village itself. As the local farmer was now unable to leave his farmhouse, his son and daughter-in-law came on to the coach to meet Dorothy, possibly for her the most emotional moment of the tour. Conversation quickly flowed between them since the farmer was able to give much information on the happenings on that fateful day. He stayed on the coach and accompanied us to the farmland area of the crash site and we were joined there by the local mayor, who was invited on to the coach to meet Dorothy. It was moments such as these that Ron and I, who were in the seat immediately behind, realised that on this tour we were really close to a most significant 'chapter of modern history', something which neither of us had anticipated but, believe me, will not be easily forgotten.

Quite remarkably the day had gone so very quickly - we had done what seemed to be an awful lot - and as dusk fell it was time for us to return to our hotel, a return almost in complete silence, so deep were our thoughts of the bravery of friends half a century before.

After dinner there was time in the evening for Brad King, of the Imperial War Museum, to 'entertain', which he did with video about the Amiens raid and about the plane - the Mosquito - which was used most successfully by the RAF. There was much discussion - indeed a most lengthy discussion - since even by Holts' standards this was a marathon session which quite unbelievably continued into the early hours of our third day.

Even at this late hour some members of the party afterwards found some interesting relaxing entertainment in a local night club until 4am so it was rather remarkable that no-one was left at the hotel when we departed at 8.45 on our last day.

A short visit was made to the Grevillers/Achiet airfield which, during World War Two, was used by both the Allies and the Germans. From there we moved to the Mur-des-Fusilles in Amiens where we met a former Resistance fighter at the site where they were shot by the Germans. A plaque on the wall indicates that five of them gave their lives on 31 August 1944 'For the Liberation', just before the Allied liberators arrived.

Soon after leaving the Mur-des-Fusilles we had a coach stop at a newspaper/tabacco shop where our leader collected several copies of the local newspaper, *Le Courier*, which included an extensive article, together with photographs, of our activities on the 50th anniversary day. A headline described this as *Visit by Ancients* which drew an earthy comment from one of our party involved with the raid - 'Christ,' he said, 'they've called us Ancients!' - which was almost appropriate since most us were in the 'seven-o' club.

Although far too many prisoners - 37 in all, were killed in the raid there were many escapees who had been given the chance to avoid certain death by a firing squad. The Resistance network was vital to the Allies since at risk was the postponement of the Normandy invasion planned for June 1944. Inevitably any delay would have given the Germans precious time in the development and use of their deadly V weapons which may have seriously delayed the outcome of an Allied victory.

We travelled on and while many among us had their heads in *Le Courier* we were sharply reminded of the previous day's ceremonies as we again passed Amiens Prison where the flags were still flying and where our wreaths were still lying outside the main entrance gates. Then in only a few seconds, as we proceeded a little further on our outward journey, we approached the St Pierre Cemetery and as we came alongside the entrance gates Dorothy, looking to her left and towards the area of the CWGC grave, was heard to say a dramatic farewell...'Good-bye, Pick' - most significant since it would seem unlikely that she will make another visit. A moment to remember for Ron and I as we may have been the only ones who heard this last farewell to a loved one.

After lunch in Arras we visited the CWGC where we gathered at the RFC/RAF memorial for a short ceremony to be followed by the rather grim experience of the Mur-des-Fusilles where many, very many, plaques indicated that local Resistance fighters and other dignitaries had been shot by the Germans during their occupation until the 'Brits' arrived in the autumn of 1944.

Throughout the tour several in our party made some very interesting and thoughtful contributions about this most spectacular visit to Amiens Prison on 18 February 1944, in particular Ian McRitchie. Although a little older now than he was and having come from Melbourne, Australia, for the tour, he gave us several thought-provoking contributions which, at times, almost created a feeling for us of being there. As a pilot he led the second flight against the guards' quarters at the west end of the prison, holing the wall and destroying the barracks. His aircraft was brought down by ground fire.

In 1944 for security reasons there was an eight-month delay before an announcement of the raid was released. Mosquitos had made the attack on Amiens Prison in a 'one-off' operation to release a large number of inmates including, hopefully, many of the Resistance fighters who were condemned to death by firing squad. A few who had recently been imprisoned knew the secrets of the forthcoming Allied landings and as they were under severe pressure from interrogation by the Gestapo, it was felt vital that an attempt be made to release them, despite the knowledge that some unfortunately would become casualties.

The following is an extract from *And the Walls Came Tumbling Down*, by Jack Fishman, a contribution by Alf Jenkins…

Pickard's Ghost

The Mosquito raid on Amiens gaol led by Gp Capt Pickard of 'Target for Tonight' fame is well known. The object of the raid was not simply to allow imprisoned Resistance fighters to escape. By February 1944 the Resistance in that part of France had suffered devastating blows, with wholesale arrests and betrayals of groups, and because of this the Allies would suffer from lack of intelligence concerning the V bomb sites and also lack of back-up after the invasion which could place the whole of the Overlord operation in jeopardy.

Moreover, only two days previous to the raid Raymond Vivant, kingpin of the Resistance in northern France, with invaluable knowledge of the D-Day plans, had been imprisoned in Amiens. Therefore, to raise morale and improve the effectiveness of the Resistance it was essential to give him a chance to escape.

Although the story of Guy Gibson and his dog, Nigger, who was killed on the eve of the Dambusters raid is well-known, the story of Pickard and his dog Ming may not be so. Ming, an English sheepdog, was given by Pickard as a puppy to his wife Dorothy as a wedding present. An uncanny sympathy between Ming and Pickard developed. Dorothy noticed how restless Ming became whenever Pickard took off for a raid, how between take off and return she would settle down to sleep and how, when his return was expected, she would sit outside scanning the sky from side to side.

In June 1940, returning from a raid on the Ruhr, Pickard's plane was forced down in the North Sea and was missing for several hours. At 3.20am Ming tugged Dorothy's bed clothes and, thinking that she wanted to go outside for the usual reasons, let her out. Ming refused to come in but sat outside scanning the sky. Later in the day Dorothy sat at the end of the runway with Ming watching the planes returning from their search for Pickard. Late in the afternoon Ming suddenly went to sleep. It turned out that Pickard and his crew had been found in the afternoon and that it was exactly at 3.20am that he had crashed.

Pickard's wing that was to make the raid on Amiens, 140 Wing, was based at Hundsdon. By a coincidence, Hundsdon was the former country house of Sir Cedric and Lady Hardwicke, Lady Hardwicke being Helena, Pickard's elder sister. Cedric Hardwicke is well remembered for his many film appearances, and his son, Edward, is also a well known TV actor, one of his roles being that of Dr Watson to Jeremy Brett's Sherlock Holmes.

Because Dorothy could not be with Pickard at Hundsdon, he had left Ming with his adjutant at Sculthorpe. On the evening of 18 February with the rest of the wing back and Pickard still missing, Dorothy received a telephone call from Sculthorpe asking her to go there as Ming was terribly ill, although two vets could find nothing wrong with her. When Dorothy finally arrived she found Ming prostrate on the floor, vomiting blood. 'Pick is dead' said Dorothy.

Eight years later, Dorothy who had moved to Rhodesia, was woken one night by Ming whimpering. Letting her out into the garden, she heard four sharp whistle blasts just like those Pickard used to make with his fingers to summon Ming. She walked round the garden calling out 'is anyone there?'. She returned to the house and found Ming, who had been ill for months and too weak to stand, sitting on her haunches, her head moving from side to side, just as she used to when waiting for Pickard to return from a raid. Dorothy heard the four whistle blasts again. Ming raised her head higher, stared at the sky - and fell dead to the floor.

When Dorothy looked at her newspaper the next day she was startled to see the date - the previous day had been 18 February, the anniversary of the raid.

9

Battle of Normandy, France

It has been a privilege for me to travel with Holts' Battlefield Tours on a large number of occasions since 1984, several times to Normandy and indeed my first tour there was for the 40th anniversary of the Allied invasion.

Over these years I have listened thoughtfully to the habitual 'instructive and thought provoking commentaries from their guides and guest speakers'. No-one can possibly not be enthralled by such a tour, which to my mind, describes a military operation which was 'do or die', to say the least. The Normandy Landings would be very high on any list of major battles in which British forces have ever taken part. Everyone, everywhere, seemingly had an involvement of some sort in this final effort for victory against Hitler's Germany.

The first day of the invasion - 6 June 1944 - has been well described as 'The Longest Day' which, together with the many weeks of Allied forces containment in Normandy, provides a story which necessarily is a very long one.

The Holts' party for the 50th anniversary consisted of 20 coaches, Capt Paul Snook being our tour leader, covering the period of six days from 4 to 9 June 1994.

At the time the British forces and some Allied soldiers were evacuated from Dunkirk in Northern France in late May/early June 1940, the Continent - more-or-less - became Hitler's Europe. Some lines of a well-known WW1 poet (and fellow Salopian), Wilfred Owen, in his work *1914* include these words - significant also for the dark days of WW2 in 1940.

War broke, and now the winter of the world
With perishing great darkness closes in.
The foul tornado, centred at Berlin,
Is over all the width of Europe whirled.

After only nine months since declaring war on Germany in September 1939, Great Britain found itself standing alone in its fight against the

German tyranny which took hold of the European continent. The immediate priority for Great Britain was the defence of the country. In the air the RAF did just that. The Royal Navy continued, despite heavy losses, to maintain sea routes. The Army and the civilian services were extremely vigilant. Without any doubt the situation could not have been more desperate. Quite unexpectedly, however, help came eventually from two of the world's most powerful nations. Russia and America became our Allies when, respectively, they were attacked by Germany and Japan.

Only after more than two years, in the last quarter of 1942, did Britain have its first significant gain, success in far away North Africa at El Alamein. Although after this most famous battle in the desert the Allies continued to make steady progress against the enemy it was nearly two more years - June 1944 - before they embarked from many harbours around the coast of southern England to attack Hitler's European fortress.

However, by this time the Allies had resolved certain key issues -

- After the debacle of the Dieppe raid in 1942 when the Canadians suffered heavy casualties, it was clear that any attack on a port area would be costly, if not unsuccessful, for any landing parties;
- The overwhelming superiority at sea and in the air must be established and preserved;
- The weather, including the tides, must be favourable;
- The date and exact location of the invasion must remain a secret;
- Deception plans would be essential simultaneously. The Supreme
- The Supreme Commander for the Allied invasion of North West Europe was Gen Dwight David Eisenhower (United States of America).

Gen Montgomery, who was appointed 'Head of the Armies' supported the view that the original area planned for the landings was too narrow, and he also emphasised the need for a much larger number of assault troops.

In the event the 50 miles of the Normandy coast stretching from the west of the River Vire to east of the River Orne was chosen for the frontage of the assault.

With 'Monty's' larger force, the length of coastline was divided into five sections, one assaulting division each, with the American 1st Army covering the beaches codenamed Utah and Omaha and the British 2nd Army covering the remaining three beaches codenamed Gold, Juno and Sword. In addition, two American Airborne Divisions were dropped at the western end, and one British Division at the eastern end, to secure the landing beaches while the frontal landings were taking place. The Americans were conveniently located to cut off the Cotentin Peninsula which included the port of Cherbourg.

In anticipation of an Allied invasion, Hitler had ordered the fortification of the French coast, many thousands of soldiers and conscripts had constructed, and were defending, the 'Atlantic Wall'. The German commander in the area, Field Marshal von Runstedt, disliked the idea of a fixed forward line, preferring to strongly hold key areas including ports. Infantry and armour would be in reserve available for counter-attack. However, Field Marshal Rommel, who was given command of an army group, believed in defeating the Allies on the beaches, saying that: 'the first 24 hours will be decisive'. Thus Rommel set about defensive and coastal work with gusto and he deployed the German Army reserves covering the landing beaches. When Hitler discovered the differences of strategy between his two field marshals, he decided that command of the armoured forces should be split between them but those under von Runstedt's command - the reserve - could not be used except with his personal permission. Subsequent events proved this to be a costly strategic mistake.

In war deception weapons can often be decisive, indeed without them the Allied invasion of Normandy may not have been a success. Anyone in the southern counties of England in the early months of 1944 would have realised that an attack on the Continent was imminent - there was simply too much material and men around everywhere to suggest otherwise.

To deceive the enemy in these circumstances a phantom army operating in south east England was perhaps not too difficult for the invasion planners to set up. This imaginary 1st Army Group was put under command of the disgraced American general George S Patton. It was reinforced by establishing a series of signal centres which sent messages to each other about fictitious troop movements.

In the air, by flying twice as many bombing missions in the Calais area as in the Normandy area and by moving American and Canadian troops into Dover and Folkestone areas, the enemy was persuaded that any invasion would be made from Dover to Calais, this being the narrowest part of the English Channel.

Further afield, another deception was created by an actor impersonating Gen Montgomery carrying out an inspection of troops in the Gibraltar area, suggesting that the invasion would be launched on the French southern coastline instead of the northern one. This visit was reported by enemy agents in nearby Spain.

At the time of the invasion itself, dummy airborne troops - known as 'Ruperts' - were dropped over a wide area to confuse the Germans as to the strength and exact location of the Allied attack; silver foil was dropped

A scene on Queen White Sector of the British Sword Beach: wounded at the edge of the water while a few yards away others are moving forward without hurry. In the background can be seen the landing craft and the tanks of 'A' Squadron, 13th/18th Royal Hussars in support. ***(IWM B 5114)***

to confuse the German radar system; misinformation was used to disrupt enemy plans and, as the German signal code had been broken, the deception plans themselves could be adjusted whenever necessary.

After many months of preparation, and some delay because of bad weather conditions, the armada set sail from many ports around the English southern coastline, landing the Allied Armies in Normandy on 6 June 1944, preceded a few hours before by the airborne American and British troops.

The sixth of June was quickly described as the 'Longest Day' full of heroic events from dawn to dusk. Any other description would fail to emphasise the happenings of one of the most historical days, if not the greatest, in British history.

On that day Allied casualties amounted to approximately 11,000 while

21 ARMY GROUP

PERSONAL MESSAGE FROM THE C-in-C

To be read out to all Troops

1. The time has come to deal the enemy a terrific blow in Western Europe.

The blow will be struck by the combined sea, land, and air forces of the Allies—together constituting one great Allied team, under the supreme command of General Eisenhower.

2. On the eve of this great adventure I send my best wishes to every soldier in the Allied team.

To us is given the honour of striking a blow for freedom which will live in history; and in the better days that lie ahead men will speak with pride of our doings. We have a great and a righteous cause.

Let us pray that " The Lord Mighty in Battle " will go forth with our armies, and that His special providence will aid us in the struggle.

3. I want every soldier to know that I have complete confidence in the successful outcome of the operations that we are now about to begin.

With stout hearts, and with enthusiasm for the contest, let us go forward to victory.

4. And, as we enter the battle, let us recall the words of a famous soldier spoken many years ago:—

" He either fears his fate too much,
Or his deserts are small,
Who dare not put it to the touch,
To win or lose it all."

5. Good luck to each one of you. And good hunting on the mainland of Europe.

B. L. Montgomery
General
C-in-C 21 Army Group.

1944.

SUPREME HEADQUARTERS
ALLIED EXPEDITIONARY FORCE

Soldiers, Sailors and Airmen of the Allied Expeditionary Force!

You are about to embark upon the Great Crusade, toward which we have striven these many months. The eyes of the world are upon you. The hopes and prayers of liberty-loving people everywhere march with you. In company with our brave Allies and brothers-in-arms on other Fronts, you will bring about the destruction of the German war machine, the elimination of Nazi tyranny over the oppressed peoples of Europe, and security for ourselves in a free world.

Your task will not be an easy one. Your enemy is well trained, well equipped and battle-hardened. He will fight savagely.

But this is the year 1944! Much has happened since the Nazi triumphs of 1940-41. The United Nations have inflicted upon the Germans great defeats, in open battle, man-to-man. Our air offensive has seriously reduced their strength in the air and their capacity to wage war on the ground. Our Home Fronts have given us an overwhelming superiority in weapons and munitions of war, and placed at our disposal great reserves of trained fighting men. The tide has turned! The free men of the world are marching together to Victory!

I have full confidence in your courage, devotion to duty and skill in battle. We will accept nothing less than full Victory!

Good Luck! And let us all beseech the blessing of Almighty God upon this great and noble undertaking.

Dwight D Eisenhower

during the Normandy campaign from 6 June to 31 August the total casualties - killed, wounded, and missing - were over 200,000, The enemy casualties were 400,000, half of whom were prisoners of war.

On the invasion day itself the Allied forces were generally successful. In the eastern sector British airborne and glider-borne troops, dropped some hours before dawn, quickly captured the river and canal bridges, destroyed three other bridges in the vicinity of Benouville, and silenced the Merville coastal battery. In the western sector the American airborne troops promptly entered St-Mere-Eglise and progressed towards Carentan.

In the area of Utah Beach the Americans met little enemy resistance and quickly linked up with their airborne troops. However, at Omaha Beach they met strong enemy forces and suffered heavy losses. At Gold Beach British troops were soon in Arromanches and advanced inland about 10km. The Canadians at Juno Beach, who were supported by British armour, had success at Courselles and established themselves in similar depth. The British on Sword Beach lacked infantry support and failed to reach Caen by several kilometres.

Afterwards the Germans were able to bring up reinforcements along the whole length of the Allied bridgehead as bad weather, including a gale for several days and nights, prevailed in the area.

Although it appeared that the Allied invasion had reached stalemate, Gen Montgomery, through a series of attacks, successfully attracted the enemy to the British 2nd Army front where there were at one time seven and half of the eight German Panzer divisions in Normandy.

In the second month of the landing - July - there were several determined efforts to break out of the bridgehead. Operation Goodwood in mid-July was preceded by a large armada of Lancaster bombers aimed at Caen and Falaise. Operation Spring, towards the end of July, was again in the Caen area. At the end of July Operation Bluecoat aimed at Aunay-sur-Odon. The Americans during this time had been fully occupied in the Cherbourg Peninsula since it was vital to have port facilities without delay.

On 6 August the Germans made an attempt to cut off the Americans from the British in the area of Mortain. Monty immediately ordered the Canadians to attack in the Falaise area which enabled the American 1st Army, in a pincer movement, to advance behind the Germans resulting, more or less, in the annihilation of the German 7th Army by 19 August.

As head of the Army forces, 'Monty' had planned for the Normandy landing as follows...

First US Army

a To assault;

b To capture Cherbourg;
c To develop operations St Lo;
d After capture of the area Cherbourg - Caumont - Avranches, to advance southwards, capture Rennes and reach out to the Loire.

Second British Army

a To assault;
b To protect First US Army while it captured Cherbourg;
c To secure airfield sites south east of Caen;
d In subsequent operations to pivot on its left and offer a strong front against enemy movement towards the lodgement area from the east.

More or less this plan was a success. With hindsight it was much slower in achieving vital targets; eg the airfield sites, than was hoped, nevertheless, the Allied overall advance through northern France was much quicker than anticipated - indeed the German Army subsequently rarely made a counter-attack.

On any Holts' tour of Normandy - a comparatively small area of northern France - there are many highlights of great interest including...
The beaches where Allied forces landed - known as Utah, Omaha, Gold, Juno and Sword;
Pegasus Bridge - replaced by a similar one in 1994 - and the adjacent river Orne bridge, together with the most famous cafe, Gondree, in an area where 6th Airborne Division landed;
The Merville Battery;
Courselles and Graye-sur-Mer;
Pointe-du-hoc;
Arromanches and the Mulberry harbour;
St Mere Eglise;
Bayeux;
Caen;
Museums at Pegasus, Arromanches, Bayeux,Caen and St Mere Eglise;
Cemeteries at Bayeux, Ranville, Hermanville, Douvres-la-Delivandre, Rye and several others.
The National Cemetery at St Laurent (American) and The Cemetery at La Cambe (German).

The former canal bridge at Benouville was renamed Pegasus bridge in honour of the British Airborne Division whose Regimental emblem is the immortal winged horse of Greek mythology. This was the first bit of continental Europe, in the vicinity of the bridge, to be liberated.

Wally Parr, Col Tod Sweeney, Wagger Thornton, MM and Paul Snooks.

The Allied invasion began a few minutes after midnight on 6 June 1944 when airborne troops landed in silence to capture an area between the two rivers, Orne and Dives, much of which had been flooded by the Germans as part of their defence against Allied landings. The role of 6th Airborne Division was to protect the landing forces from an armoured counter-attack by the Germans whose reserves were in the area east of Caen.

In the landing area were seven bridges. Five of them over the River Dives were destroyed so allowing the marsh to be used with effect by the British troops, while the remaining two bridges - the Caen Canal and River Orne - carrying the main road from the sea to Caen - were successfully captured intact and held to facilitate reinforcements. This first action could be well described as 'The Battle of the Bridges'.

During the hours of darkness several actions took place beginning with the small force of gliders which dropped on the two bridges at Benouville; shortly afterwards there was the main parachute drop in the area of the marshland and finally the main force of gliders - 72 in all - carrying anti-tank armament, transport and heavy equipment.

My Regiment landed in Normandy in mid-July 1944. On my return visit there 40 years later in July 1984, the Holts' tour party first visited 'the bridge'. There we were met by Maj John Howard DSO, Oxford and Bucks Light Infantry, officer in charge of the advance glider force. On a lovely bright sunny day we sat on the grassed area on the south side of the bridge

The cafe at Pegasus Bridge.

in an 'O' group and listened intently to his reminiscences of this most eventful landing upon which so much depended.

By capturing the bridge his troops were certainly the first to achieve their objective. Indeed they claimed to be the first of the Allied forces to land in Normandy. John Howard's glider came to earth at 90mph, careered across a small field and crashed through the enemy's wire defences. In the pandemonium a platoon moved forward some 20 yards on to the target, a Mills bomb dropped into the pillbox from where a machine gun had fired, then on to the pillbox on the other side of the bridge. Casualties were inevitable and they included the platoon commander, Lt Brotheridge, who is buried in the churchyard of the nearby village of Ranville. This action was completed in about 15 minutes but the 150 men had the task of defending the area until reinforcements came. Adjacent to the bridge is the cafe which became famous as an airborne memorial. Its original name Buvette de Tramway was quickly changed to Pegasus Bridge Cafe Restaurant and it was on the forecourt where John Howard habitually sat giving his autograph. He signed a postcard for me which included the words… 'This was the first house in France to be liberated during the last hour of 5 June 1944 by men of the Oxfordshire and Buckinghamshire Light Infantry in the British 6th Airborne Division under the command of Maj John Howard'.

In recent years both the bridge and the cafe have been very much in the news. This most famous bridge has now been replaced by a similar one to allow bigger ships to use the canal on their way to the port of Caen and for heavier lorries to use the road. The cafe was in danger of closure because of a bitter feud over its fate between three French sisters when their mother died following her husband's death a few years earlier. The two elder daughters were in disagreement with the youngest one who wanted to sell. At the sale the two elder ones were successful and so became joint owners of the Gondrei cafe. They keep it more or less as it was when owned by their parents.

Next to the cafe is the museum which has many war relics, models, maps, and photographs, and some of Maj Howard's personal items, including his bullet-holed steel helmet! However it is understood that the museum situated alongside the cafe is now to be re-sited nearby.

While on a battlefield tour some time later, the Holts' tour party was leisurely meandering in the 'Pegasus' area when three 'old' friends were discovered - Lt Col 'Tod' Sweeney, Wally Parr, and 'Wagger' Thornton, all three having dropped at the same time as John Howard.

'Tod' was a platoon commander who remembered that shortly after landing with his platoon they found the River Orne bridge already captured.

A short time later there was a car and motorcycle crash between the river and canal bridges. A German major, who was the commander of the two bridges, had been drinking the night away with his girlfriend in nearby Merville. When captured he said: 'Shoot me, I've lost my honour'! Found in his car were bottles of champagne and a variety of ladies' underwear, so no-one was quite sure which honour he had lost!

Again there was another unusual, with hindsight amusing, incident when it was noticed that some anti-invasion 'asparagus' poles were being erected in the vicinity by a slave labour gang who were later identified as Poles. When John H heard of this he said: 'Go and tell the silly-bees that they were no longer necessary'. However, the Poles said they must put them up as 'the Germans would be back to see that they had done so by four o'clock that afternoon!

A most serious, critical, happening, as described by 'Wagger' Thornton who gave us a vivid account of how at a most crucial moment he successfully used a PIAT (projector infantry anti-tank) to knock out the leading German tank as two of them were about to come down the straight on their way to the canal bridge. He was with his platoon which had successfully captured the River Orne bridge when, within minutes, the rumbling of tanks was heard and Maj Howard ordered them to the T-junction near the canal bridge.

Crawling along a hedge he got to within 30 yards of the junction where he saw two tank commanders get out and exchange words before getting back inside. As the first tank moved slowly down the road he fired his PIAT, made a direct hit, and there were fireworks everywhere.

The second enemy tank beat a hasty retreat. One round from 'Wagger' avoided a disaster. Charles Thornton was awarded the Military Medal for his bravery on this occasion.

Wally Parr was able to recall that an enemy gun was captured on the south side of the canal bridge. It was then used by the airborne troops to fire at the nearby chateau and water tower occupied by the enemy. When it was realised that the chateau was in use as a maternity unit, the fire was directed on to the water tower. The snipers there were suitably liquidated - with one of their own guns, of course.

'Tod' told us that before this momentous airborne landing they had obviously trained hard in the UK, capturing/destroying bridges in circumstances similar to those likely to be met on the day of action. Some interesting points included: 'If the enemy had blown the bridge, we must land inside since, as far as possible, everyone must be together'. They were well loaded to be decisive, having a map of the area like a handkerchief, money, drugs, chewing gum, morphine and a ration pack. At that particular time they carried these things including drugs without too much thought but he wondered whether some of the present day soldiers would have considered doping themselves with some of the Army gifts. They each had a hacksaw and a fly-button compass. Among their brass flybuttons, one was magnetised with a little spike on top to indicate north and this was normally kept in their 'housewife' since, if it was placed in a normal position, it might indeed cause a very nasty wound!

A very receptive audience listened when he recalled his own D-Day experiences. His glider landed about 400 yards short of the drop zone. In pale moonlight he had seen two bridges so he opened the door to land quickly, otherwise all his friends would be an easy target for the enemy as the glider was running along the ground, as happened later on the Rhine Crossing. However, opening a door on landing had never been done before and the slipstream made this quite difficult for him. Fortunately his batman had the presence of mind to hold his belt and by so doing avoided a very embarrassing drop by him on some Normandy cows. The platoon landed safely and rushed to the nearby river bridge with the intention of taking it. At that time it was single lane and seemingly longer. However, he found that another platoon commander, Dennis Fox, was already very calmly in situ. Tod remembered saying, 'Dennis,' are you all right? Are you all right?', with heart panting. Dennis, not being without a bit of humour, replied:

'Yes, Tod, but I haven't seen the umpire yet'! (On training exercises while in the UK, platoon commanders always looked out for the umpire, someone with a white arm band - since they gave a good, or bad, mark accordingly.)

During the commemorations for the 50th anniversary the airborne veterans and others returned no doubt to be with friends and to be present at the special ceremony at their cemetery at Ranville. To say the least there was plenty of activity around the Pegasus area on this memorable day of our visit. The new bridge was lifted to enable a large boat to pass through and a number of helicopters flew overhead, resembling in some way the gliders of half-a-century before.

The Germans under command of Field Marshal Rommel, had strong fortifications in readiness for any attack by Allied forces. One such strong point was the enemy battery at Merville, a short distance from Pegasus bridge.

A special airborne force of 700 men were trained to drop in close proximity to capture the enemy position. Only 150 men of this force had arrived at the exact drop zone two hours after landing and this comparatively small party reached the battery area just 11 hours before the proposed firing by ships offshore including *HMS Arethusa*. Many of the supporting glider parties became casualties. However, a diversionary force made an attack sustaining 70 casualties, leaving only 80 officers and men for the main attack. Enemy casualties were also heavy - out of 130 defending the battery, only 22 were taken prisoner. The German army artillery battery at Merville was one of the best examples of defensive positions along the whole of the Atlantic Wall. It commanded the estuary of the River Orne some 4km to the north-west and was able to fire beyond it but provision had not been made to do so except inland on a road junction in Ouistreham. The guns were housed in casemates of very thick reinforced concrete with earth on top and at the sides and proved impenetrable to many RAF bombardments. The position was defended by an anti-aircraft gun, several machine guns, a partly dug anti-tank ditch and a very thick barbed wire fence between two minefields. In addition to the 'resident' troops the enemy had two infantry companies stationed nearby who were on call.

And so it was just before dawn on D-Day that paratroops bravely assaulted this heavily defended coastal battery. The much depleted force attacked with such ferocity the enemy were shocked and went to ground and didn't fire their guns on their target Sword Beach. The paratroopers' achievement made a significant contribution to the success of the D-Day landings. During the following morning, however, the Merville guns were believed to be in action. Two troops of No 3 British Commando attacked that afternoon but were repulsed with serious losses. Thereafter the Royal Navy and the RAF ensured the silence of the guns by pouring fire on any observed movement in the battery. Thus neutralised, the guns gave no more trouble. With the rest of the Wehrmacht the German unit withdrew in retreat in mid-August.

A successful landing was made by British and French invasion forces on Sword Beach despite the area being within range of enemy big guns at Le Havre. The D-Day task for the invasion forces was to proceed swiftly inland, to capture Caen, and to link up with the forces on either side.

The Germans had been pounded by warships from the sea, other ships were moving towards the shore carrying barrage balloons, and beforehand the RAF had destroyed the enemy big guns on shore.

When action commenced at about 7.30am on D-Day the tanks came quickly ashore looking for targets. Among them were some of Hobart's 'funnies' - 'D/D' tanks. These were Shermans which had duplex drive enabling the engine power to be transferred from the tracks to twin propellers and by erecting high canvas screens allowed them to float until on shore when the screens were jettisoned. There were 'Crocodiles' - Churchill tanks which had been modified as flame throwers towing a fuel supply as a small trailer. Sherman tanks, known as 'Crabs', carried flails to clear minefields and other beach obstacles - a sort of military 'Hoover'. There were several other 'funnies' available for special circumstances. The flail tanks were some of the first to land, thrashing the beach with their chains, clearing the mines and anti-invasion defences, as they moved steadily forward to the various exits. When it was observed that the enemy was accurately shelling the landing area, it was realised that they were using the barrage balloons, which had been put in place against low level air attacks, as markers for their guns. The balloons were removed. Soon the Commandos came ashore and proceeded to Oustrieham, thereby allowing the assault troops to move off the beach. These forces managed to get within about 6km of Caen but were forced to withdraw through lack of infantry support. The landing at Sword had not been without casualties, however, and 426 were reported killed on that day.

A particular landmark here, which still remains, is the house/hotel - a fairly large property adjacent to the beach. On the 5Oth anniversary tour were Dr Leslie and Mrs Rosemary Rendel Baker from America. Dr Baker well remembered many of the things which happened to him on D-Day. By about noon he had moved inland to Hermanville where a dressing station was set up. The only medications available to them were contained in a 26lb rucksack. However, some transport arrived later in the afternoon enabling two dressing stations to be set up which included a surgical unit - a surgeon, an anaesthetist and five assistants. Initially there was one blood transfusion service with about 100 bottles of blood and 420 bottles per day thereafter.

Unfortunately, one surgeon was sunbathing somewhere in the bay, where he stayed all night, seemingly a very unhappy man. The guns of the British Warspite and the Germans in the Merville direction were firing at each other, so there was a cascade of shots overhead. Fortunately a young relief surgeon and his party arrived at about 8am, but when he mentioned that he was 'the relief', he was told: 'Forget it, you are the surgical chief'! Sterile dressings had been brought over in Jacob's biscuit tins, about 10 of them, and together with other minimum necessities, including ether, they worked throughout the day and night.

In the first three days they dealt with 1,025 casualties, in a week about 1,700. The surgeons mostly dealt with belly wounds - the men had their bowels sewn up within about six hours. Other casualties were cleaned up, given sulphonamide tablets - the antibiotic of the day - and were sent off to a holding ship just off the beach and sent back to Southampton.

Some problems occurred with French civilians and their children. A medical orderly, who had six children of his own, was given the task of looking after these crying youngsters. The following morning he had made arrangements for them to go to Southampton. They were unaware of what was happening to them - they thought they were going to a French hospital.

As part of a beach group, 1,600 vehicles and 22,000 troops were landed on the first tide. Dr Baker was in the area for about eight weeks while the battle continued and was within six miles distance when the bombing of Caen took place, being within range to see bombs landing - for him quite an experience.

Later around Caen the troops were suffering from battle fatigue. The Corps psychiatrist was with his unit and he himself changed from being a surgeon to a psychiatrist. The troops had been pinned down for several days in trenches, lacked real food and had no rest. They were allowed plenty of sleep, were given good food and shortly afterwards some vigorous exercise - soccer. If there were not enough patients to make up a team, then the medical orderlies were called upon. Some of the orderlies suffered when playing against the rejuvenated patients, some of the Army's tough guys.

Next to Sword Beach came Juno Beach. The landing at Juno was the task of the Canadians supported by British armoured forces. The Canadians suffered many casualties in the bitter fighting there, not only getting off the well-defended beaches but also in the streets of Courselles and Graye-sur-Mer, before advancing inland to their target, the Caen-Bayeux road. In addition, their task was to close the gap with the forces on either side of them, since these gaps of several miles left the British landings open to attack by enemy tanks.

When getting off the beaches the Canadians were ruthless on some occasions. The enemy was dealt with severely, six PoWs were discovered behind a sand dune having had their throats cut. Could this have been some sort of reprisal for cruelty meted out to them at the time of the Dieppe landings two years earlier? Later at Abbaye de Ardenne during our 50th anniversary tour we discovered that several Canadians were buried - while PoWs they had been murdered by the Germans. Was this a reprisal for the Canadian action on the landing beaches?

Donald O'Hara, accompanied by John Allison, were close friends while on tour. During a lunchtime spent at Courselles-sur-Mer they had walked the beach area, Donald having landed with the Commandos at H-hour on 6 June 1944 in support of the Canadians. This return visit had been most nostalgic for him and when thinking of those who were not so lucky as him, one is immediately reminded of those words…'But for the grace of God go I'.

Also as a friend returning to the Normandy beaches for the first time was Dr Lloyd Divers. Arriving off the Arromanches beach, Lloyd well remembered the unnerving experience which he had of having to remain on his invasion transport offshore for 24 hours before landing. As a young medical officer in the RAMC he was attached to an Army base hospital during the North West Europe campaign.

At Graye-sur-Mer, Gen Charles de Gaulle, leader of the Free French forces, which included an 'army' of Resistance fighters in France, stepped ashore on 14 June 1944 following the earlier D-Day landings. He was a young army officer and politician who had repudiated the Vichy regime which operated from the unoccupied French zone where the Petain government collaborated closely with the Germans. There was some local dispute with the local authorities in Courselles about where precisely he did disembark.

To satisfy both communities it was suggested that a cross be placed in the River Seulles which flows between them or for a change in the boundary so that the memorial site selected for the cross would run through the centre of it. His landing however had been shifted from Courselles to the beach at Graye-sur-Mer for security reasons and this was confirmed by two French generals who had accompanied him and the British map of operations for the day supported this view. A memorial - a 60ft high Cross of Lorraine - was placed on a patch of sand near the beach at Graye-sur-Mer. It is in polished aluminium and is illuminated by a giant 'V' at night. A visit to Normandy was made by King George VI just two days later, 16 June 1944, coming ashore at the same point. About a month later, in mid-July, my own Regiment landed on the same beach at Graye-sur-Mer being a replacement for another tank regiment which had lost heavily in the Normandy fighting. Our arrival off the Normandy coast, as recalled by 'Jim' Boardman, was in bright clear sunlight and would remain in the memory for all who saw it. Shipping everywhere, unloading of supplies and reinforcements, battleships pounding away with their heavy naval guns, and the constant noise of aircraft moving out over target areas and returning. Some 300 yards offshore the LTIs dropped anchor, and flat square rafts, powered by two outboard engines on the corners of one side, came alongside. We transferred to these and were ferried ashore on to dry land. A short march up Juno Beach at Graye-sur-Mer, to a refreshment point at the north edge of Banville, carrying a large sign 'The Ritz' where tea was provided; a further short march to a dispersal field and we were over stage one! Our thoughts were...Where are our vehicles?... How long would we stay inactive?... Meanwhile we were busy swatting May bugs and playing cards!

Next along the coast was Gold Beach where heavy enemy artillery pounded down on the British forces. However, by nightfall on D-Day they had taken five square miles, got to within a mile of Bayeux, and almost reached the Caen-Bayeux road.

Vital for the success of the invasion as a whole was the capture of Arromanches since the 'Mulberry' prefabricated harbour was to be established there. This specially constructed harbour consisted of four miles of piers and six of floating roadway from 15 pier heads. They were towed across the English Channel in sections and submerged the day following the invasion. Each enclosed more than five square kilometres of water with a breakwater of concrete caissons each five storeys high and weighing 6,000 tons.

The harbour had taken less than a year to construct, less than a fifth of the time it took to build Dover harbour which had half the capacity.

Ten days later the 'Mulberry' was battered in severe gales and after three days started to break up. But the weather changed for the better and consequently the harbour was used extensively until the port of Cherbourg became available several weeks later. The American landings were to the west of the British forces at Omaha and Utah Beaches.

At Utah Beach they were most successful despite landing some 1,000 yards off target as this happened to be a much less defended part of the coastline. On the first day the Americans advanced six miles and had met up with their airborne troops. The Germans, however, had flooded large areas of the drop zone and many of the paratroops, weighed down with heavy packs, plunged straight into these flooded marshlands and were drowned.

The monument at Utah Beach was erected by the American Battle Monuments Commission with the approval of the French government. It commemorates the achievements of the American Forces who fought in and liberated the Cotentin Peninsula from 6 June to 1 July. It consists of a red Baveno granite obelisk surrounded by a small, developed park overlooking the historic sand dunes of the nearby beach.

A short distance away is Pointe du Hoc where there is a memorial in the battleground area where the 2nd Ranger Battalion scaled the 100ft cliffs on D-Day morning, 6 June 1944, to seize this fortified enemy position which controlled the landing approaches to both Omaha and Utah Beaches. The memorial consists of a simple granite pylon atop a concrete bunker with inscriptions in French and English on tablets at its base. The battle-scarred area remains much as the Rangers left it on 8 June 1944. Omaha Beach soon become known as Bloody Omaha since the landing there almost became a disaster for the American landing forces. They found that in the heavy seas their floating tanks went down like stones while so fierce was the enemy artillery that the assault was almost abandoned in the early hours of D-Day. However, by nightfall they had made a landing, had gained some ground, albeit only as far as the nearby coast road. Needless to say it had been tough going for the Americans who suffered very heavy casualties.

On our 50th anniversary tour we visited St-Mere-Eglise, the first town to be liberated by the Americans and where a paratrooper had feigned death for several hours when his parachute landed on the church tower from which he was left dangling until he was rescued by his countrymen.

We visited the Normandy American Cemetery Memorial located on top of the cliff overlooking Omaha Beach. 14,000 originally buried there were returned to America at the request of their next-of-kin but more than 9,000 still remain.

The Omaha Memorial at Colleville-sur-Mer is most impressive, consisting of a semi-circular colonnade with a loggia at each end. There is a 22ft bronze statue, the 'Spirit of American Youth', a most thoughtful tribute to those many thousands who gave their lives. Around the base of the statue is the inscription *Mine eyes have seen the glory of the coming of the Lord.* American President Bill Clinton was among soldiers and statesmen of the Allies that defeated Nazi Germany who had gathered for the 50th anniversary of D-Day on misty Normandy beaches to commemorate the invasion that eventually brought Hitler's armies to defeat. He paid tribute to those who, 'When they were young saved the world' and he stressed the responsibility of the younger generation to continue the ideals of those who fought on the Normandy beaches. To visit the length of coastline which includes the Utah and Omaha Beaches as we did on tour, one immediately realises that those who scaled the cliffs such as Pointe-du-Hoc did so at the time in terrible conditions with wreckage and dead comrades almost everywhere. For many it was an impossible task. There are several monuments and plaques at Omaha which recognise and remember the units and servicemen of D-Day, including a monument for the 29th Infantry Division in which one of our touring friends, Bernard Ratel who was accompanied by his wife and family, was serving on that day. The whole touring party needed no persuasion to gather round the memorial while Bernard placed a wreath on our behalf on this most memorable anniversary occasion.

Under cover of intense naval and air bombardment the Allied forces, consisting of American, Canadian, French and British landed on the various Normandy beaches in the early hours of D-Day. In this greatest amphibious assault ever, there was a heavy price to pay. As at the Omaha Cemetery, where thousands of American servicemen are buried, so too there are many thousands of war dead buried in other cemeteries throughout Normandy. For the British, special 50th Anniversary Commemoration Services were held at five of them, the service at Bayeux Cemetery was attended by HM The Queen while other members of the Royal Family attended the same Order of Service elsewhere. At Bayeux some of my Regimental friends are buried and at their graves those famous of all words always come to mind...*They shall not grow old, as we that are left grow old. Age shall not weary them, nor the years condemn. At the going down of the sun and in the morning, we shall remember them.*

Not all casualties, however, result from battle. In a most tragic event two days after my Regiment arrived in Normandy three members lost their lives including Padre JA Newson who is buried in the Bayeux Cemetery. On this day the weather was fine, we were close to the sea, so troops crowded down to the beach for a swim, a 'wash-down' and to rinse through a few 'smalls'. In point of fact, the area chosen was dangerous for bathing, for there was a strong under-tow and treacherous currents swirled about the rocks. The troops were taking advantage of an especially hot day, some

Canadian soldiers were bowled over by the heavy rollers and in a moment were in the gravest danger. Attempts at rescue were made at once, but even the strongest swimmers in the Regiment could make no headway and the men who tried to form a chain were beaten down and swept away.

At the time I was one in a small group of non-swimmers who were at the far end of the beach and who were not in the sea. It was only on our return to our harbour area did we become aware of the awful tragedy. We were all stunned by the happenings. Throughout the North-West Europe campaign we did not have another Regimental chaplain.

For the 50th anniversary my party attended the special service at Douvres-la-Delivrande War Cemetery where more than 1,000 British troops are buried. Princess Anne attended the 40-minute commemoration ceremony, having landed by helicopter in a nearby field. During the service were prayers, readings, the hymns *O God, our help in ages past* and *Praise, my Soul, the King of Heaven*, and a bugler sounded the Last Post and, after two minutes silence, Reveille. When the service ended wreaths were laid, one by the Princess, who on making her way out of the cemetery proceeded slowly past veterans, relatives, friends spending time talking to many of them. It was all very friendly and most thoughtful. As we left the cemetery, the local people lining the route showed their appreciation by clapping heartily as we veterans, with medals proudly on display, proceeded to the rendezvous with our leader. While in Douvres village, Princess Anne took an opportunity to visit the memorial where she laid a wreath.

Most of our party also made a special visit to the village - to the local bar - a visit which was due to circumstances beyond our control.

We had assembled at the RV point for our coach returning from Hermanville. A prolonged period of waiting ended when a motorcyclist came along to tell us that there was a hold-up as a coach - not ours - on its way from there had found its way into a ditch. Seeing our plight at the RV point some local residents from a villa opposite generously supplied some drinks (tea) and offered hospitality. But when our leader (Karen Ingleby) suggested a visit to the nearby local bar, there was an immediate exodus thereto.

Promptly on our arrival, our newly found friend, Dr Lloyd Divers, gave the barmaid a verbal prescription for some gold coloured liquid (cognac) but before this had hardly reached our tongues our leader appeared at the entrance…'Coach here, get on or else!' (or something which meant that). As old soldiers we were all too much aware that 'an order is an order' and soon we were on our way to Arromanches for the visit by the Queen. There were no problems en route - we were tail-end Charlie - as everyone was ahead of us in view of our earlier delay. However, we did arrive in plenty of time for the anniversary of our lifetime at Gold Beach.

The main event of the 50th anniversary commemorations for the British was held at Arromanches in the afternoon of 6 June 1994. The weather on this most memorable of all occasions was dull with some slight drizzle at the outset. The parade of veterans formed up on the sands of this Normandy beach at Arromanches known to the troops as Gold Beach. On parade were thousands of old soldiers - six deep - who were informally inspected by members of the Royal Family. We were in a position near the slipway to the sands - a vantage point indeed to see the Queen's arrival in an open-topped Land Rover.

She was greeted by a 42-gun salute by the destroyer *Edinburgh* and the assault ship *Intrepid*. Five Army bands played as she took the salute, the march-past lasting 20 minutes. As old soldiers ourselves this very special commemoration was a treat which we will never experience again. It was a time to remember, to remember that on these same beaches 50 years before the struggle to liberate the Europe Hitler had conquered, had begun. HM the Queen, speaking to the 12,000 veterans, told them: 'Veterans of the Normandy campaign you deserve your nation's thanks. May we, your fellow countrymen, be worthy of what you did for us'. It was a time too for the British veterans and their friends to feel proud of their generation - to have overcome all the odds stacked against them - and left no-one wondering why the scale of D-Day commemorations was so vast. 'This has brought the past into the present,' said the Queen, 'may it also be an inspiration for the future'. May her words never be forgotten.

As HM the Queen addressed the very large crowd on the Arromanches beach we looked back and remembered our young, some very young, friends from many countries - Britain, America, Canada and France, who were killed or wounded on those beaches and in the landings on the Normandy coast. It was not too difficult for our thoughts to reflect on the experience of those who were among the first waves of servicemen who were given the Herculean task of liberating the continent of Europe. D-Day - 6 June 1944 - was a long day, the longest day of battle in any war, during which there were many deeds of heroism.

The Victoria Cross, the premier British award for conspicuous bravery in the presence of the enemy, was instituted in 1856 by Queen Victoria. Steve Bench confirmed that in the North-West Europe campaign there were 11 VCs awarded in 1944, and nine such awards in 1945. Despite the indescribable heat of battle on invasion day, along the many miles of the French coastline, only one award of a VC was made. Company Sergeant

Major Stanley Elton Hollis of the Green Howards, risked his life on many occasions on that day, destroying several enemy positions and removing the enemy, which enabled assault troops to get ashore and to advance inland.

After the afternoon ceremony we met at a point on the fringe of Arromanches. Because of the large crowd of veterans and friends we, along with them, had a very long wait before our particular coach was called forward. After approximately five hours we were able to leave which allowed us to return to our hotel in Caen just a little before midnight. We had on this memorable day been present for the commemoration of The Longest Day which had also been *the longest day* of a Holts' tour.

Arromanches has a very important museum including a diorama and models of the Mulberry Harbour and the landing beaches. Across Normandy there are many museums - the larger ones are at Bayeux, Caen, Pegasus, and St Mere Eglise. The most modern one is the Museum of Peace in Caen which was opened in 1991. The Caen Memorial, on the site of one of the bloodiest battles in history, takes you on a compelling journey from the dark years of war to a vision of peace. The sights and sounds of Europe's descent into war and Hitler's rise to power are experienced. So too is the fear of daily life under German occupation and the terror of those sent to concentration camps.

One of the highlights of the very memorable Holts' tour was the presentation on our last day of the very special medal as Normandy veterans. There were 11 of us in the group which included Americans and Canadians.

In his letter to us the Secretaire General, Jubile de la Liberty (1944 - 1994 Normandie), stated: 'I have the honour and pleasure to inform you that the Commemoration Medal, created by the Regional Council of Normandy, will be presented to you at the Abbaye Aux Dames in Caen. I reiterate the consideration of the Regional Council of Normandy for your personal commitment during the Liberation of our Province.'

At the Abbaye we lined up on parade, with others, and the medal was presented by the Mayor who gave each of us a 'kiss and a cuddle' (why didn't we have the Mayoress!) and a blessing as follows...'On behalf of the President of the Republic I present you with this token of our appreciation of your assistance in producing our Liberty.'

In addition we were later presented with a medal certificate signed by Le President du Conseil Regional.

After the ceremony there was a vin d'honneur for veterans, relatives and friends. Before leaving our hotel for the Abbaye one of our group had been presented with the Croix-de-Guerre for some exceptional exploits in France before the Normandy invasion. The medal had arrived by post and was given to the recipient by the hotel receptionist! No vin d'honneur, no nothing - not quite the usual way to honour the brave!

While we are very much aware of the depth of sacrifice, daring exploits, and the vital contributions overall made by the flyers in the RAF, both bomber and fighter crews, throughout the war years, nevertheless, the RAF had a significant ground role too.

On that day of all days - 6 June 1944 - the Normandy seaside site of Arromanches became history. Winston Churchill, in his legendary and courageous manner, declared that in order for Allied forces to set foot on French soil, they would need to construct an artificial port. 12 days after the Allies had landed, the port Mulberry was in full operation. 115 enormous blocks of reinforced cement were submerged under water, and 60 sunken warships of varying tonnage, together formed a giant semi-circular breakwater measuring 12km which extended the length of several nearby communities. Four floating piers, measuring a total length of 5.7km were positioned in the centre of the port and joined to the mainland, completing this gigantic feat of military ingenuity.

A close association at invasion time between the Mulberry floating docks and personnel of the RAF Mobile Signal Unit emphasises the role of such a critical operation. A friend, Derek J Pitchford, was there with RAF MSU 5274B and in his *Memory of the Year 1944* has, to my mind given an absorbing account of their special role of which so many of us in the Normandy campaign were totally unaware.

An RAF memory of the year 1944

After passing out at RAF Compton Bassett, Wilts, as a wireless operator, that is being able to read and send the Morse Code at 18 words per minute, plus other technical detail, I was posted to RAF Chigwell, Essex, not knowing my fate. I subsequently passed out at 20 wpm, quite an achievement. While there I was assigned to one of the first RAF Mobile Signal Units ever to be deployed known as 5274B. The unit was complete with vehicles later to be waterproofed containing wireless equipment (receivers and transmitters) aerials, cipher, cooking, water bowser, generators, tents etc. plus approximately 50 personnel of all ranks including three officers named Meade, Moorehouse and Moody. We also had two despatch riders with their motorbikes.

We were deployed along the south coast living at all times under canvas, setting up the wireless equipments, becoming fully operational for short periods of time and then moving on to a new destination going through the same procedures. In May 1944 we were moved to an embarkation area, at

Horsham not knowing the invasion was but a few weeks away. At the beginning of June 1944 the unit was moved to Gosport and loaded on to a small naval landing craft moving out and anchoring off the Isle of Wight. The Channel at that time was full of shipping - large and small craft all waiting for the signal to proceed with the invasion of France on 6 June 1944. All the Allied aircraft joining in were marked with white stripes on their wings for identification purposes.

After landing in Normandy, seasick, we made camp in an orchard near to the beach overlooking the coastline. All the boats flew barrage balloons from their bows many of which were destroyed by enemy action or electrical storms.

The unit 5274B was given the enormous responsibility with others of the defence of the Mulberry floating docks at Arromanches by plotting the movement of all Allied and enemy aircraft entering the sector or zone of the floating docks. To achieve this 5274B was attached to the Mobile Operations Room set up and camouflaged in a large crater. Morse signals were received in code on certain radio frequencies and entered on a blackboard in white chalk of all aircraft in the vicinity of the floating docks. These messages were decoded and plotted on the large map by the RAF operations personnel. I cannot recall from memory who were the originators of these signals or messages. We had to wear full battledress at all times in the ops room. I was on duty early one morning when 3,000 Lancaster bombers raided Caen and its surrounding area and again I was on duty when a further force of 300 Lancasters bombed Caen in order to enable our fighting forces to break through the German resistance. This was eventually successfully concluded.

Following the breakthrough the unit 5274B proceeded to Amiens and then on to Paris where we joined up with the American forces in the liberation of the French capital. While in Amiens I visited the grave of Gp Capt Pickard, shot down in his Mosquito aircraft on a raid to free Resistance prisoners from the jail.

Other memories I recall are -

Going to Bayeux for a shower bath in the mobile bath unit. The water was either too cold or too hot, no happy medium. Also going to the same town to have our uniforms fumigated.

The splendid Trojan work of the amphibious vehicles called 'Dukws' which unloaded stores constantly from vessels alongside the floating docks and brought them ashore.

Going down to the beach to beg bread from the massive American LSTs as all we lived on were biscuits and small packs of vital necessities.

Receiving a copy of the message given by the Allied Supreme Commander, Gen Eisenhower, which commenced with the words…'We are about to embark upon the great crusade for which we have striven for so long etc. etc.'

For our participation in the defence of the Mulberry floating docks the unit was awarded one medal and seven Mentions in Despatches. To show no favouritism the names of all the 5274B personnel were put in a hat and drawn out. I was not one of the lucky ones.

The successful Allied campaign in Normandy led to the eventual freedom of the whole of France. Their leader, Gen de Gaulle, however had not been held in the highest esteem during his sojourn in England and indeed he showed little gratitude to the British people at the time of the liberation. Suppose that if Normandy, or at least some portion of it however small, had been generously given to Britain by France for playing a large part in removing the domination of their country by the Nazis, it would have represented a wonderful gesture by de Gaulle to Winston Churchill, close ally and friend of the French people.

Maybe too it may have been that such 'small seeds' would have resulted in the two countries developing a close, indeed a very close, relationship with deeply beneficial advantages for both in the subsequent affairs of the continent of Europe.

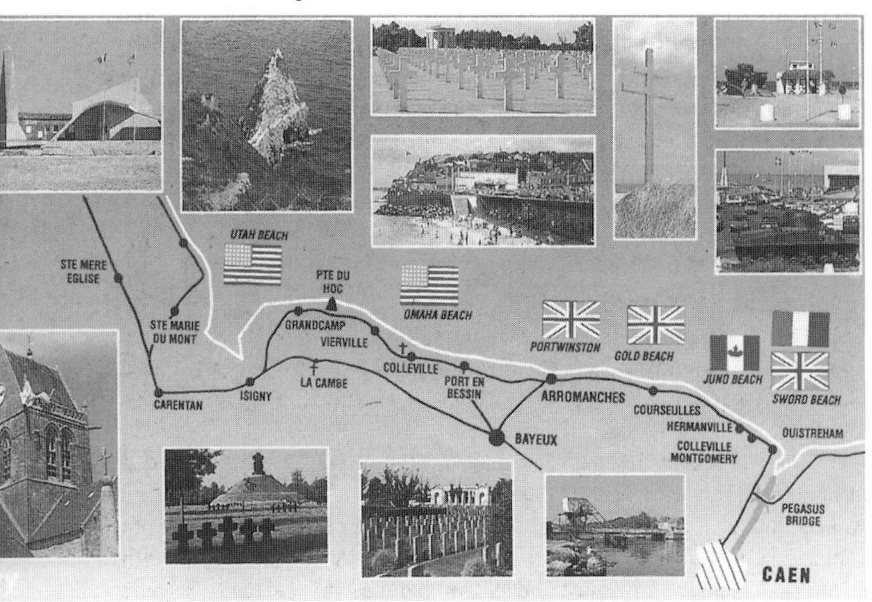

10

Normandy and Northern France

During the years before the Normandy invasion, the 5th Royal Inniskilling Dragoon Guards were in 28th Armoured Brigade which formed part of the 9th Armoured Division, the 'Panda' Division. Early in 1944 it became generally known that neither the Brigade nor the Division were to remain as an Army formation.

Two of the three armoured regiments in the Brigade, the 15/19 Hussars and the Fife and Forfar Yeomanry left to join other Divisional units, leaving the Inniskillings all alone and, at that time, with nowhere to go! There were the usual rumours as to the Regiment's future role, the foremost being a posting to the Far East; another was that squadrons and/or troops and/or officers and other ranks being posted to Normandy as replacements for other units. Needless to say these were not acceptable to us. Eventually, all rather hurriedly, the Regiment received an order to mobilise for service overseas. In mid-July 1944 we arrived in Normandy not knowing what our role was to be. Again, eventually, we discovered that we were to relieve the 4th County of London Yeomanry in 22nd Armoured Brigade of 7th Armoured Division, the 'Desert Rats'. Shortly after our arrival we received news that the Corps Commander, the Divisional Commander and the Brigade Commander were being replaced! Perhaps word of the 'Skins' arrival had reached them - well, anyway, we were assured that it was none of our doing.

It is often said that unfortunately they were in the wrong place at the wrong time. This is more or less what happened to 4th County of London Yeomanry in the early days of the invasion in June 1944 when in the area of Villers Bocage. The Short History of the 7th Armoured Division contains the following record...

'At half-past five the next morning (13 June) the advance continued through Briquessard and Amaye-sur-Seulles. Villers Bocage was entered without incident, although the 11th Hussars and the 8th Hussars had both contacted enemy on either side of the centre-line. A Squadron of the 4th County of London Yeomanry and A Company of the 1st Rifle Brigade then pushed on according to plan towards the high ground to the north-east of the town. In order to clear the traffic on the roads behind, the column had to move out comparatively closed up, and it was this that gave a Mark VI tank, which suddenly appeared from a side road, its opportunity. Its first shot destroyed one of the Rifle Brigade half-tracks, thus blocking the road, and then at its own convenience, it destroyed the remainder of the half-tracks, some Honey tanks of the Reconnaissance Troop, four tanks of Regimental Headquarters and two OP tanks accompanying the squadron. Escape for the tanks, carriers and half-tracks was impossible, the road was blocked, obscured by flames and smoke from the burning vehicles whose crews could only seek what shelter they could from the machine gun fire, and our own tanks were powerless against the armour of the Tiger, with limitless cover at its disposal. Meanwhile A Squadron in the lead, with the Commanding Officer, were cut off. Their last wireless message, received at half past ten, reported that they were completely surrounded by tanks and infantry, that the position was untenable, and withdrawal impossible. Relief was equally impossible, as, in addition to the burning tanks and vehicles, the road was blocked by the same Mark VI which commanded all approaches.

What had happened was simple enough, namely, that the anticipated counter-attack by 2 Panzer Division, much delayed by our own and the United States Air Forces, was at last on its way. Both sides were using Villers Bocage as the most important road-centre south of Bayeux, and the Division, advancing from the north, had met the German armour coming up in the opposite direction. As a result, there followed the brilliant defensive battle of Villers Bocage which, although it obliged us to withdraw some seven miles, cost the enemy casualties quite disproportionate to this gain.'

It was quite by chance that the German Tank Commander, Wittman, had confronted the Desert Rats resting. In a Tiger tank, with its 88mm gun giving it superior fire power to the British tanks, he knocked out the first vehicle in the line and was then able to destroy 25 tanks of the 4th County of London Yeomanry. Later Wittman got his come-uppance when at Falaise shortly afterwards he was killed by Canadian and Polish forces. He is buried in the German Cemetery at La Cambe.

On any battlefield tour of France the Holts' itinerary invariably includes visits to various CWGC cemeteries while, additionally, there may be requests for special visits. Sometimes a cemetery may be small, just a handful of graves; sometimes there may be hundreds of graves; and there may be thousands in a few of the cemeteries.

On occasions it may be observed that many men were killed on the

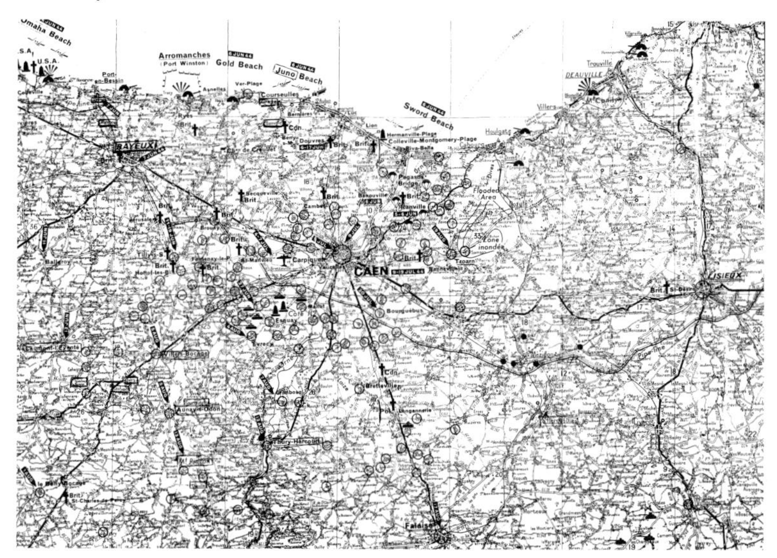

same date or thereabouts suggesting that a battle in which they fought probably occurred then and there, while many headstones bearing a particular regiment would undoubtedly indicate it had been deeply involved in heavy fighting in the locality. As part of a battlefield tour it is not unusual to visit a German cemetery. When I visited the La Cambe Cemetery and saw Wittman's grave, my thoughts wandered to the effect that this one man had on the role of my Regiment in July 1944 and on my own life in the Army. His exploits at Villers Bocage had resulted in the assignment of my Regiment as a replacement for another at that time. Would my Regiment have served in Normandy and the North West Europe campaign; would a posting to any other theatre of war have been our lot? Thoughts go on and on.

One of the NCOs with my Regiment at the Normandy landing was 'Jim' Boardman who was in Reconnaissance Squadron. Some time later he became Regimental Sergeant Major and subsequently was commissioned in the Army Air Corps. On retirement from the Army he became Secretary of the Regimental Association. Among many activities he has organised tours for members of the Association. It would not be easy for anyone to surpass this one which he had arranged for Normandy and Northern France as a special 50th anniversary.

The hazards of being at the sharp end in Reconnaissance were not very comfortable to say the least as Jim vividly reminded us while on this tour 50 years after 'we were there'.

The Allied invasion forces were contained by the Germans in Normandy from 6 June to mid-August 1944 until the 'break-out' at Falaise. Fortunately for my Regiment we were only there for the last month of this period. Very briefly, the Regiment landed on 18 July, subsequently took over tanks/ vehicles and moved up into the line on 31 July as part of 7 Armoured Division and were immediately involved in the fighting to 'break-out' of the beachhead.

Diary dates indicate that from 1 to 13 August the Regiment was continuously in action in the general area of Coulain - Villers Bocage - and Aunay-sur-Odon in the area of Mt Pincon.

After a rest day on 14 August, the following two days, 15 and 16 August, involved operations in the river Orne area before moving to east of Caen on 17 August. Immediately afterwards the advance through northern France via St Pierre-sur-Dives, Livarot, Lisieux, Thiberville, and Boissey-le-Chatel (26 August).

The Association tour covered the five-day period 24 to 28 August. Jim's account is as follows:

'Forseeing the many problems which would be encountered during the celebration of D-Day we opted to revisit Normandy in late August and so revisit some of the villages on the actual day of their liberation. This proved to be a most successful and memorable experience and permitted an almost troublefree four-day tour through the Bocage area of Normandy and almost to the Seine. We also felt rather bogus in claiming any glory from those who had landed on D-Day because we had in fact not landed until 18 July to join the 7th Armoured Division and to take part in the break-out. There was still hard fighting to be done; we were fresh and well-prepared.

Day 1

Despite rail strikes, a friend with a broken leg and a variety of pills for ills, a 51-seater coach left Dover for Calais at 8am on 24 August. Some of us had not met each other since 1945. We arrived in Caen in late afternoon. There was a quick tour of the beaches and in particular Juno Beach where we had landed 50 years earlier. We were the lucky ones to return. A visit to Bayeaux War Cemetery was the first of an emotional journey. Some of our early casualties were buried there or recorded on the memorial because they had no known grave.

Day 2

The following day we set off on our old centreline from Bayeaux to Cahagnes, Courvaudon Aunay-sur-Odon and Mt Pincon, the objective for Operation Bluecoat. One of our party requested an additional stop at a small village called Jerusalem. He had been a member of the 24th Lancers, a wartime armoured regiment which had been disbanded at that point. Some of his friends were buried there. I had also read a moving story of the death of a padre who had been officiating at the burial of another padre. A shell had killed him. Both were buried side-by-side. Our friend had then been transferred to the 'Skins'.

The two Army padres buried at Jerusalem, CWGC, Chonain, lie side by side. One was the Rev G Nesbitt who had also served with the Eighth Army in North Africa. He was attached to 8 DLI (Durham Light Infantry) and was killed in action on 5 July 1944. The other padre was the Rev Cecil Hawkesworth, Curate of St Peter's, Croydon. He had already served in the Sudan, Eritrea, and with the Eighth Army in North Africa. In 1944 he was attached to 6 DLI and was killed as a result of an accident on 7 July 1944.

A special visit to Jerusalem CWGC had been requested by Mr D Stewart. He had served with the 24th Lancers and now wished to visit the three graves of two officers and one man, all of whom he knew well. Mr Stewart recalled...

'The 24th Lancers was a wartime regiment, formed in 1940 and disbanded at Jerusalem in 1944. It was in 8th Armoured Brigade, attached to 50th Division, and landed in Normandy on D-Day. 4/7 Royal Dragoon Guards were then the leading Regiment and the Sherwood Rangers also formed part of the Brigade. In the Jerusalem area most of the fighting for 24th Lancers was around Tilly which controlled a crossroads along the approach road to Caen, and the fighting continued for several weeks. When they landed on D-Day 8th Armoured Brigade had, as its objective on the first day, the town of Villers Bocage but this was still not taken when the 24th Lancers was disbanded. Tilly changed hands several times and in the process was thoroughly destroyed. When the 24th Lancers were disbanded he was sent on a course and, fortunately for him, eventually a posting came for the 'Skins'. '

After this thoughtful visit to Jerusalem CWGC we journeyed on to the area of Caumont.

After passing through Caumont the tour party halted just a short distance on the Cahagnes road from which point Maj Pat Whitmore MBE described the first Regimental battle position, 2 August 1944.

'Behind us the sea, about 30 miles away. A long way to the west is the sea again, a huge peninsula which we called the Cherbourg Peninsula but the French knew it as the Cotentin Peninsula.

'The Regiment had been in a harbour area north of Caumont which had been liberated three days after D-Day but the battle had gone backwards and forwards and therefore it was still in the front line when we arrived.

Jim Boardman's granddaughter

'The whole battle area could be seen from our vantage point - Caen was about 30 miles to the east; St Lo was about 30 miles away in the other direction; and we had gone in from the coast. The Canadians, the Poles, the Dutch, and some British were still holding Caen; we were in the centre and the Americans were on the right. The Americans found an easy way through St Lo towards the sea - done a fork - gone up to Cherbourg - and down to Avranches which is where the Brittany Peninsula extends. Then the Americans halted and faced Paris, a distance of about 130 miles.

'Immediately in front of us on our right was the valley of the Orne (a big river) which flows through Caen and a tributary to it is the Odon. In fine weather could be seen the spire of the new church at Aunay-sur-Odon - remembered by many at the time as a large heap of ruins; and the hill beyond it, Mt Pincon - a Regimental battle honour.

'We came down the road, Recce leading, and shells were falling in the valley. On our left about five miles away was Villers Bocage which was very much in the front line. The road went left and then right and on the next crest was the village of Cahagnes, never to be forgotten, a heap of ruins - masses of dead cattle all over the place, houses flattened, but a vast crucifix was still standing just on the left side of the village.

'Over the next crest we came to a big road fork - one road going to St Lo, the other to Granville on the coast. HQ Squadron stopped nearby; A Squadron went on the road to Villers Bocage; B Squadron on the right of the road. What happened next is a story to be told by Capt Derek Philo.'

When on the recce for the tour Pat had asked some of his friends from the local community to please slaughter a few cattle in June - let them rot - so that on this 50th tour the party would have a real smell of the days of battle. When they joined our coach party he questioned them about his request and told us "I'm afraid they haven't done it"! So we continued to enjoy the freshness of the Normandy countryside.

Jim continues...

'We moved forward to the next point of contact, Cahagnes. This village had been fought over by British and German troops and changed hands four times. As we entered in 1944 it resembled a scene from the Somme Battles of 1916. Cattle lay dead and the smell was revolting. Only the crucifix hung crazily from the cross among a pile of rubble. I remember wondering how my father had survived the four years of war in that war of horror. We had planned to give a presentation on a slope facing south and where we ought to have been able to see the objective as a low hill slightly higher in the range in front of us. In 1944 the objective was of little importance to forward troops, the immediate problem was to get across the next field! There was a drizzle and visibility was too poor to permit this so a presentation of the situation was given in the coach. We were joined by a party of French locals, the Mayor of Cahagnes and some of his council and the Commandant of the French veterans, the equivalent of our British Legion.

'There was an exchange of greetings before we were invited to a lone grave which the local people had tended for 50 years. Just one grave with an account of the action which had killed the occupant. Lt JG Marshall-Cornwall, Grenadier Guards, had alighted from his tank to hand over prisoners and had been sniped. The French had asked that he should remain where he was at first buried. They had a great pride in this personal act. It was to be only one of many we would witness in the following days. He will remain there with pride of place for many years after we are forgotten, almost like the tomb of the unknown soldier. We were all touched by their sincerity. There followed an interchange of souvenirs and we moved on.

'The Commandant asked us to call at the home of a local farmer who we had met on a previous visit. Although I and a friend had made a visit in April of this year to let the villages know what we intended, we had no idea whether they would partake. We had made a programme and sent a copy ahead. More than that, I thought that there might be the odd issue of calvados but was concerned that this would be insufficient to satisfy the needs of some members of the party, particularly those with diabetic problems. I need not have concerned myself. At every halt there was a mini banquet.

'We moved forward half a mile to a point where the farmer lived and where one of our party had led a troop of Cromwell tanks. He had moved cautiously forward onto a cross roads, seen mines on the road, tried to reverse but been hit by a well camouflaged 88mm gun at a range of about 100 yards. The effect was devastating. The round entered the co-driver's hatch and went out through the driver's side killing both men instantly. He had been struck heavily on the head and was lucky to escape with the other members of the crew.

'Capt Derek A Philo, who was with our party, recalled his experiences of that fateful day at Query on 2 August 1944.

'I must have had one of the shortest combatant careers in the Regiment. We started off in the morning. A Squadron was in the lead. Recce came up to what, at that time, was a much smaller T-junction. Ray (Irwin) was coming up the road; one of the Recce tanks went back; it went off the side of the road, went over a mine, and Ray got all the bits in his face. He was left there.

'At this point I was called to come forward and come round the corner. This is where I think that we all started learning, although we had been training a very long time. There was confusion over the wireless, talking about a crossroad, but in fact was a T-junction so I was not at all sure what crossroad I was looking for. In fact, I was on the actual spot. Thoughts went through my mind wondering what to do next - *I don't like it - I don't want to go* - but somebody has to stick his neck out. One of the lessons learned was that as it is vital to be quicker on the trigger than the enemy, go out with all guns blazing. Sometimes when that is done some comrades in the infantry are around and they would not like it. So having looked at it, I said to my Troop Sergeant Archie Carr you stand firm and I would go quickly over the T-junction and once across on the other side I would have a good view up the road. At this particular time the ground in front was covered thick with several inches of dust. I could not see a thing but when we got halfway across the road, all of a sudden, my driver Eddie Booth saw what I had not seen, there was a line of pencil box mines in the middle of the road, deep in dust. The tank stood on its nose; I said, let's get back - we were in a classic trap. The enemy gun was only a short distance away tucked into the side of the road by a barn. By the time he had got the tank back into reverse, we found ourselves the first people in the 'Skins' looking up the barrel of an 88m the wrong way. The shot hit us in the front - straight through the two chaps Eddie Booth and Billy Hodgson in the front - the tank stopped - its turret would not move - I threw out some smoke as we had been told to do - and this was everywhere - so we could not see and we could not breathe. The impact of the shot had not only gone through the front of the tank but it had also dislodged the lid in the turret and the lid was on me. I was out momentarily but by that time Tubby Johnson was on his way up. We got out - walked back - saw the doctor who said 'drink this - get in the ambulance'. I didn't see Tubby and Epps again. They disappeared.

Afterwards I was in hospital for about a fortnight. Suddenly they came round and said, 'Anybody want to go out' and I said 'I've had enough of this'. I would not have minded if they had back-loaded me to the UK but they didn't!

'I then found that I was one of two junior officers, two sergeants, and 24 others with rifles, stenguns, pistols, all sorts of people who had come from everywhere. We were joined by a captain and a sergeant major who had flown over from England and the group became No 204 POW Unit.

'It says a lot for the organisation because we were told to go over to a field. Two drivers went down to the beach, picked up two lorries after reporting to 'so-and-so' and within that day we went back to the beach having collected barbed wire, pit props, sledge hammers, cooking equipment and all the appropriate gear to run a POW cage. It was all available down at the beach. By the time we had got all this lot assembled, it was getting dark so we had a brew up, put up a couple of tents for ourselves and kipped down.

'I did not know where we were but I heard that there were over 100,000 prisoners at Falaise. At about 4am along came a jeep with two redcaps in it and they asked if we were No 204 POW - well, we have got 2,000 prisoners who will be here at 6.30am.

The captain and the sergeant major had been doing this in the desert - collecting Italians, then losing them, so they were quite experienced at it. They told us not to worry - get some breakfast, so we did.

When the prisoners arrived we marched them round the field in fours and when they became an absolute solid block, they sat down. POW staff were told to walk around with their rifles and to look busy. The German officers had been taken away. The senior NCOs had to find men who were cooks and 40 other men were given a diagram and told to start building the cage. They built it beautifully. When the cage was built, all the POWs were allowed to stand up. I still feel that it was so impressive to have someone present who really knew what they were doing. Eventually the POWs were back-loaded into lorries, went down to the beach, from where some went to England, some to Canada, and some to America. They were shipped out as quickly as possible.

I was later posted to the unit where we first got our tanks and having stayed there a short while, I got back to the 'Skins' in December 1944.'

Freddie 'Trooper' Gibbons remembered that...

'On the first night of Regimental action, the Luftwaffe came over dropping flares which we thought was marvellous because we could see to put the petrol in our tanks. But suddenly they splattered us with anti-personnel bombs. I remember this episode very well. While getting the petrol cans at the back of the tank, a button came off my trousers and while cursing about this, all of a sudden I was aware that something was coming down which seemed to me to be snowflakes all over the show. Something hit me over the head, it must have been a stone, causing a red mark I found later on.

'I crouched down for about 10 minutes unable to get to the petrol cans until eventually it stopped. I got in the turret again and they bombed us again. I don't think - and it was surprising - there were any casualties arising from the raid.'

Sergeant Sam Hayward confirmed the story pointing out that…

'It was the first real action of any sort - a big shock - for the whole Regiment in the area.' To him the falling debris looked like sparks, possibly phosphorous. All this happened just about going dark time - about midnight (BST). According to Gibbons there was very little night time then as it was necessary to be up at about 2.15am to receive the 'netting call' for the next day. The scene was most grotesque.

Jim continues…

'I walked ahead to our farmer friend to see what in particular he wanted us to do. He invited me in. 'I have 51 people with me', I explained 'That's all right, bring them in,' he said. Tables and chairs were prepared in the garden but the rain was falling hard. We all crowded into his sitting room while his wife cooked pan after pan of small cocktail sausages. The farmer

Mrs Bradfield, Col W Bradfield OBE MC and the local mayor.

The above photo was taken in August 1944 of an 'A' Squadron tank handed to Derek Philo by the young man standing in front. Who are the four crew members Archie Carr is talking to?

came in armed with a seemingly unending supply of champagne. It was still only 11am and we had a long way to go! It was with some difficulty that I managed to get everyone back onto the coach. It was also an indication of what the next three days would be like!

'Courvaudon would be our next village. This is a small complex of farms and small houses on a hillside north east of Aunay-sur-Odon. In 1944 we had lined up in battle formation intent upon charging down the reverse slope to capture Hamars. The fields and trees have hardly changed in 50 years. We were met by the dignitaries of the village and many banner bearers of local groups. The village band, about 12 strong, led us to their memorial where wreath laying and speech making took place. We were all presented with a special medal struck by the village. The mayor led us to a well kept barn where the most wonderful buffet was awaiting. We were wondering how such small villages could raise funds to pay for such splendour and where in England would a village of perhaps 100 inhabitants be able to arrange such an event. We in England of course have never suffered as these people did and therefore have no real deep gratitudes as the French have. The spread would have been a credit to any regimental cook sergeant at one of our regimental balls, Waterloo or Balaclava.

'Despite my warnings about the liberal issue of calvados, a few of our members were beginning to show the effects. I had been the regimental sergeant major in the early 60s and now was the time to use some of the well used phrases to extract the unwilling to get on the coach! My own memory of this place came back to me during a previous visit in 1983 and when with six friends we had set out to retrace our route. I had remembered that in 1944 there had been a lot of smoke coming from the next field. At the time I suspected that one of our tanks had been hit, but it had been at least 100 yards away and someone else's war. One tended to concentrate on what was the immediate threat. We had met the local mayor who informed us that his father had tried to get the pilot of the Spitfire which had crashed there out of his burning plane. A small piece of the jigsaw of war was completed.'

Aunay-sur-Odon had been bombed so heavily that only the church spire remained to indicate where the centre of the town had been. The rubble had been bombed. No roads were useable and a new route was bulldozed round by armoured dozers. For those who witnessed such destruction, the sight of rebuilt towns showing no signs of the damage is a real pleasure and reward. It is a mental satisfaction and indication of a happy ending to a horrific experience. I had two sons and a grand-daughter aged seven in the party and I wondered if they could visualise such horror when standing in a lovely peaceful field overlooking such delightful countryside.

Day 3

One of our members had been in the 6th Airborne Division and landed by glider in the Pegasus Bridge area. I promised him that we would try to fit in a visit even though the original bridge has now been replaced by a new but identical one. He had carved his initials on the old one. The stories of the air drop and particularly those glider landings leave me in wonder and admiration for the troops who took part in them. In my latter years of service I had served in the Army Air Corps and appreciate some of the problems of flying. To fly across the Channel in the dark and being towed by a bomber which is being shot at and to expect to find a landing at a place where you have never been before belies belief. The odds of success must be about five per cent. The single story of Maj Howard's glider which had the task of being the first to land and to capture the bridge is but one story. Once cast off there was only one way to go and that was down. There was certain to be a crash landing at something like 100mph and after that there would be a battle to fight for many hours before relief. The major's sergeant pilot cast off, saw a ribbon of light which he hoped was the Caen Canal and put the nose down. He landed with the nose of the glider through the wire which was there to defend the bridge. Neither James Bond nor Indiana Jones could improve upon that. Our friend had been in the 12th glider to land. His story emphasised the tremendous security level that we had all been part of. He had no idea of his point of departure in UK and was uncertain about the point of impact. He had spent his one hour forty minute flight being buffeted by the turbulence of the towing aircraft and trying to tighten bolts which kept the tail attached to the body. He need not have bothered because the craft was smashed to splinters on landing.

On 24 August 1944, we had fought through the heavily defended town of Lisieux, an important rail centre. I had changed my vehicle to a small Daimler scout car and was in a troop of three vehicles trying to get to the Basilica, a dominating feature resembling Saint Paul's Cathedral. Perched high on a hill it dominates the area. I remember having the greatest pity for the infantry we were working with. We respectfully referred to them as PBI (poor bloody infantry). I witnessed a platoon of the Queen's Regiment destroyed one by one as they attempted to move up towards the objective. I had tried to take the Sten gun from a dead corporal because mine had a bent butt. As I rolled him over, the gun went off and a burst of fire missed me by inches. Once at the base of Basilica, the shrine to Saint Teresa, we reported. The orders were to try to get to the high vantage point in the dome and check that it was not being used as an observation post by the

Local mayor, Derek Philo, Archie Carr and Jessie Carr.

enemy. My officer told me to move off and followed with his Sten. There was a circular stairway of some 270 steps which at no point gave a better vision than six feet. I have never climbed a circular stairway without being instantly reminded of that stressful climb. There were no Germans there, or at least we didn't see any. I climbed the same stairway with my sons on this occasion but some of the same feelings of stress were there. When we arrived at the base in 1944 there stood a group of German POWs who were being searched. On this occasion there were sightseers who were full of admiration for the beauty and splendour of this wonderful building. Only we who witnessed the horrors and carnage 50 years earlier could think of other matters.

In 1944 we had made an advance of 20 miles to Saint George-du-Vievre on the following day. The chase was on and the Germans were retreating for the remaining crossings over the Seine. Small pockets of resistance caused us casualties but there was a feeling of victory in the air. It was dusk as we approached on foot through the wooded area leading to the village of St George. We were very tired and had a petrol problem with one of the carriers. To add to our concern, an American Thunderbolt fighter was circling us. We stood by with our yellow smoke should he peel off and make an attack. He flew away. We sighted something through the gloom and thought it was a tank. None of us were feeling like a battle and decided to withdraw and report. The following morning an infantry platoon supported by a troop of our tanks advanced to check it out. They found that our appreciation of the object was correct. At a range of about a hundred yards it fired at the party but missed. The HE round struck the ground and flying debris caused some casualties before it was knocked out. During a visit in 1984 we learned that St George-du-Vievre had been a strong centre for the French Resistance, the Marquis. When we had landed in June, they had thought themselves strong enough to come out into the open and fight in the belief that liberation would come quickly. It had taken us ten weeks to reach this point. In that time the Germans had rounded up the group, led by a female doctor and the chief of the fire brigade, and shot them. We also learned that our commanding officer had been contacted and requested not to attack the village, they preferred to liberate it themselves!

This probably accounted for a detour with which my troop of the Reconnaissance Squadron was tasked and which would find an alternative route to the next village of Saint Grégoire-du-Vievre. It was early morning on 25 August and I was the leading vehicle. We came to a road block which consisted of a fallen tree on top of a trailer. I dismounted and went forward to take a closer look. A civilian came running from a nearby house waving his arms and indicating that it would blow up. He pointed out the explosives and informed us that he was a member of the Resistance. This we thought was an excellent excuse to call a halt while the engineers came forward to clear it!

Our commanding officer had other plans and over the radio told my officer to take a man and proceed on foot through the woods on a pathway on the map. The object being to get tanks through without running into an ambush. With the road block where it was, that seemed to be the intention of the enemy. My officer looked at me because I was already on the ground and said: 'Come with me.' I suggested that it might be a good idea to take the Frenchman with us, he knew the area and seemed fairly at ease. It was agreed and we set off. I think the realisation of the stupidity of this venture dawned upon both of us at the same time and I was not surprised when he suggested that one of us should return to get a back-up vehicle and so speed the operation up. The blow came when he informed me that he would return and collect one while I plodded on! I would have preferred to have done that instead of venturing into the unknown with a man who I could not communicate with and to a very uncertain terminal point. As a corporal I would also have the responsibility of saying 'yes it could be done' or 'no it was not possible'. The track was earthen and could conceal mines and the wood was thick and could have covered a regiment of infantry or even tanks. I could only consider that the track would hold up if the other factors were none existent. I have measured the distance of this walk on a number of previous visits and found it to be well in excess of a mile. It was still very early as we entered the village. There was a deathly silence which was not a good sign. My French friend seemed quite happy and gave me much confidence. He shouted something. Probably, 'Get out of your beds, your liberation is at hand'.

The whole village erupted and descended upon me. I was led away to a house where tables were set and a reception was ready. Toasts to England,

France, De Gaulle and Churchill all with liberal doses of calvados gave me a tremendous ego trip. I kissed most of them at least once and some several times. One of the party who spoke English asked where my friends were. It dawned on me that I was holding up the British Army while having a party and that my troop officer would surely arrive and find me spark out on the floor. I made my farewells and returned. I was somewhat put out when I arrived back and found that my leader was stood with the vehicles and looking somewhat abashed at my return. I was fairly full of calvados and asked why he had not come to meet me. 'I didn't think you would come back,' he answered. Now, exactly 50 years later, I decided to re-enter the village in the same way and I invited any of the party who wanted a pleasant walk to join me. All but the one with a broken leg decided to have a go. While walking I pointed out the overgrown route of an old railway line. In 1944 I was concerned about this. The trees had been cut back only sufficiently to permit an engine and whatever it pulled to pass. I had thought then that it probably led to a V1 launching site. During our return in 1984 we had learned that this line had played a major part in the survival of the Resistance group because they had placed a telephone line under it and the Germans had never discovered it.

We had called briefly at this village in April of this year to inform them that we would call in to commemorate their liberation. No other communication had been made, hence we were uncertain about the reception on this occasion. As we came up my old track we found the village bedecked with flags, tables were out and perhaps 100 people were waiting. There followed an almost identical reception to my solo party of 50 years earlier except that I had friends with me and could get the speech making done. Presentations were made and we moved away. The thought persisted in my head...if only we could have known 50 years earlier that we would return in such happy circumstances?

Time, when trying to stick to a programme is always the problem. Friendships with locals and even a sprinkling of English people who have taken cottages in the area were wanting to talk. Until now I had concentrated on the places where I knew what had happened and I had the feeling that I was giving the impression that I was alone. In 1991 I had a book published and had been over this ground to ensure its accuracy. Incidentally I called the book *Tracks in Europe*. This had certainly been one of them.

The next objective was the crossing of the River Risle at Pont Authou, a small village with two bridges very close together. The area behind the crossings was heavily wooded and on a steep bank. The leading troop approached as the first bridge blew up. They fired at the retreating Germans but were unable to prevent the second bridge suffering the same fate.

The Risle is a deep river about 20ft wide and a problem for tanks. One of our members present on the trip had his story to relate here. He had led his troop of Cromwell tanks downstream for about a mile and found a wooden structure over a dam near a mill. He reported the find over the radio. The problem was, would it take the weight of a tank? The only way to find out was to try it. One of his crew who was also on our trip offered to swim under it and check for demolition preparation. He was told to sit tight. The old bridge has long been replaced by a more robust concrete affair but I still wouldn't wish to take a tank over it. Our friend 'Archie' ordered his driver to move forward and onto it. It held and he passed over. The three other tanks in the troop followed and were able to move ahead. That bridge was later to carry the whole of the 7th Armoured Division. We have referred to it as 'Archie's Bridge' ever since.

Sergeant Archie Carr recalled...

'During a Regimental advance an important road bridge was blown up by the enemy as we approached it. We were sent out - Squadron Leader Gibson said, one troop go to the left; one troop go to the right, and see if you can find a bridge for a crossing.

'We found this bridge - which is not the original - so if you do step on it, be very careful, because ever since then it has been sacred!

'For 50 years there has been a secret kept about this wartime episode. Maj Bernard Fitzsimmons, was my wireless operator, and when we got to this bridge for a proposed crossing - which was then a wooden one, just sleepers - he said: 'Well, what I think we had better do is to let me

Sam Hayward, Peter Rose, John Etherington and Syd Shepherd pictured at Archie's Bridge.

get out of the tank, swim underneath the bridge, and see whether there are any limpit mines attached to it'.

Dougie Fowles was my gunner and he said: 'No, that weir is much too strong', and so I would not let him go. Eventually we decided to go across, come what may. Also in the crew were 'Messrs' Gulliford and Methley, both well-known members of A Squadron.

'Well, as everybody now knows we made it to be followed by all Desert Rats (7 Armd Div). Bernard also had a secret. As an 18-19 year old, he often wondered how it was possible sometimes to recall some of their experiences after a lapse of half-a-century. However, as recalled by Archie, he did remember what happened at this particular spot. Archie could 'give him' 20 years in 1944 and could probably do so now!'

It was just as well perhaps that Archie was not going to ask him to swim the crossing now to look for limpits on the underside of the bridge. There were no ladies present in 1944 and on this tour he had completely forgotten to bring his bathing costume with him!

We spent the night on the high ground above the Risle and were resupplied. There was a visit from a loan German aircraft and flares lit up the area. We had been caught by a similar visit in the earlier days. The illumination was a blessing at first because we could see to fill up our tanks and issue the rations. Suddenly the whole area was saturated with small anti-personnel bombs. None came on this occasion.

Jim continues: '26 August was to be a day to remember for me and to cost the lives of five members of the Regiment and the wounding of nine others. I was one of them. One of our squadrons was sent to capture the village of Boissey-le-Chatel. They found it held quite strongly and there was much firing. My troop was to investigate some buildings on the main road to the north of the village. To my relief I was given the task of liaising with the tanks and set off at a fast pace to get closer to them. The other two vehicles in the troop were to search the farm buildings. One of the tank commanders waved frantically and indicated that I should join them. The verges were mined and this was a chance operation. He was urgent about it and we crossed the field and parked beside him. He informed me that I had just passed a German gun which was behind a hedge but pointing in the opposite direction to my approach. The barrel was protruding through the hedge but in a ditch cut for it. It could not traverse. I had no option but to return in the same direction so asked him to give it fire. There was no response and we set off. Once on the road we saw heavy black smoke rising from the point where I had left our troop and as we drew closer, what appeared to be a body in the road beside one of our vehicles which was burning. The ammunition was exploding and we had to get past. It was a case of keep your head down and hope. As soon as we were level with the vehicle we also blew up. My driver was killed instantly and I was somewhat shaken. His feet were trapped under the pedals and I could not move him. I had a broken nose for sure and a lot of blood was down my front. I thought of my limited medical training and that vital four and a half pints which could kill me. I pulled the driver onto my seat and stepped out. There were no wheels on the scout car so that was easy. My boot fell off because the explosion had burst the stitches. My foot swelled quickly and I knew that I had a walking problem. I grabbed my Sten gun and hopped towards the farm. Somewhere there should be another vehicle. I was met by about six Germans. There was no time to consider whether they were about to give themselves up. I aimed at them and pulled the trigger. There was a loud click. The magazine had been blown off in the explosion. I had a complete collapse of hope. I was unafraid because I had expected something like this to happen for weeks. Now I knew what my end would be and all the stress left me. I turned my back on the group and hopped away. I don't know what they did but it must have occurred to me at some stage that I had a chance. I fell into a ditch and remained there until I saw the missing tank from my troop returning. I was evacuated and returned to the UK until the following January. The tank which I had left in the field drove forward and was struck by a bazooka. The crew were killed.

In April when visiting I had given the mayor a copy of my book. We learned now that until then they had thought that they had been liberated by Canadians. One of our friends had been buried in the local churchyard of Boissey-le-Chatel and his grave was very well looked after. The now well-used procedure of flags and calvados followed by presentation and speeches followed. We were also given a document which gave us a welcome in English and a transcription of a diary kept by a woman in the next village. This gave a day-by-day account of the events of the days leading up to our arrival. This document is to be found in later pages.

Boissey-le-Chatel on 26 August 1944 was the day on which Cpl Bill Peat and Cpl Ron Wright of A Squadron were awarded the Military Medal when they dismounted from their tank and destroyed with their Sten guns an enemy Spandau post and two parties of enemy infantry enabling the crew of a knocked out tank to get back.

Day 4

The last day of our eventful travel was to attend a ceremony for a whole day at a small village the size of Tarporley, called Bourneville. I, with a friends, have visited this village on a number of previous occasions and so was better prepared for what would happen. On one of our visits they had unveiled a memorial to the Regiment which will remain on their memorial for ever. There was a reception at the Marie (town hall) followed by a march to church and a Catholic service in French. It didn't matter. There followed a gathering at the memorial, speeches and then a very moving event. Two small children aged about three had sat by the memorial dressed in traditional Norman clothing. The small boy was fairly bored with the whole affair but sat it out. At a given word, they pulled a sheet away to reveal yet another wonderfully carved replica of our old Regimental badge. This is to be hung in their church. The carving and painting of this is perfection.

There followed yet another medal presentation but in addition to each of us receiving one, some of us were invited to make presentations of French awards to some of their members. Two young officers and a piper had joined us from the Royal Dragoon Guards, stationed in Germany. The piper was a great attraction and added to the dignity of the occasion. The three of them also forged the link of 50 years with us and the new Regiment. Once more there was a gourmet's delight and, yes more calvados! It was a happy bunch who were pushed into the coach.

There was a quick visit to the local Resistance museum in Pont Audemer and then just one small duty to perform for another Regiment. During the planning, we had been contacted by the mayor of another village close to Bourneville and asked if we could find someone to attend the ceremony at the grave of three British soldiers who had been buried in the graveyard of a village called Saint Opportune. The men were from the 49th Reconnaissance Regiment which had been disbanded before the end of the war. No-one had visited the graves and the villages desperately wanted to hold a ceremony. We agreed. Contact was made with Charlie Chester to request relatives or friends to join us and an entry was made in the British Legion Journal. From that came a contact in Kelsall who remembered the men and knew what had happened to them and then a phone call from the widow of one of the men. She desperately wished to be with us and to bring her brother. Our coach was full and we had no way of taking her with us. The mayor of Saint Opportune then arranged to pay for both of them to travel to Le Havre. He would pick them up and accommodate them and return them. It was a wonderful gesture and typical of the treatment throughout the tour. It was a very moving service at the graveside and the poor lady, almost 80, found it all too emotional to permit her to lay her wreath. The village gathered and both French and English unashamedly wept for her. This was, after all, what we had come to remember. A tired and quieter party returned to the hotel in Rouen, duty well done.

The real reward for us all was to see France free and restored to its original glory. For us will remain the memory of those days. *Vive la France!*

Day 5

We left the hotel in Rouen early (7am) travelled via Calais and Dover, arriving in London in the early afternoon (2pm). A memorable, thoughtful, friendly tour.

Speech by the Sous-Prefet de Bernay at Bourneville

Translated by Maj Pat JS Whitmore MBE

'There is a call for celebration of a special kind in the arrondissement of Bernay this week. We remember that it is exactly 50 years ago that all our towns and villages were liberated thanks above all to you, our British allies, and thanks to you, men and women of the Resistance. If it is a week of rejoicing, it is also a week for contemplation.

'The joy we feel is akin to that which our elders, our parents felt when allied troops entered our towns and when the Fifth Royal Inniskilling Dragoon Guards entered Bourneville chasing out the enemy who, for more than four years had been in occupation. And if the joy that was felt then was so intense, if one uses such a word as 'liberation', it is because the people of this region and of the entire country were freed from an immense yoke - the yoke of enemy occupation. It is of course true that not every town or every village suffered equally under the occupation; some suffered more, some less. But each one suffered the same humiliation, the same absence of freedom, the same privations and the same fear of having to comply with every whim of the occupying forces who were capable - as everyone was well aware - of going to any extreme. Indeed the story of the liberation of our country bears witness over and over again to frenzied, irrational and barbaric acts having no military or any other justification: we have only to think of Tulle or Oradour.

'Let us remember those young Normans, members of the resistance, who were tortured to death on the eve of the Liberation and whose monuments stand in our fields and woodlands as reminders of their tragic end.

'The act of relieving us from such a yoke and freeing our land from such an occupation deserve our homage and our gratitude. It imposes upon us a duty to preserve intact the memory of it. Homage, thanks and recognition of this debt to you gentlemen of the 5th Royal Inniskilling

Dragoon Guards and members of the Resistance; and with you, let us remember the fallen. You dedicated your youth and vigour to the service of that sacred mission on the outcome of which our life still depends today, and if we - that is to say men, women and children of 1994 - are able to live out our lives in peace and under democratic rule, it is thanks to your having entered the fray; it is thanks to your courage and sacrifice.

We must not forget, now or in the future, that what was at stake was nothing less than confronting totalitarianism and dictatorship with freedom and democracy.

'You have proved that when democracy mobilises its forces and realises that it is being vilified and abused, when it sees that its detractors are profiting from its essentially peace-loving nature, it is capable of overcoming the most loathsome and barbaric dictatorships. The proof of this lesson must assuredly remain inscribed in all recorded history.

'Thank you for giving this lesson which has made some latter-day dictators think. Thank you for the victory which you won and which has allowed us to live in security, proud of our civilisation - for democracy is indeed a civilisation, the civilisation of Liberty.

'It is now up to us, men women and children of today, to keep this lesson alive. You have left us a heritage, we must preserve it. We who have profited from this peace honourably won, it is our duty to safeguard it. Peace is a blessing which cannot be measured. But there is no peace of which we can be proud if it is made without honour. Because we forgot this truth in 1938 the world had dishonour and war, as Winston Churchill foretold. Peace demands vigilance; let our guard drop and the condition in which peace thrives will decay by our neglect. Peace needs to be nourished and cultivated.

'And indeed peace has never been maintained by the mere recital of its name. Peace cannot be maintained by just wishing for it, however ardently. Peace is maintained by tolerance, by international justice, by the determination to uphold the rights of nations and by securing a balance of power so that no-one shall come onto the international stage claiming to be morally or materially the strongest. Peace means that no nation shall use its strength against another for its own ends. In the last analysis peace is maintained by making oneself respected and therefore by seeing that one has the means to achieve this end.

'At the beginning of the speech I said that this was also a week for contemplation: let us consider the soldiers of the allied nations, of the 5th Royal Inniskilling Dragoon Guards, of our own people who fell in battle so that liberty might be established in our nation. Let us consider all those civilians who were caught up in the unavoidable battles of the Liberation. To all those dead, to all those whom history has dealt a hard blow, to the members of the 5th Royal Inniskilling Dragoon Guards who laid down their lives, we render homage. We think of you and we shall ever go on thinking of you for we know the measure of our debt.

'To forget would be an act of sacrilege. And that is why days such as this, ceremonies such as this one in which we are taking part are important events; they stand as landmarks in our collective memory and make us mindful of the men and women who were engulfed in a conflict which cost 55 million lives. But those men and women who stood firm and fought so that at the end Liberty had the last word.

'Col Bradfield, Old Comrades of the 5th Royal Inniskilling Dragoon Guards thank you and, through you, our thanks to the British Nation.

'Be assured that you have won eternal gratitude and that we shall ever be faithful in keeping alive the memory of what you did.

Thanks to our British friends.

Notes

Sous-Prefet: Represents the French Republic in a arrondissement, a sub-division of a department or county. Not a political appointment as such, in ceremonies his duties are similar to those of Deputy Lord Lieutenant of an English county. However, he plays a more active role in the administration of his area.

Bourneville: In the department of Eure and in the arrondissement of Bernay.

Tulle: the principal town in the department of Correze in central France. Scene of a particular atrocity when the SS massacred a large number of civilians in June 1944.

Oradour: the reference is to Oradour-sur-Glane, a village between Tulle and Limoges. The entire population was massacred. The men were shot, the women and children were herded into the church which was burnt down on top of them. The church and most of the village has never been restored and the charred remains stand today as a national shrine. 642 people died here, not one of them a Resistance worker. This happened on 10 June 1944. The SS unit which perpetrated this atrocious act had earlier the same day bayoneted 90 men in Tulle. A famous poem by Tardieu speaks out for all time against this crime and all such barbarities.

The liberation of Boissey Le Chatel

A complete diary account of the life of local people in the occupied part of the battle front - 11 to 26 August 1944 according to Marie-Therese

Charpentier…

'I began this diary on 11 August as this was the last truly quiet day under German domination. The situation on the front towards Caen seemed to have stabilised for several months. Moreover, we received scant information from the Journal de Nouen while the news reported by the English wireless reached us in a very distorted state.

As the vice tightens around us, the days and especially the nights become more agitated and dangerous, but we try to carry on life as normal.'

11 August

A splendid day. It was decided today that we would treat the children to Mother's Day tea, postponed owing to the landing. Mme Tapissier, the notary, organised it and asked Edith if she could use her courtyard for the occasion. The children enacted historical events of their own invention: Charlemagne and the schoolchildren, Joan of Arc on the day of the consecration.

At bed time, (10.30 pm), machine-gun fire very close to us made us jump. The Germans were firing at a woman whose lights were too visible. No damage.

12 August

The movement of the Americans is becoming clearer. This time we seem to be in the frying pan! The Americans are reported to already be at Chartres.

We had just retired for the night when two violent explosions shook us. A V1 had just flown overhead and had the wit to explode in the countryside far from the houses, at the edge of Bonneville. All the stained glass windows of the Church of Bonneville were blown out along with a few windows at Boissey.

13 August

Jean has arrived. He is also very worried about the situation. People are frequently the target of machine-gun fire on the roads. The trucks carrying parcels from Elbeuf to Paris have stopped running since the Americans are so close. They are said to be at Versailles and Evreux, but it is impossible to know for certain. The night of 13 and 14 August was terrible. Continuous machine-gunning and bombings. Aircraft fly overhead ceaselessly.

Finally, at 3.15am, we heard a bomb fall very close by. Half an hour later, Edith is telephoned. The bomb fell on the small house of the gardener of the castle where two refugee families are staying: the Ferrera (Portuguese) and the Loiseau de Sotteville. The house is squashed. Jean leaves immediately to help with the clearance work. When Edith arrives, a small girl had already been removed from the rubble: she has a broken arm and head injuries, causing her considerable pain. Gradually, everyone is removed; Mme Loiseau was dead, one of the little Ferrera girls had suffocated, probably a few minutes before being removed from the rubble because her sisters asserted that she was moving and was still talking only minutes earlier. The legs of one of the Loiseau were found, the body had disappeared under a heavy flagstone; apparently she had been reduced to a pulp. But when a hand was removed from the rubble, she responded to the pressure. Jean and four other men from the village tried to lift the flagstone. In vane. It is too heavy. The flagstone is then smashed with a mallet. Barely had the pieces been removed when the child straightened herself and asked 'where are my sisters?'. She is unscathed.

The clearance and rescue work continue during the rest of the night under torch light. One of the older boys is seriously wounded. He needs to be taken to the Elbeuf hospital along with the little girl with the broken arm. Jean again volunteers to go and requests an ambulance on his motorbike. He obtains one with some difficulty; thanks to him, the two wounded people are in their beds in hospital at Caudebec-les-Elbeuf at 8am.

After this hectic night, everyone comes together for the usual breakfast; this is followed by mass that the vicar has not curtailed one bit. Moreover, there was little aircraft activity despite the splendid weather. As we waited for lunch we noticed odd smoke trails in the sky. They must have been preceded by aircraft flying straight ahead, but the wind had deformed the furrows. It was very pretty. We began to eat under the trees. In the middle of the potatoes: the drone of nose diving aircraft immediately following by the moaning of many bombs all dropped together is very impressive; it feels like the sky has collapsed on our heads. However, everyone remained calm and we unhurriedly took the children into the kitchen. The bombs kept pouring down. The children were not too scared.

Meanwhile, Edith drove her motorbike at full speed to the scene of the accident. It seems to have occurred at St Denis. Of the 300 bombs dropped on the road junction and on St Denis, some were very small since, as Edith quaintly put it, she could have picked up the crater in her two arms, but by some amazing stroke of luck, there was no-one on the road or in the fields that were killed.

Only one woman standing behind the door of the house tore her arm near the shoulder. An enterprising neighbour made her a sling. Edith only had to dispatch her to Caudebec-les-Elbeuf.

Jean and Helene no longer want to sleep in the house. They fear a fresh bombing. So the Homberg tribe leaves us around 8pm to go and sleep in

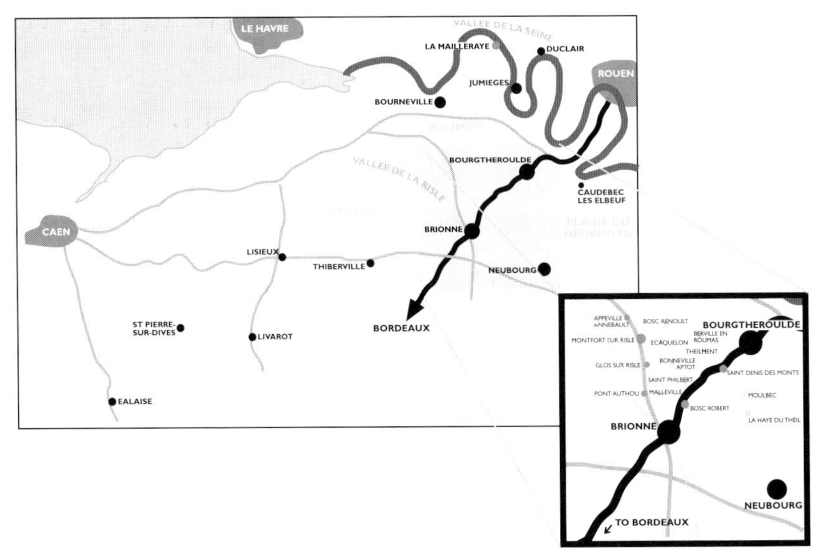

the woods near Pont des Vaux.

14 August

At 7am the Hombergs re-emerge looking pale and drawn after spending a rough night. The sound of bombs grow louder in the woods and are really close to the Berville road which the convoys now take on their way to the front. However, these convoys are now scarcer; one sees more trucks carrying ammunition and fewer harassed infantrymen.

This evening Edith assembled some lady volunteers to set up a first aid unit at Boissey. The hospitals are full after Sunday which was a very trying day for our sector (several dead and wounded at La Haye du Theil, Malleville, Brionne and Pont Authou) and it is more difficult to obtain ambulances.

An entire chicken-house of clucking ladies met at the Mayor's House at 8pm under the chairmanship of the village cockerel. I appointed M Préveret as chairman.

Finally, everything is organised. A room is found with five beds and bedding. Everyone offers to bring furniture to furnish the infirmary or old clothes to serve as compresses and bandages.

15 August

The morning is spent in worship. Jean then goes off to build a hut in the Tilly wood. We are invited to visit it after lunch. The weather is very stuffy and worsens during dinner. There is a very violent and very short storm. A clap of thunder falls on the transformer. As a result, after having only three quarters of an hour of electricity every evening around 10 pm we now have none at all.

16 August

Jean has left. This morning the victims of Sunday's bombing are buried. Tonight for the first time retreating convoys drive along the main road. We have started to cut bandages and compresses out of old clothes.

17 August

The vicar maintains his afternoon catechism and a few boys then come and play in the courtyard. We continue to cut compresses.

Montfort was bombed this afternoon: we saw aircraft nose diving into the valley and the bombs shook us. In the evening we received details from a member of the library which is requisitioned to guard the Glos Tunnel. Half of Montfort is razed to ground; as planes have dropped many bombs into the river, this has created showers of water which have wet the rubble and drenched the rescuers working with mud up to their knees. There is talk of a dozen dead.

The adjacent commune of Appeville has just been bombed too. The first torpedo hit the Gourlins house (Madeleine Lefebvre). She had just put her youngest three babies to bed (she has ten children) when she heard the aircraft passing. She was enjoying watching the planes with her sisters Elizabeth and Monique through the corridor window when they saw the bullets flying. Immediately afterwards there was an explosion very close to them; as they opened the door of the children's room they saw a gaping hole. However, Marie-Claude (four years old) at once slithered out of the rubble saying that she was not wounded. Dominique, whose iron bed had withstood the shock, was also unharmed, but the youngest, Emmanuel (20 months old) was found with his chest crushed by plaster and bricks. This village was hard hit: two deaths in a few seconds and only the church remains more or less standing.

The night of 17-18 August remained in everyone's memory as the hardest. We had barely gone to bed (I personally was sleeping) when a series of explosions rocked the whole house. It was so violent I thought Boissey was being bombed, but the series of eight blasts began over and over again. Edith had put on her cape and had gone for a stroll on the village square. The men had assembled there to exchange views (some bet on a plane, others on a cannon). The vicar reassured the population.

Around midnight or 1am the explosions became more intermittent. We later learned from the Lefebvres, who had spent the night around a hay grinding wheel, that the explosion came from an aircraft that dropped bombs four by four under each wing.

We had not heard anything like it the other nights. The little Hombergs went to bed and we joined Edith at the gate. She was watching a German convoy pass and exchanged a few words with the officer who was going to the front and who looked very weary. 'War is sad, Madame. Leave quickly'. 'You are going to bomb us,' Edith replied bluntly. 'No, it is two o'clock in the morning - finished now'. He was right. We were able to sleep a few hours. The bombing started again around 5am but we no longer heard the eight blasts as before.

18 August

At breakfast we discussed what safety measures to take and Helene asked me to go to the Glyselens whose farm is very isolated and request the shelter of a stable. I therefore spent a part of the morning preparing our sleeping quarters with the help of Therese to carry the straw. During the afternoon, Jean arrived saying that there was no longer any way to cross the Seine and that the boats were now only used for the Germans who no longer concealed their retreat. We had supper very early and loaded the children into the cars with blankets and belongings for the night. When it was time to leave a plane dropped a few bombs on the large trolleys filled with hay by the cemetery. Almost immediately, some people came to fetch the stretcher from Edith's house because a man was thought to have been wounded, but fortunately it was only the carter who had collapsed under his load and who had remained stretched out there, afraid that the plane would return.

The adults did not get much sleep. That night clusters of parachuted luminous balls again descended slowly towards Neubourg. It is a beautiful and impressive sight. A few bombs were also dropped, one quite close on the Rouen to Bordeaux road, we could hear the Germans cursing and the horses stamping the ground while the convoy reorganised.

19 August

While we are in open country, we can see a string of planes flying at high altitude. Then one of them dropped two black loads: the pilot and his parachute. The plane then nose dived for a few seconds and crashed into the Theillement wood. The English pilot was immediately taken prisoner and he had the composure to offer cigarettes to the Krauts around him. The rest of the day remained quiet. The German retreat gathered pace. The vicar has decided to dismantle the stained glass windows of the church and to replace them with straw.

20 August

The next day the weather is again superb. We return to attend great mass at Boissey. The children are tired from the journey and the short nights since Nono wakes everyone up at the crack of dawn.

In the afternoon, the children lie down in the hay to rest; we then go for a stroll by the farm. There we see a carter that the Germans had requisitioned the day before to carry ammunition, but he was released at Serquiguy and there the Krauts must have headed off towards Evreux. That farm worker was lucky since others who had been led off the night previously in the direction of Caen had to abandon their horses and carts and flee, since the Germans wanted to draft them into their army.

We again return in the evening to sleep at Bonneville. On the way we again see a fight between aircraft. One plane, in flames, fell on Ecaquelon.

21 August

The children and myself are much too exhausted and everyone has blisters on their feet. We decide to sleep in a real bed in our own house tonight. As we were beginning the cooking, the courtyard was invaded by retreating army trucks. Fortunately, they only stay three hours because a counter order is suddenly issued. However, almost all this time the officers and men remain in the kitchen making themselves coffee and food. The entire village is more or less invaded by the troops. Mme Toque, our neighbour, houses the officers who paid us three visits. On one visit, a tall distinguished fair-haired man, resembling Napoleon II, spotted Jean's motorbike, even though Jean had tried to hide it in the lounge. Noticing that he was eyeing it up, Jean camouflaged it under branches in the garden behind a large stone.

During the night, the field is invaded by a screaming group of 50 horses and 80 soldiers who rotate the tank continuously from midnight to 5am to water their animals. During the day, we also discovered a cannon and seven or eight trucks stationed in the courtyard. All the buildings have been searched and looted, including all the preserved eggs, all the fruit, both ripe and unripe, all the potatoes, the milk and a hare killed by Simon as he was mowing and which was all prepared on a plate. There is nothing more to eat and we have 80 hairy rogues in the courtyard! You should see the way they are dressed: no longer in uniform, breeches in shreds, old tapered trilby hats on their heads and beards a week old. Walking through the study I find that our pales are full of green pears. I call Edith and coldly we take back all our pears, then I conduct an inventory of the soldiers' bags to see whether they have not pinched too many things. I find some very fine balls of wool and large pink and blue rolls of elastic for garters. Where on earth did they pinch those? I cannot find my camera, the game of happy families or Jean Claude's football.

We spend our day chasing up our belongings and the kitchenware. The

Germans make several meals, dress the wounds of their horses, sleep and clean themselves up.

Yesterday's distinguished officer has suddenly entered the lounge; failing to find what he was looking for he calls us over: 'Where is the Monsieur who had a motorbike?'. Denise and I replied together: 'Gone…to Rouen'. 'When will he return?' 'We don't know, perhaps Saturday…perhaps in a month's time…there is a lot of work'. The officer did not insist and left empty-handed.

The remaining looters left in orderly fashion at nightfall. Two of them must have missed the departure because an officer on horseback returned to call them shortly afterwards. They hid and had to sleep in the study. We heard them chatting and drawing water around midnight.

The number of mule carts, small tanks and caterpillar vehicles is staggering. We can also see soldiers on foot, on bicycles or in labourers' carts. They continuously file past all night and almost as regularly during the day. They are all around us, on all the roads and all file down the Berville road in the direction of the La Mailleraye Jumieges ferry or Duclair.

22 August

A night without bombing, but the convoys prevent us from sleeping. In the morning, everyone is blurry and discouraged. The courtyard is enough to make you sick and the air is fouled by the smell of horse droppings. We muster up courage to thoroughly clean up: the droppings, the straw, egg shells, smelly woollen socks, greasy shirts and dirt paper. We work all day under the watchful eye of a decent horseman that Jean recovered from the Germans and who is called Bayard. At 4pm the cleaning is almost completed and it begins to rain.

The English are reported to be at Pont l'Eveque and to have landed at Honfleur; the Americans are reported to be in Paris.

24 August

During the night there is bombing over Bosc-Robert with bright lights of parachuted rockets. The Germans are panicking and arrive in Boissey in such streams that a traffic jam forms and it takes half an hour for the flow to start moving again. We walked down to the square and chatted with some people. Edith was very afraid that a plane would detect the convoys and make a meal of both them and us.

I rose at 6am (no one is able to stay in bed at the moment). I wanted to see the German disarray which continues to be a picturesque sight. I saw them this morning taking out the slate board from the cafe to point with chalk the direction of the Seine. It was less of a laughing matter to see several trucks, including an anti-aircraft vehicle, entering our yard.

Mass had barely finished when the anti-aircraft vehicle began firing on a few lurking English planes and the roof of the church was well and truly peppered. I quickly return to the house and find Denise hiding under the kitchen table. She thought it was a bombing raid and as she had gone upstairs at the sound of the first blast and had seen Monique asleep, her one thought was for Monique's safety.

At midday the trucks shook, tearing down a few fruit trees and demolishing the gate. At 1.30pm, the anti-air vehicle tried to move off but the ground was so soggy that it got stuck in the mud, its wheels spinning out of control. Jean, who was eager to see it go to the devil, was needed to help free it.

The afternoon is almost calm. The weather is clearing a little. We can see an English plane descending straight on the anti-aircraft vehicle which is next to the cemetery despite a terrible shot which produces a shower of sparks and bombs it. It must have aimed accurately because it is no longer audible.

25 August (Friday)

Wonderful weather, but at dawn the Germans install a canon at one corner of the square. The English are reported to be at Houlebec (6km) and Brionne (12km): the cannon has also drawn much closer over night. We are going to interview yesterday's German officer who is seated on a bench in front of the cafe: 'Where are the English?'. 'We are the English, Madame'. 'Oh, then you won't use your cannon?'. 'We will fire if the Germans come'. 'And are the Germans far?'. 'Very far, there is no danger, Madame'.

We nevertheless decide to put the children in a safe place during the brawl that we sense is impending. We take provisions for a full meal, some sewing work and some books and we load up Monique's car. With Edith we decide to head in the direction of the English and to stop at the first farm to ask for shelter for the day. The five children, Aunt Denise, Stop and myself therefore set off in a caravan train. We stopped one and a half kilometres from Boissey at the Carpentiers. The Carpentiers gave us a very warm welcome and Aunt Denise leaves us there to go and tell Edith that we have arrived.

The planes are lurking a great deal. They can be seen nose diving over St Denis, then one descends to unleash machine gun fire right over Boissey. The children are quite upset and kneel down on the grass to recite a dozen rosaries. We put them in the press-house since the situation is worsening. Machine gun fire and shooting can be heard one or two kilometres away. A little later a group of some 20 Germans turn up. They make food in the field and rest. The officer seems very nervous. He stalks up and down like a bear in a cage; then they bring a wounded man whose leg has been shot right through by a bullet and seems to be suffering a lot. The Germans have requisitioned a car to take him away.

Edith leaves by bicycle around 4am on a call out. She is still trembling with emotion because on her way to give her cancer patient a morphine injection in St Denis (the way she takes each day), she wanted to visit a wounded woman whom she had been told was as little further away on the main road. She looked for her in several houses but could not find her. The Germans found her ploy very suspect and summoned her. One of them said: 'You are a spy,' grabbing her wrist. Another studied her Red Cross arm band and seal. They called a truck but at that moment a cluster of English planes appeared and opened machine gun fire on three different occasions. Everyone falls to the ground on their stomachs. Edith is in the middle of the Germans. But in the few seconds that separate each machine gun shot, Edith jumped from tree to tree while having the impression that she was leaving dead bodies around her. She herself does not know how she found her bicycle and kept it with her. As soon as the machine gunning stopped, she re-mounted her bicycle waving her white handkerchief with one hand. But a plane again nose dives almost over her to machine gun a truck which had already been knocked out a few days previously and had remained in the middle of the road. This is the plane we had seen nose diving on Boissey.

We then discuss tactics. Edith prefers that we stay put over night since the English cannot delay now and the Carpentiers let us use the small room. I therefore leave with my Edith to look for a few provisions and night effects in Boissey. Jean is reading quietly in the garden while eyeing a group of Germans who look like scoundrels, particularly the cook, an escapee from Stalingrad who always holds a gun in his hand. He has threatened our intrepid Stop who barked at him.

Barely had I returned from the Carpentiers that the brawl became very fierce and very close to us. The Germans stationed in the courtyard hastily took up arms and left. At five o'clock all hell broke loose. As the farm did not have a shelter, all the children were called back into the common room and I tell them a fairy story: Good Little Henri. The children were not in the least bit worried and whenever I stopped to listen to the explosions they asked: 'So what did Henri do? What did the jinni reply?'. When the story was over, we took some sewing work with us. The battle was still raging 1-200 metres from us. We could see the illuminated outline of the bullets and we could hear them whistling. Finally, we began to prepare dinner. During a lull, Genevieve Carpentier and myself went looking for a few bales of straw in the barn as we were particularly eager to see what was happening. We noticed a few Kraut soldiers hiding behind some wisps of straw and some other German soldiers coming towards us brandishing strange instruments: these were meant to cut the telephone wires. On the road opposite us, a building was burning with a lot of smoke.

Night began to fall. We had milk soup and hard-boiled eggs for supper. The brawl had resumed, still very close to us. While we were at table a very young German arrives and asks for civilian clothes to hide. The farmer is very fat, he has nothing to fit the little Kraut who explains to us that he is only 18 years old and that the English are fat, greasy and tall and scare the life out of him. While we talk, two other Germans turn up to ask for a house for a wounded man. At once the little Kraut has disappeared out of sight; we find him after the others have left hidden under the dairy table. Genevieve Carpentier tells him to follow her and goes and hides him in an isolated building used as a woodshed. We put the children to bed: the four eldest sleep on the floor on mattresses in the small bedroom. Monique sleeps on the bed that I will share with her. The battle is less intense and a little further away. Together we wait for the arrival of the English until 10am, then each of us return home and try to sleep.

Meanwhile, the situation at Boissey was calm: the soldiers had vacated the courtyard, unfortunately taking Bayard with them. Jean wanted news of his wife. He did not know that Bonneville had been liberated. He had already tried to go there at around five o'clock but there was too much machine gun fire in all directions. Jean therefore set off at nightfall; he tried to cross the field but was stopped by a German patrol unit who believed he was a spy and did not accept his explanations. They put a shovel in his hand and forced him to dig a grave. Jean thought it was for him, but it turned out that they are burying the body of a German soldier. Jean's ordeal was not over yet. He had to start digging a second grave. This time it could be his turn. At that moment the Germans raced off in their trucks; after the last of them had left, Jean heard a violent explosion only a few feet away.

Apparently, the Germans had set fire to explosives to protect their retreat. However, Jean dares not move at first. He fears a trap or a pistol shot if the Germans see him dashing off. Only when he realises he is alone does he dare to leave by crawling under some barbed wire and returns to Boissey with his shovel on his shoulder.

What exactly happened at St Philbert near the Carpentiers' farm that day is hard to say. Two farmers, Mr Decaux and Mr Dannet, had noticed in the morning a German officer in a brand new suit (something one no longer saw). Both of them had separately noticed that he spoke correct French but with an English accent. He had asked a series of questions about the activities of the neighbouring villages and had been very interested in an ammunition truck that had remained there. They thought that they recognised this officer as one of the English who had climbed up into the first tank and had set fire to the ammunition.

A battle and body to body fighting had taken place there: the Decaux stable caught fire later (around 7am), Mme Decaut was blinded in one eye by a piece of shrapnel. The farmers wanted to go and fetch Edith but had to wait until the fighting moved away. Finally they crossed several German blockades and reached Boissey. There they felt obliged to report to the Mayor first. Their comings and goings attracted the attention of the Germans who locked them in the church for an hour. Only at around midnight were they able to alert Edith who went upstairs to take care of Mme Decaux and only returned in the early hours since they were afraid of letting her leave again. The blockade had been dismantled by that time. Edith did not meet a soul in Boissey, but the battle was imminent.

Bonneville was already liberated. It had happened quite easily. One hour in the shelter for the Gyselens, Helene and her children, while the battle wages at the farm adjoining the Rouen to Bordeaux road. The English were beginning to fire in the direction of the Gyselens' farm when a brave youth crossed the field in front of them waving a white towel. He tells them that all the Germans have fled. The tanks then advanced (it was about 4pm). The first tank in the line stopped at the church and the officer got out to question the farmer living next door. To his question 'are there Germans here?', the other replied raising his finger towards the bell-tower covered by two Krauts holding machine-guns. But they did not even fire and came down to give themselves up (the farmer in question told me this).

26 August

Inevitably we come to the famous day of 26 August which saw our liberation.

It had been a silent night for us, apart from a few explosions. The last, at 5am, partially woke up Monique who started crying. At once the entire bedroom emerged from its sleep, but I demanded that everyone remain lying down. I myself got up at 6am when Genevieve Carpentier arrived. At that moment, we saw English tanks passing some 200 metres from us and heading in the direction of Boissey (they had the wit not to take the hollow road which was mined, but to cut across the field in front of the Bouler farm to join the Bonneville road).

Around 7am I got the children out of bed and we served breakfast with the Carpentier family. 'Are the English here?', the children 'Not yet,' I tell them, 'but I think we are liberated and to celebrate I'm going to give you some blackberry jam'. The nippers yelled with joy and I begin making the sandwiches when Mr Carpentier informed me: 'Yes, liberated, just look at all those Krauts entering; their uniforms are bizarre'. Indeed, a few soldiers entered in khaki jackets and gripping machine-guns; others climbed the hedge and moved forward cautiously. 'They are not Germans, but Tommies,' I said to the farmer, and I run in front of them shouting: 'English or Americans?'. They replied: 'Canadians'. We then led them to our prisoners whom they rounded up and they then searched the farm. We naturally began to chat with them, but their French was rudimentary so that it was simpler to talk English.

They offered us cigarettes and the farmer offered them brandy, but they were not very enthusiastic as they had just had breakfast. Everything about them surprised us - their uniforms, their caps covered with a net for camouflage and designed to hold an individual bandage, their lack of stripes...one told me that he was a commanding officer. I vainly looked for gold or silver stripes on his sleeve. He seemed to be dressed exactly like the others. Then he showed me a square measuring a few centimetres on his shoulder representing a crown. This was enough to show his rank.

The Canadian soldiers continued to walk around us and to search the farms. They found nine Germans hidden in the wheat bags.

Another commanding officer arrived and asked me whether the farmer would let them use one of the rooms as their HQ. The farmer was delighted to oblige: he would have taken the shirt of his back, and the farmer's wife kept repeating: 'We are liberated, liberated at last'.

In next to no time the dining room was emptied and the headquarters set up; immediately all kinds of vehicles entered the courtyard, while some 40 cannon stood in line outside the hedge pointing in the direction of Boissey and Bourgtheroulde. As an added precaution, we locked the children in the granary while the vehicles arrived and also to allow the Canadians to install their telephones in peace. Francois soon took advantage of the situation to climb into the lap of a Canadian and to begin an animated conversation with him in pigeon talk, a conversation punctuated with offerings of biscuits, caramel sweets and chewing gum!

His sisters come downstairs and began gossiping. The commanding officer in the HQ shaved with a rubber bowl attached to a wooden cross. All his instruments were brand new. Zabeth watched staggered and said: 'I wonder where he could have pinched so nice a mirror.' Genovefa indignantly replied: 'You are stupid. The Germans pinch but the English never steal'. I translated this to the officer who smiled and replied: 'Quite true'.

After this, I no longer had anything to do. All the children passed from one set of Canadian arms to another. I began to iron the farm's clothes while listening to the wireless that Mr Carpentier had uncovered as soon as the Canadians arrived and which was broadcasting news on the liberation of Paris. A lieutenant arrived and leant against the window sill to listen to the broadcast. He spoke good French with an awful accent and he looked like Ronald Colman.

All the Canadian soldiers are volunteers (the one who spoke to me was an American from New York, but he had been serving with the Canadian army for the last four years). He showed me the insignia on his beret: a cannon surrounded with laurel leaves with the motto: 'Ubique fas et gloria ducunt'.

I had the chance to see their HQ maps at close hand. They were superb. They were in colour and drawn to a large scale (5cm:1km). Quite a change from the pages of the post office calendars that the Germans had been consulting in recent days! The Canadians place a mica sheet over the map on which they indicate with a thick pencil their firing line: this could change from hour to hour without dirtying and obscuring the map.

Around 1.30pm, I could stand it no longer; I again went to see the officer to ask whether I could go into Boissey: 'I think everything is all right,' he said, 'but you know that we are firing and that the Jerries are firing back. There's a 99 to 100 per cent chance that everything is OK, one chance in a 100 that you will be killed by a shell; it could happen on the road or in the field where we are now'.

I passed in front of the 30 cannon mouths that were spitting fire. The servers all shouted out to me in joy: 'Bonjour, Madame' - all proud to say something to me in French. No one on the road, of course. 200 metres before the house, I noticed the intrepid Stop trotting perkily along, his ears pricked up.

At the bend in the road, I noticed the middle-class family house; I was so pleased to see it intact. Next to it, however, the press-house was in flames.

Edith was in the dining-room eating chicken and custard. This is how she told me about the liberation of Boissey.

So it was that at five o'clock on the morning of 26 August Edith had returned from her visit to the Duclaux. The situation was calm, but throughout the night the Germans had been at work. They had cut down trees along the road running along Edith's courtyard to block the tanks; the two remaining roads on this side had been mined.

At 6.30pm the first tank appeared at the corner of the Bonneville road. It fired a shell which bored a hole in the bakery. Seeing that there was no return fire, the Canadian got out of his tank. He looked joyful and confident. He turned his machine around, perhaps to alert his comrades that the village is poorly defended, but at the cross-roads he struck a mine and the tank jumped. An ammunition truck which followed had to jump too. Nevertheless, the two vehicles completely blocked the road for the others and this is why the Boissey battle lasted so long.

This noise worried Jean. He forced everyone to descend into the shelter. Inside people spent three quarters of an hour reciting the rosary. The explosions of the ammunition truck are so frequent that Jean believes that the Canadians are cutting a path through the hedges and expects to see them arrive at the back of the courtyard. He wants to go to the granary to look for a French flag or a piece of white cloth and plant it on the shelter to show that there are no enemies inside.

Around 8.30pm as the battle rages with a vengeance, we see Stop arriving whom Denise had carried to neighbours the previous day. He drags the piece of rope that he broke and delights the family. Then Simon arrives and informs us that the press-house is burning. The whole thatch roof is already in flames, but Simon insists that we move everything that can be moved.

Everyone sets to work. We roll Jean's car outside, the casks and some of the bottles, all under a hail of bullets. Edith finds that this is madness and begs us to stop, but the others are in a frenzy and continue until it becomes unbearable owing to the flames.

Aunt Denis alone has remained in the house and is doing the washing up. She goes to the gate as she dries a saucepan to see what is happening. She can see a German near the church aiming his rifle and he cries out to her: 'Go away madam, we will kill you.'

A further short stay in the shelter. Then Edith wants to return to the farm to look for some milk. It is impossible to pass owing to the fire at the blockade point. So she remains chatting at the Solaires. During this time, Aunt Denis continues her housework and tidying. Jean had already left some time earlier for Bonneville. He has succeeded in getting through and had just returned in time for the liberation. Edith returned from the Solaires about the same time to announce that Canadian tanks had entered the village.

Boissey le Chatel was completely liberated from the German occupation before midday on 26 August 1944.

(Note: Since the diary gives details of the problems for those civilians caught up in a battle area, it has been given in full.)

11

Battle of Arnhem, Holland

'It will be all over by Christmas'. Those very familiar words were being uttered by everyone. But most disturbingly for all for us, it was not to be. After Normandy and the speedy pursuit of the Germans by Allied forces throughout northern France and Belgium my Regiment, more or less had reached the border area of Holland. The Battle of Arnhem quickly followed.

At this memorable of so many memorable times 30 Corps, under command of Gen Brian Horrocks - and at this particular point few servicemen in the north west Europe campaign, if any, would acknowledge that they were in any other Corps - was to take part in Monty's last 'heave-ho' against the enemy.

If this rapid thrust had not been pursued, no doubt those with hindsight would have questioned why such a 'war-winning' plan had not been evolved by 21 Army Group.

On the afternoon of Sunday 17 September in overcast weather an incoming noise drew our attention skywards where to our astonishment we were witnessing the beginning of a massive air armada, hundreds of planes with gliders in tow, which seemingly continued indefinitely. This was the first indication of the big Allied airborne drop to capture three bridges in Holland - at Grave over the River Maas, at Nijmegen over the River Waal, and at Arnhem over the River Rhine.

The operation was codenamed 'Market Garden' - market representing the airborne part and garden the land forces. By capturing these three key bridges a way would be opened for the British 2nd Army to outflank the Siegfried Line and the Ruhr area and so win the war before the end of 1944.

Day followed day but the news of the airborne drop was far from uplifting. Despite a most valiant effort, herocially fought, by the airborne troops, within a period of just over a week we were able to see for ourselves the battle weary, bedraggled survivors who had blackened faces so as to be invisible as they withdrew at night in small boats to make their break-out across the River Rhine in the Arnhem pocket.

The break-out was ordered by Maj Gen Roy Urquhart, commander of the 1st Airborne Division, once he realised that there was no hope of success. He was not prepared to surrender to the enemy and he decided to escape with about one quarter of the original force of 10,000. Many were taken prisoner - 6,450 in all, while 1,350 were killed in battle.

Until then the North West Europe campaign had proceeded quite successfully. The Arnhem operation however was a failure and many reasons were later given for this.

The planners of the 'Market Garden' operation had underestimated the strength of German units, some undergoing a refit in the area at the time including powerful Panzer forces which easily outgunned the landing troops who were armed with only light weapons. Intelligence sources had forewarned the Allied planners of these enemy dispositions and had confirmed too that the enemy had every intention of defending the Scheldt, the Antwerp port area.

Shortly after landing the Airborne Commander, Gen Urquhart, was himself cut off from his headquarters while in the front of the action when making a personal reconnaissance. Thus the overall command was severely weakened at the most critical time.

The landings took place at Ginkel Heath, in an area some six to eight miles from the bridge at Arnhem. Most airborne troops are aware that it is their role to drop on, or in close proximity, to a target area. They dislike being used as infantry.

Because of the likely German anti-aircraft fire in the Arnhem area and other difficulties, the whole airborne force did not land on the same day. It should have been a single lift. By the time the Polish troops were flown in 48 hours later the enemy was waiting for them having captured an officer in possession of the appropriate Allied orders. After some 4-5 days there was a shortage of ammunition, food and water, for the airborne forces.

The operation would have been carried out more easily if the port of Antwerp had first been opened up. As it was all the supplies had to be brought up from the Channel ports.

Wireless communications were poor - at times they were non existent. The relieving land forces failed to make the link up which was planned to be in two to four days. The advance should have been more adventurous and determined on occasions. But although 2nd Army forces failed to reach the airborne troops at Arnhem, some of whom under Col Frost were holding the bridge over the river Rhine, the operation as a whole was not considered to be a complete disaster since the American Divisions did successfully secure the two bridges en route over the rivers Maas and Waal.

German photograph showing the scene at one of the bridges at Arnhem after the attack. ***(IWM HU 2127)***

Those of us who were in the vicinity at the time considered that perhaps the greatest problem of all was that the relieving land forces were unable to make the vital progress required since the Dutch cobbled roads - unlike the roads of today - were totally inadequate for heavy equipment - tanks, artillery, and so on - so rarely was there any room for manoeuvre when such vehicles broke down or suffered a 'knock-out' by the enemy. With hindsight a 'super highway' - an autobahn as in Hitler's Germany - would have considerably helped the mobile columns to make such a long, daring, journey to the Arnhem bridge which, in the circumstances prevailing in the autumn of 1944, proved to be 'A Bridge too Far'.

For instance, when in Normandy, tanks and indeed most vehicles were able to move across country if that was thought desirable whereas in Holland the terrain was such that once off the cobbles, it was into the dyke!

Success in an operation as big as Arnhem does need to be preceded by some diligent homework not done in haste - this more than any other factor was glaringly apposite in September 1944. The gamble to 'press on regardless' when success would have known no limits seemingly prevailed at that particular stage of Allied operations.

Travelling with Holts on two anniversary tours - the 45th and the 50th - provided some well-attended commemorative events in an atmosphere of remembrance. Such tours are invariably accompanied by special guests. On the first occasion our fellow travellers were Sgt Peter Robinson and Maj Gen Tony Jones. The General also travelled with us on the second tour. At the Nijmegen bridge over the River Waal, Sgt Robinson's troop, which consisted of four tanks, was ordered by his squadron leader to proceed

Gen Tony Jones at Nijmegen CWGC.

to and move swiftly across the bridge - to 'go for it'. To say the least the journey was hazardous, a German 88 gun on the other side had to be taken out and so were many other enemy armed with rifles, machine guns, and grenades.

When the German general who was responsible for the bridge realised that the troop of tanks were more or less halfway across, he immediately ordered its demolition. To his astonishment and although a second attempt was made, the bridge held and Robinson's troop moved on. Eventually despite desperate enemy artillery and machine gun fire, the troop safely reached the other side. They were immediately surrounded by overjoyed American troops who were relieved to know that the half mile long bridge had been captured.

Maj Gen Tony Jones, a lieutenant in the Royal Engineers at the time, who was following the troop of tanks, had the unenviable task of clearing the crossing of demolition obstacles. Although under constant fire from Germans on the girders of the bridge, he cut wires and removed wires from mines which he threw into the river. In one of the piers at the far end of the bridge were the main explosive charges for which he had just cut the wires. The Anglo-American rush across the bridge had so surprised the enemy that they had obviously had no time to destroy it.

Lt Gen Brian Horrocks, 30 Corps Commander, described the young Lt Jones as the 'bravest of the brave' but in his view he was simply doing something for which he had been trained.

It was late in the evening by the time that Robinson's troop had made their successful crossing. Nevertheless, the local American Commander strongly felt that having got armour across the Nijmegen bridge, the tanks of the British Guards Armoured Division should make haste to the Arnhem bridge to relieve the paratroopers there, a distance of some 11 miles. However, the British infantry had not caught up with the tanks because of various enemy attacks along the route. The American infantry were not prepared to support the British armour because of lack of resources, so the advance stalled. Thus there was never to be a link-up between Allied land

Lonsdale church, Arnhem.

forces and the airborne troops at Arnhem.

The enemy had made good use of the formidable forces that fortunately were in the Arnhem area when the initial assault landings were made and he was quick to reinforce them before the troops of the British 30 Corps were able to penetrate the area.

As is well known, Operation Market Garden was accordingly described as a 'Bridge too Far'. At Arnhem our party was privileged to see at Ginkel Heath an airborne drop by some 200 paratroopers. Present at the 45th Anniversary among many distinguished officers and local civilians was Col Frost who made an epic stand with his troops for several days at the bridge which is now named after him.

During the tour a visit was made to the bridge - a very special visit indeed since we were able to walk the crossing. When the Germans left the area in October 1944 they demolished the bridge to hamper any Allied advance so after the war it was necessary to erect a Bailey bridge until a new one in the exact style of the blown bridge could be built in 1969.

Next we attended a special ceremony of remembrance in nearby Airborne Square, exceptionally well attended by veteran airborne servicemen but also by large numbers of Dutch people.

It is a feature of all such events for the local people to have such a depth of interest which they explain shows a very long standing appreciation for their liberation in 1945 and, which it is believed, is never forgotten in Holland since young people are made aware in their education of the events of 1940s and annual ceremonies of remembrance are held throughout their country,

The Hartenstein Museum is housed in the former headquarters of the First British Airborne Division which was previously the headquarters of Field Marshal Model of the German army. Here we saw a collection of memorabilia and photographs of the dramatic Battle of Arnhem and Oosterbeek in 1944 together with one of the greatest offensives by the Allied Forces to liberate Western Europe by depicted dioramas, also an audiovisual presentation and original film taken during the battle.

There was also a visit to the Groesbeek Liberation Museum which tells the history of Operation Market Garden, the struggle for freedom in the Nijmegen area. It also tells of Operation Veritable, the Second Army attack to seize the necessary jumping off area for a spring assault towards and across the Rhine. A Roll of Honour was available for reflection and remembrance which included names of all those casualties of my Regiment in the North West Europe campaign.

At the 45th anniversary our party was privileged to attend a special luncheon at the invitation of the Mayor of Nijmegen. On this occasion each of us was presented with a medallion, a reminder of the event of 1944 which indicates a paratrooper descending and a section of bridge bringing back memories of this great battle.

There was time too for a visit to Lonsdale Church; to Driel where the Poles landed and fought so bravely; and to Oosterbeek CWGC - the 'Airborne Cemetery' - where 1,775 men who died at Arnhem are buried, an area which was at the heart of the fighting.

As is well known the Arnhem sector was a defeat, a heavy defeat, for the British and Polish Airborne troops. Without any doubt the Germans won the battle but ironically in doing so they lost much more. Stalling the Allied advance in the west for a period of some 7-8 months conveniently allowed the Russians on their front to advance well into Eastern Europe and eventually at the end of hostilities in Berlin. The country was divided into East and West Germany and remained so for nearly half a century. As subsequent events unfolded the cost was dear, very dear, to the German nation.

Although strategically defeated at Arnhem, the landing troops performed heroically. With adequate support troops there could be little doubt they would have been equal to the task of capturing the bridge, as they did with such success in Normandy.

In the early days of May 1945 when the defeat of Germany was imminent, the Germans approached Monty for terms of surrender which, it is said included a suggestion that to avoid being overwhelmed by the Russians the German Army would withdraw by stages in front of the British troops following up. Monty refused to do so and demanded surrender otherwise his forces would continue fighting.

Was this response by Monty a way of reminding the Germans that they missed their opportunity of British and American domination over much more of their country some few months earlier by thwarting his 'master-plan' at Arnhem? This time the Germans gave up!

12

Frontline Britain - Dover

In 1940 Dover witnessed Britain's darkest hour. The BEF had withdrawn from Dunkirk at the end of May and early June while the RAF had sustained some serious losses having lost more than 900 aircraft. For the Germans it was not if, but when, Great Britain would surrender. This did not happen.

On 10 July began the Battle of Britain which continued for more than two months to 15 September on which date the battered Luftwaffe accepted defeat at the hands of RAF Fighter Command.

When Hitler realised that the German Air Force had failed to gain the vital superiority in the air, he also realised that no surrender would be forthcoming from Britain. He had made plans to land 60,000 troops along

The German's view of the White Cliffs of Dover showing radar pylons, and, on right, smoke from shells fired by long-range guns at Cap Griz-Nez. 8 August 1942. ***Photo by kind permission of Mr RC Hollingsbee***

the coast of south east England from Folkestone to Brighton on 21 September, his aim being to capture the whole of Kent by October 1940.

Dover is famous for its white cliffs wherein lies a concealed network of tunnels some 200ft below ground and which is known as Hellfire Corner. It was there that Admiral Ramsay masterminded Operation Dynamo - the evacuation from Dunkirk - and where key command areas, anti-aircraft control and the wartime telephone system were housed.

While many towns and cities throughout Britain suffered from Hitler's bombing raids, only Dover experienced both bombing and shelling as indicated in the paper which follows.

Only 22 miles away across the English Channel the Germans occupied the Pas-de-Calais coastline from 1940-1944 which had become part of the Atlantic wall with its many bunkers and fortifications all built by slave labour.

On a three day Holts' tour for the 50th anniversary, Terry Sutton was our special guest. He described his early lifetime throughout the Hellfire Corner years. During the four-year period August 1940 to September 1944 more than 2,000 shells were fired by German guns on Dover from the French coast. The town suffered a massive final battering from the enemy gunners near Calais and Boulogne in September 1944 as Allied troops fought their way along the French coastline. In that month alone civilian casualties caused by the shellfire totalled 41 killed and 150 injured. Damage caused to property included 150 homes destroyed; 1,560 seriously damaged; and 6,750 having minor damage. In reply to enemy shelling Allied gunners fired on German shipping convoys which were leaving the ports of Calais and Boulogne, indeed on one night the gunners claimed that 11 ships were sunk.

There were many incidents during the month of September. One shell destroyed Charlton Mill which never reopened resulting in the loss of nearly 100 jobs. On two occasions the shell warnings operated for more than 17 hours. Later Boulogne fell but in one further week the enemy made a final assault during which five civilians and two servicemen died when a shell exploded in the Salvation Army's Red Shield canteen bringing the building down. During the last two days of enemy shelling (25/26 September) there were severe casualties - eight civilians killed and nine injured, also, five servicemen killed and five injured. However, it was not until 30 September that the mayor announced that the German shelling was over. All Dovorians who had lived through the previous years were indeed very thankful for such long awaited news.

It is a feature of travelling with Holts' tours that for much of the time

British Expeditionary Force survivors landing at Dover Western Docks from destroyers, after rescue from Dunkirk, May 1940. *Photo by kind permission of Mr RC Hollingsbee*

the party is walking the ground of attack or, as happened on this tour, the ground where vital defensive action was taken. At the outset of this tour our group was very fortunate in having a friendly, exceptionally well-informed, special guide in John Reed who met us at Wanstone Farm close to the South Foreland coast near St Margaret's-at-Cliffe. He quickly proved himself to be more than a guide because he was an expert. He told us that Winston Churchill visited the area at the outbreak of WW2 and he was angered by the fact that the enemy shipping was proceeding virtually unopposed through the Straits of Dover. To stop this he immediately ordered the construction of cross Channel guns. Two 14-inch guns on experimental mountings were fortunately available and a little later two 15-inch guns arrived together with four 9.2 guns and batteries of 6 and 5.2 guns. However, none of these guns were put in a position to fire at the enemy coast but they were to deal with enemy shipping using the English Channel.

The Germans had far more long range guns placed on the French coast

The Guildhall Vaults Public House, Bench Street, Dover with, on the right at the corner with Queen Street, the coach booking office which served as a rest room during the war for HM Forces, October 1943. ***Photo by kind permission of Mr RC Hollingsbee***

than we had ourselves so it was inadvisable for us to shell territory held by them.

There were some railway guns in the area which were seen as morale boosters since they were unable to be used for any attack on the movement of enemy ships. They could have been used in any invasion of our country by the Germans since their role in designated sites inland near ammunition stores would have enabled them to bombard our own beaches and other strategic points where the enemy landed. We covered the actual ground where the various batteries were placed.

The 9.2 guns were first used at the time when two enemy warships, the Scharnhorst and Prince Eugen, succeeded in passing through the Channel but it was not known whether any damage was caused at that time. Also on site was the Guardroom for the battery. There were two big mounds for the magazines, certain areas of concrete ground where there had been an anti-aircraft battery and a specific area as an Army campsite.

There were barrage balloons in the local woods while in the immediate vicinity were the quarters for officers and men and a butts for small arms fire. There was also to be seen an old house which had seemingly been shaken up by the guns and accordingly had been strapped up by some old railway lines. It had not been used by the Army since the end of the war although it was not until 1956 that the guns at Wanstone were scrapped. That was to be the end of coastal artillery for the British Army.

Finally, it was explained to us that the guns on site were covered with camouflage netting unlike the German ones which were covered by concrete. The gunners did have much success in sinking/damaging many enemy ships using the Channel, indeed it often happened that with the aid of radar - then a secret - the guns also operated in bad weather much to the annoyance of Dover residents who were then subjected to retaliation by the enemy.

Our next stop was at the Swingate 'disused' airfield where photos were taken of two memorials at the entrance - one for the Air Force and one for the Artillery.

A friend, 'Tug' Wilson told me that he was in the Dover area in 1940 when the German Stukas came and 'had a go' at the harbour, the castle, and the town. Messerschmitt pilots escorting the bombers used to amuse themselves by machine gunning the town, up and down the High Street, at that time a terrible hazard for the local people. Tug remembered it well having been machine gunned himself from the air. He was stationed in Dover, having been called-up over the radio in August 1939 being a TA man and having just returned from annual camp. Originally stationed in the Folkestone area, he was moved along the coast to Dover 'when the balloon went up'.

Rifle and ammunition had to be carried during the times allowed out in town, generally for a few drinks. There was one occasion when the harbour was bombed by the Germans when he happened to be in close proximity. Suddenly the air raid sirens had gone, so he and a pal got down in a gutter with steel helmets over the back of their heads - noise and flying debris was everywhere. Ships ,including destroyers, were badly damaged, several were seen to be lying on their side.

In the early part of 1940 it was 'dead easy' for the Luftwaffe since they could come across almost unchallenged in a 'couple of shakes'. However, the tide turned at the time of the Battle of Britain - August/September - and often the pilots would be rescued by Army personnel. It was interesting to learn that the German flyers found it easy to shoot down the defensive

War damage in Snargate Street, Dover, looking towards New Bridge with the Royal Hippodrome Theatre on the right, September 1944.
Photo by kind permission of Mr RC Hollingsbee

barrage balloons. The Army, however, quickly outwitted them. Instead of the guns chasing after the enemy planes it was decided that the Vickers and Beaufors guns be aligned up on each balloon separately - fixed to one balloon meant that a number of guns were already on target and by this method Jerry lost several of his planes. After such a rude awakening the enemy quickly stopped 'blowing up balloons'.

During the 50th anniversary commemorations many events had been organised by Dover enthusiasts. There was a special Service of Commemoration held at the Saxon Church of St Mary of Castro, still in use as the town's garrison church, which included the dedication of a United States of America anti-aircraft unit's memorial plaque.

A convoy of World War Two vehicles toured the local towns and villages with a rally which ended at Marine Parade, Dover, being part of the Frontline Britain celebrations. Also as part of these celebrations, more than 1,000 people watched The Royal Logistics Corps Staff Band Beat the Retreat playing World War Two dance music. The music brought back many happy memories of the dances which were held in the town hall attended by both civilians and those in the Services locally.

The highlight of the 50th anniversary commemorations was the Frontline Britain 1994 Grand Parade and Dedication Service attended by many local dignitaries and thousands of veterans from all over the world who later marched along the seafront in brilliant sunshine. A memorial was unveiled by the Countess Mountbatten of Burma to the military and civilian personnel who served in the East Kent District.

The Service of Remembrance was conducted by the Bishop of Dover, the Rt Rev JRA Llewellin, who also dedicated the memorial.

The final visit for our Holts party was to nearby Capel-le-Ferne where we saw the fine memorial commemorating the four-month long period of air combat during the summer of 1940, known as the Battle of Britain, when the German Air Force attempted and failed to win air superiority in advance of their planned invasion of Britain. This national memorial to those who flew and those who gave their lives in the battle, is located on the site of a wartime artillery position on the white cliffs.

Throughout the war years and in particular during the summer and autumn of 1940 following the evacuation of the BEF from France, the famous white cliffs of Dover stood out for the whole of our country, perhaps as never before, as being the *great* in Great Britain. During that time too the nation including servicemen were encouraged by Dame Vera Lynn singing that never to be forgotten war song, *The White Cliffs of Dover* the words are as follows:

There'll be bluebirds over the white cliffs of Dover
Tomorrow just you wait and see
There'll be love and laughter and peace ever after
Tomorrow when the world is free
The shepherd will tend his sheep
The valley will bloom again
And Jimmy will go to sleep in his own little room again
There'll be bluebirds over the while cliffs of Dover
Tomorrow just you wait and see.

13

Battle of 's-Hertogenbosch, Holland

's-Hertogenbosch - in short Den Bosch - is the capital of the Dutch province of North Brabant. It lies at the confluence of the Dommel and the Aa as well as on the Zuid Willemeveart in flat pasture land which is flooded every year in winter.

It is a busy commercial town, has important cattle markets and is the home of diversfied industries which include the manufacture of cigars and hardware, food processing and brewing.

The town was given its first Charter in 1185. In October 1944 it had a population of about 50,000 but this has increased to 90,000 during the past half a century. Principally it is visited for its magnificent Gothic cathedral and where, indeed, we attended a special memorial service.

A 50th anniversary tour to Holland with the Regimental Association covered a period of six days from 25 to 30 October 1994 during which time we visited 's-Hertogenbosch and Middelbeers.

Sgt Ted Glynn DCM MM, one of the many veterans, well remembered the events of 50 years previously when all squadrons of the Regiment were busily engaged in the area of 's-Hertogenbosch at Heesch-Geffen, at Nuland, at Kruistrsat, at Rosmalen and at Hintham. For the attack on 's-Hertogenbosch in October 1944, the 5th Royal Inniskilling Dragoon Guards, an armoured regiment, was 'sub-contracted' to an infantry division, the 53rd Welsh Division, whose historical note, which follows, gives the story of the battle...

The battle for the capture of the Dutch town of 's-Hertogenbosch is regarded as the greatest battle fought by the 53rd (Welsh) Division. It took place between 22 and 27 October 1944 following the failure of the Allied ground and airborne operations at Arnhem.

The 21st Army Group under Field Marshal Montgomery was to open the port of Antwerp to Allied shipping and shorten the lengthy supply lines leading back into France and the original Normandy beachhead.

The 53rd (Welsh) Division, part of XII Corps, had landed in Normandy in late June and by June 28th was concentrated around Bayeux. Included

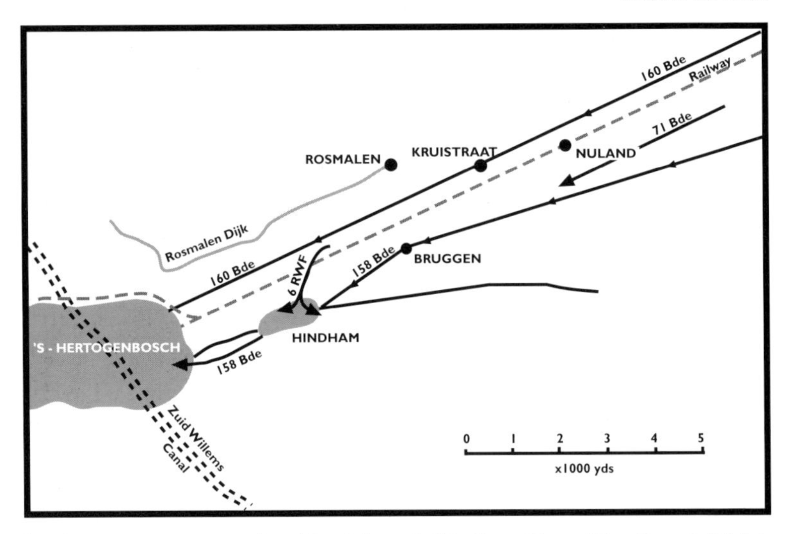

in these troops were the 4th, 6th and 7th Battalions The Royal Welch Fusiliers, the 4th and 1st/5th Battalions the Welch Regiment and the 2nd Battalion The Monmouthshire Regiment.

In the following weeks the Division blooded itself in the fierce campaign in Normandy during which Capt Tasker Watkins, commanding B Company of the 1st/5th Welch earned the Victoria Cross. By 18 August the Division had closed up to what was known as the Falaise Gap in which the best German troops on the Western Front were concentrated. The drive continued into the Low Countries, and after the failure at Arnhem the 53rd Welsh was set up tor its greatest triumph, at 's-Hertogenbosch.

To help in the bid to open the port of Antwerp, the Welsh Division was tasked in helping to protect the northern flank by advancing to 's-Hertogenbosch - a key communications centre, and clearing it of enemy. The town was strongly defended and it protected the German withdrawal and supply route for the forces still denying the Scheldt Estuary route to the Allies. Four battalions of the experienced German 712th Division held the town and its immediate approaches.

Maj Gen Ross planned to launch his attack from the east with 160 Brigade leading, supported by the 5th Dragoon Guards with tanks. The 71st Infantry Brigade was to advance south of the railway line astride the road from 's-Hertogenbosch to Hersch and the 158th Infantry Brigade was held in reserve ready to move up with the 53rd Reconnaissance Regiment and one squadron of the Dragoons to seize the canal bridges in the town, should the chance occur.

The attack commenced at 0630hrs on 22 October and by the following afternoon the Division was poised to assault 's-Hertogenbosch.

By 2200hrs the 6th Royal Welch Fusiliers had outflanked the village of Hintham, penetrating it from the west and holding it in the face of continuous attacks during the hours of darkness. Meanwhile the 1/5th Welch and the East Lancashires momentarily secured a bridge on the Zuid Willems Canal, but were to be fought off by heavy German forces who later blew up the bridge.

The East Lancashires continued their advance on the road from Hintham and by around 1130hrs had been joined by tanks from the 5th Dragoon Guards before taking up a defensive position. The 7th Royal Welch, with two further squadrons of tanks, made a rapid advance down the Hintham road and by 1100hrs had passed through the village, relieving A Company of the 6th Royal Welch.

All the bridges across the canal were by now destroyed but there was still a lock gate left intact, and in one of the most heroic actions of the battle a company of the 7th Royal Welch, supported by tanks, crossed and overcame a German post in a house on the far bank. A strong bridgehead was then established which was held throughout the night, allowing the 282nd Field Company Royal Engineers to construct a temporary bridge.

During the following morning as the East Lancashires executed a flanking manoeuvre to the south, the 1/5th Welch were pushed across the temporary bridge at the lock gate and told to clear the town to the north. Desperate fighting followed as the town had been substantially reinforced overnight. During that day the 4th Welch, from 160 Brigade, relieved the 158 Brigade's 7th Royal Welch and by that night the western edge of the town was held.

On 26 October the plan was to fling the 1/5th Welch over a partially destroyed bridge and for the East Lancashires to seize another bridge which again was only partly intact. At 1100hrs, under cover of smoke and mortar shells, but without the customary artillery barrage, the Welch rushed the bridge taking the garrison by complete surprise.

The divisional records show that the Germans continued to resist fiercely retreating reluctantly under the cover of gunfire and demolitions. But the determination of the men of the 53rd Welsh Division proved superior and by nightfall on 26 October the Germans' morale had gone. Practically the whole of 's-Hertogenbosch was in the Welsh Division's hands. Fighting continued sporadically on 27 October but by midday, the town had been taken.

There are no casualty figures tor the actual battle for 's-Hertogenbosch although the total casualties for the month, in which there was only this major action, give an indication. From a divisional strength of 12,000, 11 officers and 134 other ranks were killed and 37 officers and 668 other ranks wounded.

The captured German garrison commander later admitted that he had been ordered to hold the town at all costs but had been surprised by the determination and speed of the 53rd Welsh's advance. He paid particular credit to the resolute way in which the infantry had crossed the canal and the speed of the Royal Engineers in bridging the waterway to enable anti-tank guns to be rushed across.

Tanks advance into town via the railway line!

The East Lancs, an infantry regiment, had been most successful in their advance on the town but on 24 October they were unable to move forward without the support of tanks. The surrounding area consisted of marshy fields which were unusable for vehicles and the local roads had not been opened up. The only way for tanks to proceed into the town was by the top of a railway embankment 15ft high which would leave them extremely vulnerable to enemy guns on both flanks.

A Squadron fell for this unenviable task and after a most perilous journey of more than a mile along the railway track, the squadron reached the East Lancs. Most fortunately only one tank, the last one, shed a track. More fortunately perhaps, as became known many years later, the enemy had several guns well-placed for such a movement but at that moment had run out of ammunition. They could do no more than watch the tanks led by Sgt Albert Morris proceed along the railway line at a snail's pace to link up with their infantry comrades.

On reaching the East Lancs the tanks, together with the infantry teams, pushed on into the town to seize the only bridge still standing over the Zuid Willems Canal.

Sgt Archie Carr, who was present in our party with his wife and friends, was awarded the DCM for his skilful and courageous leadership of his troop along the railway line and the action which followed, including the determination shown by him on many occasions throughout the NW Europe campaign until that time.

Squadron Leader Maj AC Gibson MC recorded the action as follows…

Third day - 24 October: During the night, the East Lancs advanced and obtained a footing in the suburbs to the north-east of 's-Hertogenbosch, which was still held by the enemy, and as there was a rumour of enemy tanks in the area, the brigadier was most anxious to get some tank support up to them, but it was easier said than done, as all the ground north of the railway was flat, swampy and impassable for tanks, and 1,000yds away to the north, the high banks of the dyke commanded the ground between it and the railway. To the south of the railway B Squadron was advancing, and there were known to be a considerable number of 75mms and at least two confirmed locations of 88mms. The only possible line of advance for the tanks was down the railway line, which ran on an embankment for some 2,000yds, 15ft above the level of the ground and completely exposed on both flanks. However, it was considered vital that a squadron of tanks should be got into town and, after a very careful and thorough artillery plan, we advanced down the line in three parties. It was with a sigh of relief that we got to the other end.

Only one tank (Sgt Heaps) broke a track and fortunately for all concerned, this was the last tank of the squadron.

When we got into the town, 1 Coy of the East Lancs, with 3rd Troop in support, moved round the north of the pond to capture the bridge at 326465. This they did without meeting any opposition, but it was found that all the bridges on the canal south of this one had been blown, so there was little more that we could do.

However, it was necessary to gain further information on the extent of the damage to these bridges, and Lt Wallworth was unlucky enough to have a second tank hit and brewed up under him in two days, while making a reconnaissance. Fortunately, there were no casualties to the crew, and he got the necessary information. He was fired at from very close range, by a self-propelled gun lurking in some buildings on the far bank. As it was getting dark, A Squadron and the remainder of the regiment were ordered to concentrate in the area of Rosmalen, prior to a move round to the Boxtel area the next day.

So ended three days of hard and very successful fighting. The 2nd Monmouths expressed great satisfaction with the support that they had received from the squadron, and we were no less delighted with the support received from them. They are undoubtedly a fine regiment.

There was a very large contingent of veterans and their relatives from the 53 (Welsh) Division taking part in the highly successful commemorations/celebrations. My regiment, although it had played a not-insignificant part in the liberation of the town some half-a-century before, was overall a much lesser unit. It was not unexpected by our regimental party throughout the whole of our stay that a low profile be kept.

We were recognised individually by the grateful Dutch people for their liberation since we were included in the presentation of a medal for all servicemen who were there in 1944. Many special anniversary events had been arranged by the people of the town with Luc van Gent as the co-ordinator, assisted by his wife, Agnes. There was a large gathering, indeed a very large gathering, for our first commemoration, a memorial service in St John's Cathedral where a former padre with the 53 (Welsh) Division, the Most Reverend Alwyn Price, Archbishop of Wales, gave the address.

A Welsh choir and military bands contributed to the special service. Afterwards there was a silent march of some 500 metres to the Resistance Monument where we assembled with another large gathering for a short ceremony. The Dutch Last Post was played followed by wreath laying, one being laid on behalf of our regimental party by Maj Pat Whitmore. Only a short walking distance away we assembled again with our Welsh friends at their Divisional Memorial for a special ceremony and wreath laying. An excellent lunch followed and we joined local people in the evening for a liberation concert in Maasport.

We stayed at the very comfortable Nuland Motel just a short journey from 's-Hertogenbosch. One evening, having had a splendid dinner in a convivial atmosphere, it was decided to go elsewhere for drinks. As Skins, veterans never forget they were always very good at reconnoitring the surrounding area when finding themselves in new billets. It was therefore no surprise that a recce had been a priority and 'from information received' we were recommended to try the local bar which we were told was the first on the crossroads opposite. On arrival at the bar there was complete silence, curtains were drawn, indeed no sign of life whatsoever. Not to be deterred, however, the door was given a few gentle knocks but no reply was forthcoming. We were about to return to the hotel, being greatly disappointed, when some activity inside was observed and the door was opened by a young well-made lady in a slimline bikini. Needless to say our group was somewhat taken aback but nevertheless thought it was well up to Skins' standard and several moved forward making it known that we were all very thirsty, almost dying. However, although the Skins are well-known for going forward we were stopped in our tracks. Syd Swift and his 'Firefly' were absent. It was then that she realised that we were in need of a drink or two and she understood that our needs were appropriate to the local bar and were not for the entertainment provided at her establishment. Our advance party had set us up all right but a quick glance round and to our amusement we could see the local licensee much amused by our antics but he was delighted that our business was his. This evening in the bar was an unforgettable one - many, many yarns were told by veterans and friends ending in the early hours of the morning.

Much to our surprise on returning to the hotel we found many of our Welsh friends finishing off their evening's entertainment with some well-controlled singing. They were about to leave but we were told that they may have a similar session next evening. I said that I hoped I would be around to hear them sing *The Lord is my Shepherd* to the tune *Crimond*. Spontaneously they grouped and sung as only they do from the hills and valleys. A splendid evening ended for all of us - one that I will long remember.

And the following night when we returned to the hotel, we were most disappointed. It was all quiet - the choir had left early and gone to bed! Apparently 'lights out' had sounded long ago. It was church next day - for them…and for us.

We arrived at Uden on a splendid autumn morning to find local people in large numbers waiting to attend the church service which had been specially arranged for us. A feature of this service was the singing of special anthems by an augmented choir of our Welsh friends. Only a short walk away was the CWGC and here a short ceremony was held around the Cross of Sacrifice which included special singing by the Welsh Choir and was followed by wreath laying. It is a custom in Holland for children to honour the British fallen by laying flowers on the graves. Here we visited the graves of seven of our comrades buried in the cemetery. At the grave of a Regimental comrade was a very young girl accompanied by her friend. Most spontaneously Mick Hewitt removed his 5 RIDG cap badge from his black beret and presented it to her as a memento of our visit on this very special occasion.

Jean Philo, Micky Hewitt and two young ladies at Uden CWGC.

Those of us present at the time will long remember the delight on the face of this very young lady, who soon showed signs of being slightly overawed by the gift she had received from Mick.

After lunch,

provided generously by the people of Uden, our party made a 'Remembrance' visit to the Mook War Cemetery at Mook-in-Middelaar where several of our comrades are buried. They were close friends of Syd Swift, unable to be with us on tour, but who nevertheless has a depth of feeling for their loss which he included in his booklet, *Tracks in Time*, as follows...

Fate

To Larry, Barry and Hal 1944
One was a Taff, good for a laugh
In any situation.
The second kept his cool
Never played the fool
Made no protestation.
The third, tender in years
Lived with his fears
Showed no exasperation.

Three pals good and true
Daily they grew
In everyone's estimation.
The three were as one
Then they were gone
To our consternation.
Some go, some stay,
That is life's way;
Death makes no discrimination.

During the evening in the market square at 's-Hertogenbosch we had a very special treat - Beating Retreat by the Welsh Bands. And as part of the celebrations a splendid fireworks display took place afterwards at the citadel.

On our final day in the city on the occasion of this very special 50th anniversary we attended the unveiling of the Royal Welch Fusiliers Memorial at the Bastion. After the unveiling all the many groups represented formed up in their various parties for the march into the city. It was most moving that when our small Regimental party - the Regimental banner being carried by Ron Teague - was spotted by our accompanying relatives and friends and also the local people, a big cheer of appreciation came our way.

The march terminated in the city centre outside the Casino Theatre where an official reception was attended by the mayor and other dignitaries, and as on so many convivial occasions throughout our stay, plenty of food and drink followed.

On the last day of this Regimental tour we were very warmly welcomed at Middelbeers where again half-a-century previously we were the armoured regiment in support of several infantry battalions. Briefly, the local population had heard about the Allied invasion on 6 June 1944 on a radio kept in secret. They were aware that at the outset there were delays in establishing a strong bridgehead but they learned eventually that the Germans were on the defensive and consequently were making preparations to defend the Netherlands, in the area of Middelbeers they were requisitioning property including school buildings. By the time the Allied forces had crossed the France/Belgian border on 3 September and Brussels had been liberated, local people were aware that the Germans had been routed. Subsequently large groups of the enemy moved through Middelbeers and in general they began to leave the area. However by 21 September the Germans prepared themselves for battle against Allied forces. On the following day (22nd) the battle for the village began, the shelling was so heavy it was felt that much of it would be razed to the ground.

Unfortunately, during the turmoil of battle there were casualties among the civilian population. It is not often in war that a truce occurs - the most famous one probably being in World War One at Christmas 1914 - but the Regiment was involved in a truce in Middelbeers. One of the casualties was a woman, Mrs Soethout, whose story is told in the book *De Beerzen in Oorlogstijd 1940-45* by Tienus Deenen, Aloys Kemp and Frank Stalpers. (See following extracts).

Several houses had been hit by the shelling and Mr Haneveld records the following...

'One of the first shells fell near Van Eeten's textile shop on the Willibrordstraat. A woman staying with family Liebregts at that moment was injured by shrapnel.'

The woman in question was Mrs Soethout. At that time she lived on the Beerseweg in Oirschot. Mrs Soethout remembers this incident:

'Mid September 1944 the Germans wanted us to leave together with a number of other people living in our neighbourhood. The situation was getting too dangerous because the Germans were going to defend the area where we lived, against the Allies. They started constructing defensive works. We did not feel like leaving and stayed.

'After some days a German called at our house and advised us urgently to leave. I was heavily pregnant and he pointed at the risks I could run. On his advice we still left, although Hendrik, my husband, did not want to go to Oirschot because the bridge across the Wilhelminakanaal was destroyed and he would be cut off from our cattle. Moreover in Middlebeers lived a midwife and because of my situation we liked to live in her neighbourhood. The baby was expected within a fortnight. Therefore we moved to Middelbeers and would move in with Sjef Liebregts. He did not have a large family and what's more, he lived quite close to the midwife (Sister Teepen) in a house on the Willibrord Straat at the place where there is now a greengrocer's shop.

'We had scraped together some things for the baby (I was pregnant for the first time). I was sitting on the carriers of Henry's bike carrying some things for the baby and towing the pram. In this way we rode to Middelbeers some three or four days before the assault on De Beerzen.

'The assault on De Beerzen was launched on 22 September. The village was shelled. From the Kuikeindsweg the English fired at the German positions. One of the shells exploded against the front of Van Eeten's shop. Another shell hit our house. I was making the beds at that moment. The explosion smashed the panes out of the windows. I was hit by shrapnel in my left arm and my breast (in two places). Moreover a piece of shrapnel grazed my right shoulder. In spite of my injuries I managed to reach the kitchen where at that moment Hendrik was shaving. I collapsed in front of him. Sjef and Marie Liebregts were very quickly on the scene. Hendrik ran out of the house and spotted Sister Teepen in the street. She had assumed that there would be casualties among the inhabitants because of the shelling and had been prepared. She immediately came along with Hendrik. I was lying in the kitchen. My left arm was dangling beside my body. A few people went to fetch a stretcher or something that could pass for one. I was laid down on it and carried to the other side of the street, where a Red Cross post had been set up in the school. At that moment a son of Harrie Libregts (Sjef) and Mr Haneveld were there, who were both first aiders.

The shelling just went on at that moment. I stayed in the school for only a short time. Because of the continuous shelling it was thought safer to take me to the church. The walls of the church were thicker and so they could take some buffeting. Sister Teepen, Sjef Libregts, Hendrik and some other people stayed with me. There were some five of us. The parish priest came and advised us to sit closer to the church doors so that we could leave the church faster if the situation became too dangerous. The church tower was hit several times. Debris crashed down. We were covered with dust. We really looked a mess. The situation became so bad that Sister Teepen lay down on top of me to protect me. Yet I said: 'But sister, we are in the house of God.'

Later that day I was moved to the cellar under the presbytery. Towards evening I started complaining because of my injuries. A German doctor who had been sent for refused to come. In the end doctor Ruhe from Hilvarenbeek came after a telephone call from Sister Teepen. I think I was still lying in the school then.

He had come straight across the lines on his motorbike and he at once said that it would probably be the first and last time he could come. He could do nothing else but dress my wounds and give me some injections. He left some syringes behind and after he had given Sister Teepen some advice on my treatment, he rode back to Hilvarenbeek.'

Mrs Soethout was still lying in the church when fire was opened on the church tower, the situation became deadly dangerous for her and the others. Marie van Knegsel…

'The bullets really whizzed past our ears. Therefore we took Mrs Soethout to the cellar under the presbytery. It took some doing to get her into the cellar on a stretcher. In the cellar we laid her down on a number of sacks filled with hay.'

Mrs Soethout had been deprived of further medical care. In the course of the night Mr Haneveld had succeeded in calling for help from the British with his transmitter equipment. Pte Mick Hewitt was there when the emergency call came in by radio:

'I have vivid recollection of the events in Middelbeers and of the woman 'lying-in'. We had just buried Sgt Thickpenny. He had been shot through the carotid artery while he was in command of his tank. As a matter of fact it is unimaginable how much blood is involved when a man's heart is busy pumping his life out of him. We were covered in blood up to our elbows and Capt Forrester was exhausted after he had been fighting in vain for the sergeant's life for quite some time. I have recorded this because we did not even have time to wash when a message came in for Capt Forrester to pick-up a pregnant woman who was in danger of losing her life. At that stage I could not yet know that this trip meant that we would land behind enemy lines. We set out with half-track followed by an ambulance. In the outskirts of the village we encountered a German staff-car which accompanied us to the house.'

Mrs Soethout still remembers the arrival of an English doctor who assisted at her delivery. The arrival of this doctor scared the living daylights out of Jimmy Boardman…

'I had parked my armoured car on the left-hand side of the Kuikeindseweg close to the junction with the Willebrordstraat. My attention was drawn by a man who said that an injured woman was waiting for help. We heard the message on the radio that doctor Forrester was on his way. Shortly afterwards the half-track with Johnny Hines at the wheel and the doctor was following us down the road. He was driving very fast and I can still see the Red Cross flying from it. I waved to slow him down and to explain where he had to go. To the horror of my radio operator and myself, someone in the half-track waved back cheerfully and tore round the corner of the Willibrordstraat. At the back of that street the Germans had taken positions which we had been firing at just a few minutes before to support our front lines. I said to my radio operator: 'Jesus, he's had it'.'

The group drove on as far as the building of the elementary school. Having arrived, Capt Forrester got out and walked into the building.

Mick Hewitt continues…

'In the meantime the driver of the ambulance and I turned our vehicles for the trip back. At that moment I noticed for the first time that all ditches in the neighbourhood were packed with German troops with fixed bayonets and particularly unfriendly expressions on their faces. I got down from the half-track and had a short conversation with the driver of the ambulance who absolutely wanted to stay where he was, behind the wheel of his ambulance with the engine running. After a few minutes' consideration I decided that the best thing I could do was to pull a brave face. I took a tin of 50 cigarettes from the luggage and walked past the Jerries offering all of them a cigarette with my bloodstained arms and hands. They were surprised at what I was doing. But they lit the cigarettes and said 'danke'.

'After having waited for half an hour the stretcher was brought to the ambulance. It tore out of the street at about 80mph with Capt Forrester on the back seat. That was the last I saw of them. I trailed behind it with my half-track but somebody had forgotten to tell the Germans that they had let us pass. An enormous barrage of 88mm shells followed me through the street. I still thought: 'I hope those bastards will choke on my cigarettes'.'

Jimmy Boardman tells the last part of the story…

'After some moments the half-track appeared again. It was driving very fast. We succeeded in halting it. The doctor, Capt Forrester, told me: 'Nice to have a maternity case for a change - that cheers you up a bit'.

'After this Jimmy Boardman and his crew left the road and started firing at the enemy positions from the gardens on the right-hand side of the road.'

Mrs Soethout tells about her impressions of the delivery…

'When the baby, a girl, was born she did not give any sign of life. Cold and hot baths were of no avail. In the course of the morning I left the presbytery. I remember when I was being carried out that a number of

British vehicles were lined up in a row near the school while the Germans were lying in the garden behind the presbytery. Nevertheless, I was transported in a British armoured car, together with wounded British soldiers. I was wrapped in sheets which the parish priest had put at our disposal. Hendrik went along with me. He insisted on being taken to Eindhoven and not to Tilburg. The fact was that Eindhoven had been liberated.

'First we drove to Vessem. On our way the armoured car was fired at one more time. Driving through shellfire we arrived in Vessem. I was transported further to Wintelre in a normal Red Cross car and then to Eindhoven. Between Vessem and Eindhoven I lost consciousness. Hendrik banged the window. The driver stopped. Although being unconscious I heard him say: ' She is still alive.' I soon came round.

'In hospital Hendrik looked after me until 28 October. Immediately on arrival I was given a blood transfusion. It was the blood from a father. A Protestant getting blood from a father! Later we still cracked lots of jokes about it. The surgeon feared for my life. That day and night he did not give me any treatment. Covered with dirt I was lying in bed. After three weeks I gradually started recovering. At the end of January 1945 I left hospital.'

A few days later, when the Willibrodstraat was clear of Germans, the child was buried at the same time as Frans Timmers and Piet and Maria van de Loo. Mr Haneveld relates…

'At that moment nobody was left in the village. The parish priest too had been evacuated. Some German prisoners of war had dug graves. When the army chaplain started his speech it was suddenly perfectly quiet. It was a moving ceremony. The army chaplain talked about *The Lord is my Shepherd*.

'On one side of the graves there were British soldiers and on the other German prisoners of war. And between the coffins a small black coffin containing the mortal remains of Mrs Soethout's baby. Nobody could hold back the tears. Hardly had the ceremony ended when the force of arms started again. From the British as well as the German side the shells whined across the village.'

The highlight of our visit to Middelbeers was unquestionably the reception accorded us on our arrival and throughout our short stay. Quickly assembling in a nearby hall we immediately realised that among the many friends awaiting us was no other than Mrs Soethout, daughters and grandchildren.

On our coach throughout the tour I had the good fortune to be sitting on the rear seat with Mick Hewitt, a quiet, unassuming and friendly character.

It was Mick who was with Capt 'Doc' Forrester when Mrs Soethout was in desperate need of medical help.

At this most welcome gathering there were speeches by the local mayor and by Jim Boardman while Pat Whitmore gave a most lively account of Doc's dash through the front line to minister to his lady patient. Pat recalled that Regimental comrades at the time were unaware that the Germans (SS) had agreed this compassionate ceasefire. Seeing the Doc's party fly by many thought that was the last they would see of them - no-one had had time to say goodbye!

After the speeches Mick made a presentation of a bouquet to Mrs Soethout. It was a very emotional occasion for them and most thoughtful for all present. As recorded in the local book, the baby girl died so the end of the story was not a happy one. We all thought of more fortunate circumstances when a 50-year-old girl would have been present together with an extended family to greet us on this memorable occasion.

After some light refreshments we were then conducted on a tour of the local area including the church which was most interesting, indeed it would have been very much more so if only it hadn't rained. However, the weather did not spoil our visit - we returned to be provided with a high tea - a gift of a book - and when it was time to leave, some sincere handshakes of farewell. A most reluctant party left Middelbeers in the late afternoon. We were most thoughtful of their suffering resulting from the battles in October 1944 and a longer stay with our friends here would have been most welcome.

14

Battle of Roer Triangle, Holland

On 16 December 1944 the Germans gambled when they made a surprise attack in the Ardennes area of Belgium and Luxembourg with a much stronger 25 divisions against an American defensive force of only six divisions. Hitler's aim was to force a breakthrough to Antwerp on the coast thus splitting the Allied armies in two which would have caused a critical situation, so critical that the Allies may have collapsed. However, by 28 January 1945 the enemy 'master-stroke' had failed with losses of some 120,000 against those of the Americans' 75,000.

During the short period of the Ardennes offensive which became known as the Battle of the Bulge the Regiment was held in reserve. But this period of inactivity came to an end on 13 January 1945 with a new British offensive known as Operation Blackcock, designed to clear the pocket formed by the Rivers Roer and Maas. The Regiment received its orders on 22 January to capture the village of Montfort, an important road centre. When Montfort was liberated, the advance continued to the River Roer and when shortly afterwards the Regiment had cleared St Odilienberg, the final objective had been taken. Operation Blackcock was remarkable for the successful employment of armoured regiments in mid-winter over snow. Despite the cold, wintry weather conditions the Regiment had acquitted itself well. With the Roer pocket cleaned out and the Battle of the Rhineland over, it was time for the Regiment to have a short break in reserve before joining the 2nd Army force for an advance over the River Rhine, eventually to Bremen and Hamburg.

The Regimental 50th anniversary tour to the Roer Triangle was made in early May 1995, some three months later than the time of the battle in the area. Not only was it likely that the weather would be kinder then but, also, the time in the month - 5 May - coincided with the Dutch National Day of Liberation. The majority of our Regimental Association party stayed overnight at the UJ Club in Waterloo since departure from London had been arranged for an early ferry from Dover to Calais, to continue on a very long coach journey through France and Belgium to Sittard in Holland

The Roer Triangle

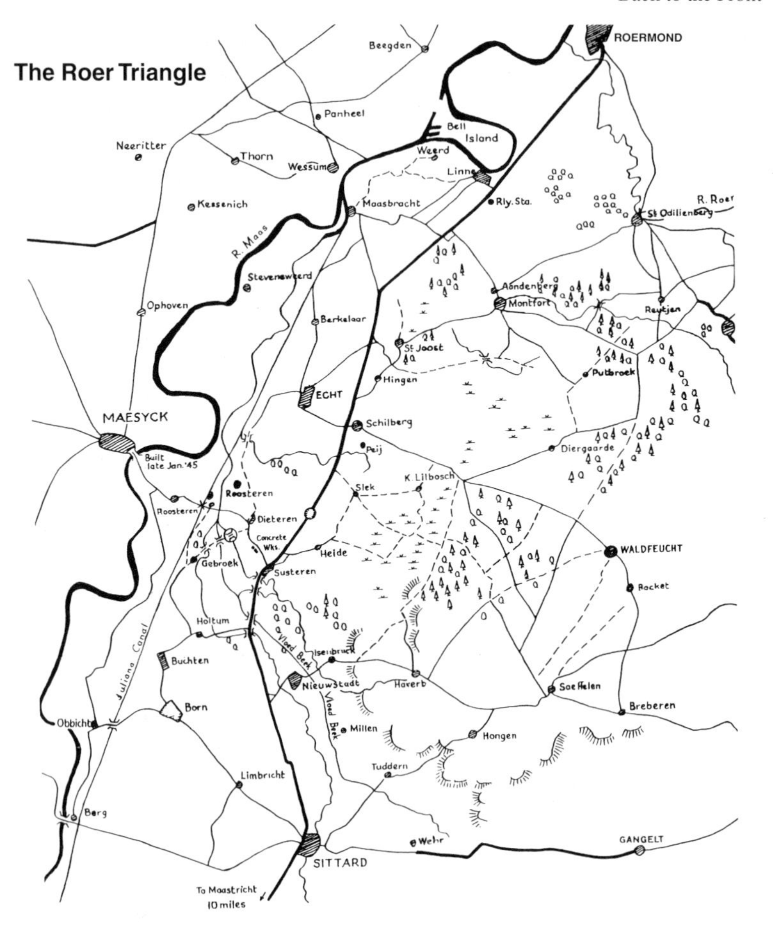

not far from the border with Germany.

In Sittard we stayed at motel Stein-Urmond, a luxurious, spacious hotel which was very much in keeping with the level of accommodation at which the Old Comrades are now accustomed to. The motel was also convenient for our commemorations/celebrations since it was in close proximity to Echt, Montfort, and St Odilienberg, the three localities which were liberated in January 1945. On the evening of our arrival - a day that had been set aside by our Dutch friends as Remembrance Day - our party assembled for a reception followed by a banquet at Bruin Cafe Spee in Echt. The restaurant, as the Jerboa Club, was used during wartime by troops of 7th Armoured Division for resting and for relaxation.

Later in the evening a special Remembrance ceremony took place at the war memorial in front of the town hall. An address was given by the Burgomaster of Echt, there was choral music by the Royal Harmony Band of Echt and by the Regimental Band of the Royal Dragoon Guards, the Dean of Echt led prayers followed by wreath laying. Lt Gen Sir Anthony Mullens KCB OBE gave an address. Last Post, two minutes silence and Reveille were observed followed by the national anthems and the hoisting of flags by members of the Dutch Association.

The Regimental Association had made a visit to Echt in mid May 1992 when, as the Regimental journal recorded, there was an unveiling ceremony, much of the finance having been provided by the Farmers Union. The unveiling of the memorial was carried out by Lt Col David Montgomery, Mr Bert Jannsen (Burgomaster),Mr Kurt Utens (Sculptor), and Capt Jim Boardman. There were in fact three wonderful memorials which will be a visiting point for generations to·come.

Capt Boardman read the names of the nine killed in action during the operation: 'Memorial Services which include the reading of names are often carried out like this but, on this occasion, these names were people who we had known well. We knew that like the rest of us, they hoped to survive. There is a thin dividing line which decides who remains on Dutch soil forever and who returns to commemorate their sacrifice.'

The three memorials - from left to right - are the Jerboa, 7th Armoured Division, Inniskilling Castle and 5 Dragoon Guards. After the Remembrance service the two bands led a march through the centre of Echt to Apollo Hall where the Royal Dragoon Guards Band played music for a social evening. A long day ended with our return to the motel in Sittard.

After such splendid hospitality by our Dutch friends on our arrival day, one hardly expected on our second day such friendly welcomes and warm hospitality. But again we were treated like heroes. This was the Dutch National Day of Liberation - Friday 5 May 1995 - and we counted ourselves as being most fortunate to be with these most kindly folk, sincere friends, who time and again made us aware of their appreciation for their liberation from Nazi Germany 50 years ago. It was also remarkable that younger people too acknowledged their freedom and the freedom of their families after several years of severe and dominating occupation of their homeland by the enemy. As, more or less, the Dutch people speak 'well-understood' English, conversations flowed freely on many occasions.

We left our hotel on a lovely spring morning and called at Echt before assembling with a well-attended crowd of local people near the Basilica in St Odilienberg. There we gathered round - plenty of photo opportunities -

Local children at St Odilienberg.

and listened to various speeches of welcome after which we entered the Basilica for a special concert by two local choirs, their final rendering of *Auld Lang Syne* was exceptional and they would have competed well with any similar English choir of similar numbers. We were all highly delighted with such splendid entertainment. We next made our way to the centre of the town where we joined the local crowd who were enjoying the lovely sunny day in a carnival atmosphere. At the end of this short break the children took part in a balloon race as hundreds of balloons were released adding much colour to the event. After luncheon we visited Montfort. Another reception by local people, music by local bands, and parades.

After a short sightseeing tour of the area which included the old Castle and the war memorial, we were provided with tea and some entertainment before departing for our hotel via Schilberg-Pey where we had a short stay to visit the church in the centre of the town. To free the town of Montfort and the local centres, heavy bombing raids were made in early 1945 which resulted in 380 civilians killed. Despite these awful casualties, they were most generous to us and we had a warm welcome wherever we found ourselves on this 50th anniversary. On the following day we left Sittard and proceeded to Paderborn in Germany to be with the Regiment for VE Day. (See Chapter 16)

15

Crossing the Rhine, Germany

Few of us - if any - in our youth at the time of the Allied defeat in France in May 1940 would, in their wildest dreams, have considered it possible that in less than five years we would be part of the Allied forces - Americans, Canadians, French, and British - planning to cross the river Rhine into Germany in a large, almost unbelievable, offensive to rid the world of Hitler and his Nazi cult.

The immediate past events had been...

- The Normandy Campaign from early June to mid-August followed by the liberation of northern France and entry into Belgium with the capture of Brussels on 3 September 1944 and Antwerp on 6 September...
- The unfortunate failure of the Arnhem operation later in that month;
- At the end of October the liberation by Commandos of the Scheldt area in Holland;
- Another setback when the Germans attacked in the Ardennes in late December in an attempt to cut off the Allied forces - including my Regiment - north of this attack;
- The Allied capture and consolidation of all the area up to the Rhine from 'top to bottom' of its length in the early weeks of 1945.

Many clearing-up operations were necessary, much re-organising to be done, essential re-equipping and the arrangement of the assault formations was possibly most vital of all activities. In the summer of 1940 never in the whole of our history possibly had the United Kingdom been so ill equipped to defend itself if the enemy had landed, yet they made no attempt to move across the Channel, albeit a more formidable obstacle than the water barrier confronting the Allies - the river Rhine - in 1945. Nevertheless the river was a formidable obstacle and, unlike battle on foreign territory, the Germans suddenly found themselves having to defend their own soil and their own people.

The events of half a century ago were described on the Holts' five-day tour from 22-26 March 1995 by Col Nic Gray. Along the line of the Rhine from the south (Switzerland border) to the north at Nijmegen (Holland), the Allied armies were in position as follows - 1st French, 7th US, 3rd US, 1st US, 9th US and 1st Cdn supported by the 2nd British. The plan at the northern end was for the 9th US Army to advance from the area behind the river Roer where it joins the river Maas at Julich to link up with the 1st Canadian Army under Gen Crerar attacking in a south-easterly direction from the direction of Nijmegen. The Canadian Army consisted of two Canadian infantry divisions and three British divisions with a further two British divisions in reserve. For such a large force of British troops to come under Canadian control was politically motivated. The Canadians had made a tremendous effort by coming to the UK to support our fight against the Germans, indeed to ensure our survival. Throughout the war they were volunteers since in their country there was no conscription and furthermore to serve overseas was voluntary.

The Canadian volunteers were very much local battalions, similar to the Pals battalions on the Western Front in the first world war. But they needed to be in the public eye so with Gen Crerar in command the reports going back to Canada were extremely favourable. Both the Canadian divisions were battle hardy. They had landed in Normandy on D-Day, they were in the break-out across France, they were much involved with the sieges of the Channel ports which eventually were taken by land forces and they were involved in some very nasty fighting in the Scheldt Estuary, all of which made them a very experienced fighting force which included the use of Buffalos, most essential for any amphibious assault and advance. Undoubtedly the Rhine still stood as the final hurdle to overcome before the battle could be taken into Germany.

By mid-November 1944 the Americans had moved out of the Nijmegen sector and their places were taken by British and Canadian troops. This area was for 300,000 of them the startline for the big push into Germany, codenamed Operation Veritable from 8 to 18 February 1945. It was also the prelude to the liberation of the remaining part of the Netherlands. Casualties during this operation were heavy for both Canadians and British as visits to Nijmegan (Jonkerbosch), at Mook and at Reichswald CWGC's clearly indicate the large number of men who made the supreme sacrifice.

The advance to the Rhine by the American 9th Army, codenamed Operation Grenade, was from 23 February to 2 March 1945. During the Rhineland battles, columns of Canadians, British and American troops reached the western end of two bridges which the Germans had blown the previous day. The Allied advance had been sudden and swift but the enemy had resisted strongly holding the line of the neck of the bend on which the town of Wesel stands.

However, the main German force withdrew at night, so by the following morning there were only a few enemy rearguard parties in the area covering road blocks.

Although Allied forces had thus succeeded in the fight for the west bank of the Rhine, instead of the three to four days originally planned to do so it had, in fact, taken 31 days, consequently the cost was high both in dead and wounded.

The German army had been able to withdraw from the west bank since the Allies had decided not to destroy the bridges. They were blown by the enemy when it retreated, all except the one at Remagen.

By a stroke of luck, the Remagen bridge was captured intact by the American 1st Army who poured across it. Unfortunately they were in the wrong place. notwithstanding its lack of strategic importance it was indeed a remarkable capture but its exploitation did pull the eyes of people away from where they should have made a crossing at the critical time.

In later military discussions it was seen that in these operations the Allies did have some room for manoeuvre in the area chosen for the attack between the Maas and the Rhine but seemingly there was no scope at all for any cleverness. The method of the Allied attack, when the opposition obstacles were encountered, had to be by frontal assault since there was no outflanking manoeuvre possible. Moreover, the choice of the attacking reserve divisions - the 43rd Wessex Infantry and the Guards Armoured - were not trained for rapid exploitation as was the 7th Armoured Division. However, the enemy point of view was that the attack was made by an overwhelming superior force which did catch them by surprise and did strike at the weakest point of their defensive position.

One point against the plan was that its success largely depended on hard, frozen, ground. But in this part of Germany and at the particular time of the year, frozen ground was largely the exception rather than the rule. Additionally, in the enemy view the Allied assessment of weather and ground conditions was unrealistic - leaving no room for tactical manoeuvre and the choice of commitment of the reserve forces was questionable.

Gen Crerar had decided to attack the main German defensive position by Canadian forces knowing that the American 9th Army was making good progress in the south and also progress was being made by the British 30 Corps as it pushed south to effect the link-up with 9th Army. A move in this direction would have cut off enemy positions enabling 30 Corps to reach the Wesel bridge over the Rhine much sooner.

The use of airborne or special forces were not included in the operations west of the Rhine while, with hindsight, other reasons were disclosed for the delay in the Allied advance.

The 15th Scottish Division was awaiting clearance of the Siegfried line when in fact the enemy had deserted the area which had already been established by a patrol and a battalion of troops having crossed a road bridge.

The 53rd Division too, having reached its objective in the eastern part of the Reichswald, could have advanced without waiting for further planning. These were circumstances where it may be thought that, having reached an intermediate objective, any commander with such opportunities has a duty to continue to attack, keeping in contact with the enemy throughout.

After the war Gen Horrocks (30 Corps) felt that the timing of the injection of 43rd Wessex Division was a great mistake. The delay caused much congestion on an already busy axis while at the same time gave the Germans the opportunity to bring in reinforcements. Often the Allied forces had too much equipment and when columns of tanks churned up the area of advance, the infantry attacks made some slow progress. The specialist armoured vehicles, however, proved successful - Buffalos for crossing water obstacles and Crocodiles using flame throwers were feared by the enemy.

During this period the Germans introduced their new plane, the Messerschmitt jet, which was making successful reconnaissance over the Allied area. Accordingly forces were brought to the area with the utmost secrecy and to deceive the enemy the British equipment and dress was Canadian.

On the second day of the Holts' tour we left our hotel in Nijmegen and proceeded through the wooded area which was firmly in Allied hands (March 1945) and had been since the 82nd American Airborne landing in September 1944. The divisions which moved through this line realised that they were passing through the actual gliders which were lying in the fields round about. We moved on from the high ground into the valley and shortly afterwards came to the border between the Netherlands and Germany. The road was relatively narrow now but some 50 years ago, in an agricultural area, was only about half of its width. They needed nothing wider since it was used by horsedrawn carts transporting the local farm produce to town.

In some of the fields were the gliders from the 82 Airborne - very scattered, having landed in difficult conditions for airborne troops in a boggy area with ditches alongside. Movement of vehicles by road was fraught with the inevitable slide into a ditch, causing a lengthy snarl up of traffic.

One of the self-propelled guns passing gliders. ***(IWM BU 2396)***

In February 1945 - the freezing time of the year - the Army generals did not consider that the ground would be other than hard, more so because the winter weather until then had been very severe.

We entered Germany along the route taken by the two Canadian Divisions and the 2nd Division was tasked to clear the road. There were many small farms in close proximity to one another. The ground on the left fell away to the Rhine but the Germans had flooded it by blowing the dams on the river, letting the water in, indeed large areas were under water at the time of our tour. On the right there were various ditches in the area of the Reichswald which formed part of the Siegfried line.

Taking over from the 2nd Canadian Division the 15th Scottish proceeded from a centreline in the nearby woods, on to the road on which we were travelling and continued along it, with the task of taking the nearby town of Cleve.

By amphibious assault the 3rd Canadian Division cleared many of the little villages up to the river, A quite nasty operation for them. A smokescreen was used to deny to the enemy the build-up of Allied forces and the impending assault across the river which, because of the sudden thaw, had risen to a level higher than for some 40 years before.

Dominating the area of our route on the right hand side was the

Reichswald, a big wood on the higher ground, giving the enemy command of the whole of the area up to the forest. There was a high little peak which was one of the major objectives of the 15th Scottish if they could get it quickly while to their right the 53rd Welsh were to advance.

We came to the village of Nutterden. At the end of the road was a church spire in Cleve. Thereabouts the forest came almost to the road. The 15th Scottish had not only to take Cleve but also to proceed through the forest - where there were no roads - to find tracks to proceed through and on to the high ground, the Materborn feature.

At this point we left the approach road to Cleve to visit the CWGC. On our approach to the town of Cleve, we saw that the houses alongside the road had little vents at ground level, purpose built for defence. The attacking forces met some stubborn resistance since at the time the roads had been badly cratered, with bricks and timber spilt over the roads and much fire and smoke.

It was on the higher ground of the Reichswald on the outskirts of the town that some bitter battles took place and where, unfortunately, there was an occasion where 15th Scottish and 43rd Wessex, who had come from the right, got mixed up and 'took on' each other.

We passed the main CWGC in the Reichswald Forest which we visited on the last day of the tour, a Sunday, for a Special Remembrance Service which had been arranged by the Airborne Division. We were reminded that travellers on tour often request a special visit, usually it is to a CWGC. On a past occasion, however, two ladies, ex First Aid Nursing Yeomanry volunteers who normally helped with ambulance duties, had asked for a visit to a hospital in which they had served in Cleve during the war years. It was located. Formerly a mental hospital, it was taken over by the Allied forces as a base hospital until, when it was no longer required, it was returned to its former use. The two ladies well remembered that the hospital trains were able to discharge patients in the hospital grounds and subsequently the wounded and sick were moved to the UK.

In this area of battle the roads were unusually straight so there was a very real temptation to use them to make rapid progress. However, these straight roads with the adjacent farm holdings afforded every opportunity for enemy fortifications and well placed defensive positions.

The forest had changed very little since the war years - the trees were of similar height and well looked after. Some were oak, many pine and others silver birch.

As we moved on we eventually reached the plain which had a ditch running across the middle. Since the war the ground had been the subject

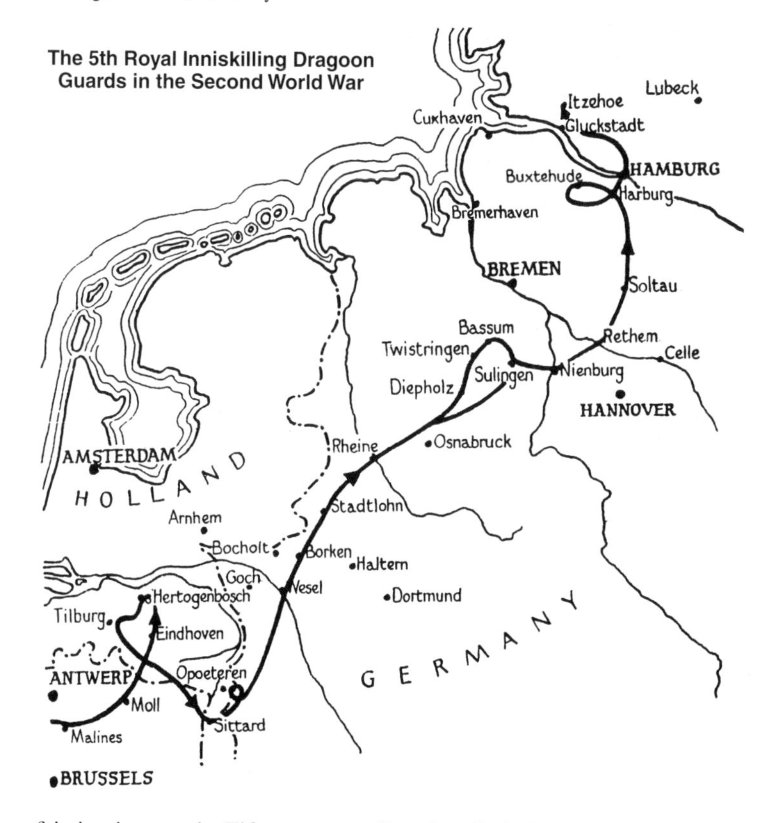

of irrigation work. Fifty years earlier the ditch formed a hazard which made any crossing by vehicles including those with tracks, very difficult for the Allied attacking troops.

The plain was the enemy's first line of defence. The second and main defensive line was the forest itself. The many small farms around had been strongly fortified, often with timber from the nearby forest. Because of the sandy soil it was necessary for many of the properties to have cellars to support the foundations. So these buildings did make excellent defences and were often reinforced at roof level by the rubble caused by Allied artillery fire. Although in their defence the enemy were able to occupy these cellars, inevitably there came a time when they had no option but to leave. However, having taken one such objective, the attacking infantry forces would be confronted by another. Once the attack had started, progress at times was often held up by the enemy, particularly from the flanks.

At this time too the attacking infantry troops had also to make advances without armoured support. Only one route was available for the whole of the 53rd Welsh Division which was a farm track for horse and cart only. There were a lot of minefields for the Sherman flails to clear but the flails damaged the surface of the farm track which together with the tank tracks loosening the surface, caused the tanks to get bogged down. The wider tracks of Churchill tanks did give some assistance to the infantry but generally they had to advance on their own.

Meanwhile Brigade HQ had moved up and by so doing into the front line suffered severely from enemy mortar bombs. Half of the vehicles were knocked out and there were some casualties. The undamaged HQ vehicles at the first opportunity were moved back to a sandpit a short distance away as this was a much safer location. The Allied position had obviously been targeted by an enemy artillery/mortar fire-plan.

During the tour we visited both CWGC and the museum at Groesbeek. The museum was set up essentially to commemorate the airborne forces at Nijmegen, at Arnhem, but particularly for the Americans who had landed at Nijmegen. Many pictures are to be seen there. Airborne forces had not been used before the second world war except by the Russians who had used them as small raiding parties.

However, the Germans had studied the Russian airborne forces during the 1930s but they preferred a much larger formation consisting of infantry, artillery, sappers, armour and all the ancillary type services in order to be a whole division when landed. The Germans therefore decided that the force would be a whole division, not simply paratroopers to be transported by air.

In 1940 they were used to great effect in France and in the Low Countries, especially on the so-called impregnable fortress at Eben Emael on the Belgian borders.

During the early part of the war the Germans successfully used their paratroopers in Holland and in France. In England at the time the possibility of them dropping on strategic targets, indeed generally, worried the population. Such an invasion by paratroopers dressed as nuns made stories for the newspapers. Prime Minister Churchill realised that airborne forces would be a very useful adjunct to any Army so he gave instructions in June 1940 for 5,000 paratroopers by the end of that year. Straightaway Commandos and other specialist troops began training at Ringway in Manchester - the first of them dropped from the belly of a Whitley aircraft. These men were formed into battalions and when they first dropped in the Italian campaign most were captured. However the next drop was successful - Maj Johnny Frost (of Arnhem bridge fame), together with a company of paratroopers, captured vital equipment from the enemy radar station at Bruneval in northern France before being brought back to the UK by sea.

Continuing this description of airborne forces, Col 'Tod' Sweeney (Holt's special guest) recalled that with 50 men he joined the 2nd Battalion Oxfordshire and Bucks Light Infantry of the Air Landing Brigade in February 1942. It was a very proud moment for them to wear the Airborne flash on their arms and to be one among some very fit men - probably some of the elite of the Allied Army.

Training was in the 1st Airborne Division which consisted of two parachute brigades and a gliderborne brigade at Salisbury Plain, the officer in charge being Gen 'Boy' Browning.

In the battle for Crete the Germans were very nearly unsuccessful. Hitler then ordered that these forces (air force troops) were no longer to be used in a major airborne role. Nevertheless, both the British and the Americans began developing airborne divisions, despite the fact that the enemy had given them up.

The British 1st Airborne Division was split up into two - the 6th Airborne Division was borne out of it. Half of the glider brigade went to North Africa with two of the parachute brigades, together with others. 1st Airborne Division went to North Africa where it was much involved in the fighting and earned it the name, 'Red Devils'. The gliderborne force later landed in Sicily - not too successfully - but at least not too unsuccessfully, and it fought its way partly up the toe of Italy before being brought back to the UK at the end of 1943 to be ready for the invasion of Europe. As part of a deception plan, of the two airborne divisions in the UK the 1st would land on the continent wherever that may be and the 6th would remain at home. But it was the 6th which landed in Normandy and returned to the UK having reached the River Seine. The 1st later took part in the Arnhem Operation Market Garden. The idea behind the Operation Varsity - the crossing of the Rhine - was threefold…

- To seize the high ground nearest to the Rhine so that once troops had crossed the river they would have a clear run through;
- To protect the troops from attacks from the north - the Americans were to the south;
- To seize the crossings over the River Issel - a small tributary of the Rhine which ran almost parallel by putting down gliderborne troops on the main crossings.

The airborne troops were to land on the other side of the river Rhine after it had been crossed by the land forces. At midnight (23/24 March) the Commandos made a crossing at Wesel, but before then the town was bombed by 200 heavy bombers dropping about 10 tons of explosives each. Two Scottish Divisions crossed the river and were soon followed at 10 in the morning (24th) by two airborne divisions, the British 6th Airborne Division and the American 17th Airborne Division under command US 18th Corps whose commander was Gen Ridgeway.

When on the ground near Hamminkeln, very near to the river Issel, the 6th Airborne Division, which consisted of three brigades (two paras and one gliderborne) had the objective of securing the bridges and cutting off any enemy counter-attack in the area.

The aim of the airborne troops was to seize the high ground of the Diersfordter forest. 5th Brigade was to guard and protect any attack from the north and to give assistance to the gliderborne troops. The three gliderborne battalions were allocated tasks as follows…

- The 12th Devons to land near Hamminkeln to protect Divisional HQ, seize Hamminkeln itself and be prepared to act as reserve. (We visited the area on tour.)
- The two forward battalions - the Royal Ulster Rifles and the Ox and Bucks Light Infantry would land near the river, on the river bridges themselves as a coup-de main operation, to seize the bridges and thereby prevent the enemy crossing and, if necessary, hold these bridges for a future break-out.

In March 1945 Col 'Tod' Sweeney was stationed at Bulford but a few days before the airborne operation was moved to an airfield in Essex.

Approximately a dozen airfields were needed for the Divisional take-off. The satellite airfields at Birch and Gosfield from which he left were empty most of the time. They could be used in a few days as all necessary facilities were readily available.

It was only at the satellite airfields that the Division was made aware of the task ahead, then briefed and met their glider pilots.

The Hotspur glider carried eight men; the Horsa - the workhorse- carried 30 men or a Jeep and trailer or a Jeep and an anti-tank gun. These pilots, although wearing red berets, were in blue uniforms - they were RAF personnel. They were trained RAF pilots - 500 of them converted to glider pilots - but after landing they were soldiers.

At the briefing the airborne troops were told that the enemy had 500 guns defending the area but these would be knocked-out by rocket firing Typhoons before the landing.

At the dispersal airfields they had no specific duties other than keeping themselves generally busy. While there one officer censoring letters discovered that one airborne corporal had written to 11 different ladies promising when he came back that he would marry them - whether he did return was unknown but if he did he certainly had to face the wrath of at least 10 of them!

The final briefing was not as exciting as that for the Normandy landing. For the Rhine operation there was much doubt in their minds but, at this time, Hitler had developed a new rocket, the V2, which was causing much devastation and many casualties in the UK, particularly in the London area. Consequently they felt that the sooner the war was over the better.

They left early morning - towed by Dakotas and bombers - 70 gliders in the Battalion - flying over the Thames estuary, Kent, the English Channel, and over Belgium. They wore fighting order - a green airborne smock - the envy of most other troops - small pack which included two 24-hour ration packs, spare boots, mess tins, socks, shaving kit and a gas cape rolled on top of the pack.

These items were considered to be sufficient for fighting for 48 hours. Food included three bars of chocolate, a hard lump of solidified porridge which when stirred in hot water resembled porridge, a meat mixture called by the troops ‘powdered monkey’, some chewing gum, some very hard biscuits and additionally four pieces of loo paper! Weapons were 9mm pistols, sten guns, rifles and light machine guns.

Once airborne the pilot of the glider, had to go where the tow plane went. Between the two was a long nylon tow rope and the glider pilot had an altimeter, a compass and a steerer.

There were 900 fighters protecting the glider armada - the paratroopers in large numbers went flying past - and they landed. While they were successful in their task of supporting the assault land forces, the airborne suffered many casualties. Not all the enemy anti-aircraft guns had been knocked-out and enemy machine guns at ground level had been able to destroy gliders loaded with troops when landing.

(During his talks Col Sweeney amused us with one or two stories of service life - two of these stories follow).

A Gen Herbert played golf on Wednesday afternoons. There was also an ADC, Dickie Herbert, who did not play. The general was a very fierce artillery gunner but Dickie was a light hearted cavalryman.

One of the officers from British troops in Berlin HQ rang up the Commandant’s Office hoping to speak to Dickie one Wednesday afternoon knowing full well that the general would be golfing.

The phone was answered and a voice said, ‘Herbert here,’. Reply from caller… ‘Ah, Dickie,’ said the staff officer,

‘Your General has made an absolute right ‘cock-up’ again’ and ‘I wish you would get him to produce proper orders instead of sending out this sort of order which he has just sent'.

Gen Herbert got a bit flustered hearing all this and by the description of his order and he finally said: 'Young man do you know who you are talking to?' and the staff officer said: 'Well, it's Dickie Herbert'. The general replied: 'No, it isn't, it is the Commandant to whom you are talking'!

The staff officer paused for a second or two and then said: 'Do you know who you are talking to, general,' and the general replied: 'No, I do not.' And the staff officer then said: 'Well thank God for that.'!

To make sure a message gets over…

A Scottish commander in Germany after the war found that drink was a terrible problem among his troops - as it often is. He thought that he would do the classical thing and call the whole battalion on parade in the gym where they would stand up and he would get up on the platform and harangue them by telling them all about the evils of drink.

To illustrate his lecture practically he had two glasses - one of whisky and one of water in front of him on a lectern. And he also had a can of worms. He picked up a worm and put it in the whisky and it died. He picked up another worm and put it in the water and it quickly wriggled about. He thought that by this he had clearly got over to his troops that whisky was bad for you and that water was good. But he wasn't sure so he said to his RSM: 'Who is the most stupid man in the Regiment?' and without any hesitation the RSM said: 'Ah, that will be MacTavish, Sir'.

So the CO had MacTavish sent forward said: 'Now MacTavish you have seen what I've done - I dropped a worm in the whisky and it died, I dropped another one in water and it lived. Now what does that tell you MacTavish?'. MacTavish thought for half-a second and then said,: 'Well Sir, if you drink whisky you'll never get worms'!

An informative briefing was given by the tour leader, Col Nic Gray, before making our visit to the Goch battle area.

As the enemy had blown the bridge at Gennep - a few miles to the west of Goch - an assault was necessary not only to take the town itself but also to build a bridge over the river Maas for an Allied crossing at a point where the river was quite high and where there was much flooding in the area. It was a formidable crossing involving the flood banks. The Commanding Officer of the Black Watch, rather cleverly, did not call upon artillery, mortars, or any other support to get his Battalion across. He did a night, silent, attack across the river, which in itself was quite a feat. It was necessary not only to get across but also to have assault craft available, boats and

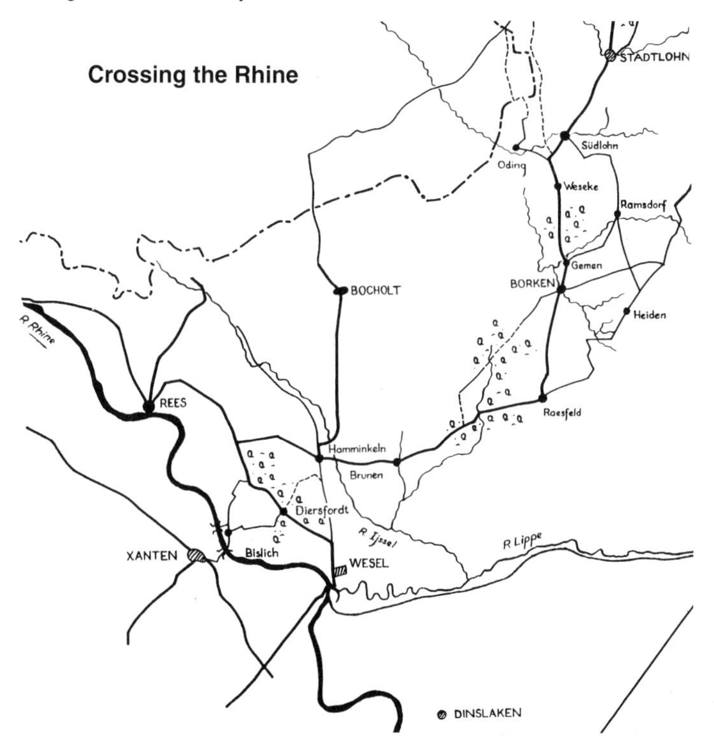

rafts of wood and canvas with flat bottoms, and they had to be paddled. The Black Watch got to the far bank but were swept quite a way down. As it was a steep bank it created difficulties until the lead man made a firm landing with the rope to attach to the assault boats.

The initial two companies of infantry got across without any observation by the enemy, it was a complete surprise. Once over they took out the enemy on the far side. The rest crossed during the night.

The Royal Engineers and the RTR Buffalos were to cross so were allowed to start their engines, making noise, and thus ferried across support weapons and the other elements of the Battalion. At daybreak the 5th Black Watch were attacking Gennep. They made some progress before 1st Gordons came in from the flanks. The two Battalions successfully cleared the area with the help of assault Engineers and 11 RTR in the Buffalos.

Within hours and notwithstanding some enemy sniping and mortar fire, the bridge was built. The approach road was flooded on either side, hence some of the enemy shelling dropped into soft ground and did little damage but shelling on to the hard surface of the road did hamper construction and caused many casualties.

The Germans launched a succession of counter attacks realising the importance of Gennep and the getting of a bridge over the river. One such enemy attack was routed fortunately because there was plenty of Allied artillery in the vicinity.

Defensive Fire SOS (DFSOS) was used during night time to deter the enemy.

The Artillery Commander, from his map and assessment of the countryside, decides in these instances which are the likely avenues for enemy attack. The guns then work out, the bearing, elevation, and charge, and the shells are loaded in preparation for action.

We visited Gennep and then proceeded to Goch on the line of the Divisions (43rd, 15th and 53rd) - and the build-up of the battle and the importance of it were described to us which included the street fighting at the time by the infantry without the support of armoured units.

From Goch we proceeded to the riverside where the theory of a river crossing was described. We crossed the river on a ferry and visited the Overloon museum. During the tour we had lunch at Nijmegen, Goch and Wesel and included in the various visits was one to the site of the crossing at Xanten, where my Regiment crossed.

My Regiment was not engaged in the operations in the few weeks before the crossing of the Rhine but we knew that the final offensive had started when, on 24 March 1945, the airborne troops passed over us in lovely sunshine.

Under command of the Regiment was a battery of 5th RHA, a company of the 1st Rifle Brigade and the 9th Battalion Durham Light Infantry. As such the Regiment led the Brigade and the 7th Armoured Division, the first armoured division crossing over the river Rhine. We crossed on the Bailey pontoon at Xanten, passed quickly through the dropping zones of the airborne troops but were held up by a blown bridge and some self propelled guns. A bridge had to be laid before advancing to the outskirts of Borken and before halting at Gemen. After an advance of some 30 miles from the Rhine, the Regiment moved on to Sudlohn, Weseke, Raesfeld and Stadtlohn. After an advance of some four days in the lead and having covered 50 miles the Regiment ended this phase of the final offensive.

At the end of April we were in the Hamburg area and by the end of the fighting on 5 May 1945 had moved north to Schleswig-Holstein. About one more day and the Regiment would have been in Denmark. As it happened, the North West Europe campaign came to an end on 8 May 1945 when the Armistice was signed.

16

Victory in Europe - VE-Day

After two days in Holland (Chapter 14) most of our third day on tour was spent travelling to the Regiment for the weekend from Sittard to Paderborn as we proceeded by Venlo, to cross into Germany, then in the general direction of Duisburg - Essen - Dortmund, all these centres being well-remembered as bombing areas by the RAF during wartime. The visit to the Regiment at the time of the 50th Anniversary of VE-Day was made at the special invitation of the Commanding Officer, Lt Col MWB Faulkner. Whereas 50 years ago the old comrades ended hostilities in Schleswig-Holstein in northern Germany, the Regiment nowadays was stationed in the area of the Ruhr in western Germany.

After a journey of several hours we arrived in mid-afternoon and, while accommodation for our party was not exactly luxurious, nevertheless we discovered some smaller rooms which conveniently housed four of us. Needless to say, with a bump, we were back in barracks! There were few dull moments since there were many, very many, stories of happenings of 50 years ago which, for me, made compulsive listening.

Tea was provided and after some 'charpoy', the main event of the evening was an all ranks dance with some excellent food and drinks available. An enjoyable evening for everyone. The following day - Sunday - was a comparatively quiet day for all. In the morning some of the old comrades party attended a family church service at St Peter's in Barker Barracks.

In the afternoon there was an excellent barbecue lunch and, later, on the cricket pitch, there were sports events which included the final of the inter-squadron tug of war competition and an inter-squadron 'It's a Knockout' competition. The day ended with entertainment and informal food and drink in the various messes.

VE-Day

Monday - 8 May 1995 - was VE-Day. There was a large congregation for the VE-Day Memorial Service - a thanksgiving service for the 50th anniversary of peace in Europe - conducted by the Rev J Coleman, Padre of 1st The Queen's Dragoon Guards and the Rev D Porter BA, Rector of All Saints Pavement, York. The lesson was read by Gen Sir Anthony Mullens, Colonel of the Regiment.

Throughout this commemorative day there was a regimental display on the squadron tank park.

A special VE lunch was provided for the old comrades in Balaclava Mess and for them followed an Anglo-German service of peace and a reception in Paderborn.

In the early evening there was a display by Pipes and Drums and afterwards a short session of entertainment. The evening concluded with food and drinks in the squadron bars and messes.

Next morning - Tuesday 9 May - the old comrades party left Barker Barracks, Paderborn, and with suitable stops and a Calais to Dover ferry, arrived back at the UJ Club in Waterloo pleasantly tired after a most memorable six days together.

The coach journey from Paderborn to Calais was indeed a long one, particularly so for some of the Old Comrades. Nevertheless, such journeys often have some items of interest and on this occasion, as we were proceeding along the French coast towards Calais, Syd Shepherd was called to 'the top table' to recall his experiences of the Regimental withdrawal in the summer of 1940. Syd, as a dispatch rider, remembered that as the Regiment reached the coastal area he was called from the Regimental rear - possibly B Echelon - by the Colonel, who gave him the task of finding a suitable 'escape' route and, more importantly, a bridge crossing for the whole of the Regiment to make its way to the beaches of Dunkirk. Syd was indeed successful and the Regiment, after some delay resulting from an assignment as an Army defensive role, were eventually allocated shipping as some of the last troops to return home to England.

By VE-Day - 8 May 1945 - the Regiment had come to a halt after having returned to the continent of Europe in mid-July 1944 and within a period of some 10 months had advanced from Normandy to Germany, not far short of the border with Denmark.

Sometimes seen is the man with the well-known poster declaring: 'The End is Nigh'! And so it was for the North West Europe campaign of WW2 which had begun on 6 June 1944. Although the campaign officially came to an end on 8 May 1945, hostilities for us had ended a few days earlier.

One of the last significant successes for the Regiment was the capture of an Admiral and 400 German Wrens who surrendered in Buxtehude in the vicinity of Hamburg. We remained in and around Hamburg for a day or so but none of us were sorry to leave there, an area of devastation almost beyond comprehension. There we saw for ourselves that the bombing by the RAF had, in many areas, reduced a great city to mountains of rubble - as far as it was possible to see - mostly smelling of many years of destruction and decay.

We moved from Hamburg into Schleswig Holstein to a point from where in about one more day the Regiment would have crossed the German border into Denmark. A daily newspaper reported on Tuesday 1 May 1945...

'The "Battle of Denmark is beginning and ending simultaneously today. As Montgomery sweeps through the German northern province of Schleswig Holstein towards the Kiel Canal and the Southern Jutland border, the Germans are scurrying out of most big Danish towns. They are moving with every means at their disposal - lorries, cars, tanks. Thousands are footslogging it southwards into the jaws of Montgomery's forces. By tonight Jutland should be completely free of German forces and there seems little reason why Anglo-American troops, and even Montgomery himself, should not be established on Danish soil tonight'.

The last wartime Regimental Newsletter continues the story of the German Army's exodus from Denmark...

'Although the war in Europe, as we know now, had another four days to run, by 5 May all fighting in northern Germany had virtually ceased, and we witnessed the extraordinary and unique sight of a German army in Germany disintegrating and surrendering.

'Hour after hour endless streams of Germans wandered along the roads into our road-blocks - apathetic and expressionless, they waited to receive our orders.

On 7 May we moved up to the western end of the Kiel Canal and established road-blocks over the bridges and ferries. Still the southward trek of the Germans continued, our prisoners ranging from the Chief of Staff, German North Sea Fleet, to Max Schmelling. What was in all those pigskin suitcases of his?

'Many were the amusing incidents that occurred while we sat waiting for the great news. How we all felt when the time came, it is not the role of these notes to record. It can simply be said that we were all surprised how calmly - almost indifferently - everyone else took the news. Visions of Denmark faded quietly away in spite of the BBC which announced us nearer and nearer to Copenhagen with every news bulletin.

'The Armistice brought little change in our routine and, with chaos prevalent everywhere, there was plenty of work for all.'

In addition to the time spent transporting many thousands of German soldiers into concentration areas (among them the German general who commanded the forces that opposed us at Ghent in Belgium) and the guarding of ferries and bridges on the western end of the Kiel Canal, the Regiment also had an abundance of work presented by the problems of the thousands of Allied nationals wandering around the Reich under the anonymity of the heading 'displaced persons'.

The defeat of Hitler's Germany, however, was greeted with mixed feelings by many in the Regiment. The scheme of demobilisation from the forces had been determined by the age and the length of service of each individual officer/other rank. Soon all those having low, some very low, numbers for their release were deservedly returned to 'civvy street', happy to know that, having done 'their bit', they would be home with their families once again.

However, the future for the younger ones in the Regiment, having much higher age and service numbers, was rather different to say the least. Not only did they realise that for them their 'home going' was a long way off but also they were to remain with the Regiment which had been ordained by Army planners for service in the Far East as victory over the Japanese had not been secured.

My own Army Book - AB 64 - confirmed that I was in the category for Far East Service and was duly signed by an officer on 6 May 1945 - two days before the German war ended. Subsequently, some of our older friends departed on their release from the forces while others were transferred to other Regiments until 'their number came up'. Meanwhile, to replace these losses the Regiment had intakes of younger men from elsewhere. But as 'every cloud has a silver lining', within the short period of three months news reached us that the Japanese had surrendered, two atomic bombs had been dropped by the United States on Japan and had 'taken out' the cities of Hiroshima and Nagasaki causing 150,000 casualties which brought hostilities in the Far East to a very abrupt end. This remarkable climax to WW2 changed the Army planners' thoughts of a Regimental posting there, indeed the Regiment remained in Germany until 1951 when it took part in the Korean War.

In the weeks and months after VE-Day there were many sad moments when older friends departed. Often their experiences, not only in the Army but their wider knowledge of civilian life including its domestic and family problems, was freely and gratefully sought by young men who had left their families for the first time at 18 years of age and, not unnaturally, found such friendly advice invaluable to them.

The first issue of the Regimental journal after the wartime years records...

'For 12 months we have occupied Germany, and it has been a period not without interest, both militarily and sporting. It has also been a period when many friends and loyal members of the Regiment of all ranks have departed to take up once again their civilian occupations. We take this opportunity of welcoming all those who have joined us to replace them.' As one would expect of a former cavalry regiment, horses became a No 1!

'VE-Day found the Regiment settled in an agricultural area unspoilt by war and apparently well stocked with a variety of horses.

'Three days before, on the outskirts of Pinneburg, a small town some ten miles north of Hamburg, three police horses had suddenly arrived at RHQ and the Regimental Stable started.

'*Pontius Pilate* and *Tommy* still survive - June 1946 - of the three that first joined the Regiment, and the sight of them seemed to transform a supposedly sane section of the Regiment into a secret cult who immediately assumed a bow-legged walk and muttered in undertones continuously of shoulders, hocks, fetlocks, and other words which had not been mentioned for nearly six years.

'For the next three weeks jeeps were to be seen driving furiously in all parts of Schleswig Holstein following the report of the 'finest 'oss wot ever was seen' on some remote farm. To cut a long story of horse dealing and intrigue short, by the middle of June the Regiment had requisitioned about 40 horses.

'A preliminary hunter trial competition held at Muhienbarbek at the end of June attracted a lot of entries and enthusiastic spectators, and it was seen that we were lucky enough to have about ten horses that, with schooling, would perform show jumping with credit.'

A motor cycling club was formed soon after the war ended when some BMWs of 250cc were obtained from captured vehicle parks and distributed among the squadrons.

'After several days of stripping and tuning, the bikes were in pretty good fettle. Soon after the Regiment went to Moll. During our stay there we were challenged by the local Belgian team to a 'scramble' meeting. The course was utterly unsuitable for our small capacity machines, being of loose sand. However the races went off well.'

'Following the return from Moll a series of grass meetings were held and when winter set in and the ground became unsuitable for grass, attention turned to 'scramble' meetings. However, generally, little in the world of sport occurred within the Regiment from the signing of the Armistice until the end of August (after VJ Day) that it is deserving only of the most cursory comment. Hampered by the unfortunate deployment of the squadrons, multitudinous guard duties, and a stifling dearth of both sports fields and equipment, cricket was given a miss. Swimming, in which most people indulged for pleasure as opposed to competition, achieved unprecedented popularity at Moll. Here the lakesides, littered with an intoxicating number of Belgian sylphs, provided a congenial retreat for the Regiment.

'The athletic season opened rather unconventionally on 19 September and after two spirited meetings closed abruptly three days later.

'Association football, played continuously throughout the summer, came into its own on a competition basis mid-way through September when all eyes followed a promisingly invincible Regimental team.

'The hockey team many times proved its worth while water-polo and cricket were later included in an ambitious sports programme. A camera club and a table tennis group were successfully organised.'

Not quite sport but nevertheless pleasant and extremely informative was being detailed as a member of a guard party travelling from Lubeck to Stettin repatriating Poles. An old German merchantman, *SS Tenerife*, had been converted to accommodate 550 passengers. Overnight in the dock area at Stettin there were bursts of gunfire, seemingly some Russians and Poles were still 'enjoying' their own war! The return journey involved Germans coming to the British zone who accepted the guards as deliverers and hence there were few problems.

On VE-Day - 8 May 1945 - in London on a balcony overlooking Whitehall, Prime Minister Winston Churchill, giving his most famous V for Victory salute, and smoking a cigar, told the enormous crowd: 'This is your victory.' To which they replied: 'No - it is yours'. How right he was, since it would be an impossible task to express gratitude to all those people, not only in the UK but throughout the world who had contributed, both servicemen and civilians who had given their lives, in the defeat of Hitler and Nazi Germany.

At this time, he told the people: 'In the long years to come not only will the people of this island, but of the world, wherever the bird of freedom chirps in human hearts, look back to what we've done and they will say: 'Do not despair, do not yield to tyranny, march straight forward and die if need be - unconquered'.'

17

Victory in Japan

The 15 August 1945 officially marked the end of the war in the Pacific which began on 7 December 1941 when the Japanese attacked Pearl Harbour, the US Navy's main base in the Pacific. The United States of America declared war on Japan the next day, 8 December.

The end of the Far East war came almost as suddenly when the USA dropped an atomic bomb an Hiroshima on 6 August 1945 and three days later, 9 August 1945, dropped a second atomic bomb on Nagasaki.

The end of the second world war had generally been accepted by many as the defeat of Germany on 8 May 1945. For the Regiment, however, preparations continued after that date for the War Office posting to the Far East. However, when it became known that a new bomb, the atomic bomb, had been dropped on Japan with such devastating effect, and a second one for good measure very shortly afterwards, it was clear that the Far East war was over and the posting to that theatre would be cancelled. To say the least, such momentous news was received with immense relief by all my contemporaries - VJ-Day several days later passing almost unnoticed as our ongoing Regimental duties proceeded and facilities for sport and short breaks from the Regiment for relaxation were introduced.

At the end of hostilities thousands of Allied servicemen were held in Japanese prison camps, maintained like slaves on the most meagre of rations, and put to work building the Thai-Burma railway. Thousands of prisoners had died during captivity while many soldiers returned home suffered from severe malnutrition and for them the lengthy process of recovery was only just beginning.

Conditions in the Japanese POW camps were most inhuman, since, in addition to lice, fleas, and bugs, men had often to contend with savage beatings and they died like flies. For failing to salute a Japanese guard, a POW would have to suffer a humiliating beating.

The defeated British Army were put to work as slaves of the Japanese building the notorious 'death railway' linking Bangkok and Rangoon. Unimaginable cruelty, torture, starvation, disease and for those men, other than the toughest, such conditions were a sentence of death. To photograph these happenings was punishable by death. The atrocious behaviour of the Japanese, it is said, caused the death of a man for every sleeper that was laid on the track. More than 16,000 Allied POWs plus 100,000 Asian forced labourers perished on the 257-mile railway which was built under the lash, gun and bayonet, in a period of 16 months which the Japanese engineers had predicted would take at least five years.

In the early days of August 1945 the Americans dropped atomic bombs on two Japanese cities bringing a sudden and ignominious defeat for the Japanese.

The 50th anniversary of VJ-Day itself fell on Tuesday, 15 August 1995 but a special series of commemorations took place around the country on the following weekend - Saturday 19 August and Sunday 20 August.

In London an ecumenical service took place on Saturday outside Buckingham Palace, the salute being taken by HM the Queen after a march down the Mall by veterans. Tributes were paid to all those who took part in the second world war - Army, Royal Navy and RAF ex-servicemen, Merchant Navy, land girls, emergency services, Home Guard, air raid wardens and many more.

On Sunday evening in a more solemn vein, Beating Retreat and Sunset Ceremonies were held in Cardiff, Carrickfergus, Edinburgh and London.

But there is a price to pay for every war. Indeed during the 10 months of fighting from Normandy to the end of the North West Europe campaign 160 officers and men in the Regiment were wounded and 57 loyal and gallant members died in battle.

The second world war was a horrific war being fought across six of the world's seven continents and all its oceans. Not surprisingly there were 50 million human beings killed, many millions more were wounded in mind and body.

The Commonwealth War Graves Commission (CWGC) records that in the 1939-45 war the number of identified burials and cremations together with the number commemorated on memorials to the missing, total 580,000.

Throughout the world there are 8,052 burial places which contain only 1939-45 war graves and 7,162 which contain graves of both 1914-18 and 1939-45 wars.

Members of the Regiment were often feted by the Belgians when serving in their country as their King, HM Leopold III, was Colonel-in-Chief for 46 years until his death in September 1983.

One of the places of interest in the Belgian town of Ypres is St Martin's cathedral, the access to which is reached across some of the few remaining old cobblestones of the town. In the cathedral high above the south door is the British Army and RAF Memorial to King Albert, a rose window which includes 'V' DG - the 5th Royal Inniskilling Dragoon Guards.

Wording of the memorial plaque hung on the pillar of the nave crossing in St Martin's cathedral, Ypres...

To the glory of God and in honoured memory of Albert I King of the Belgians, Knight of the Garter Field Marshal of the British Army and Colonel in Chief of the 5th Royal Inniskilling Dragoon Guards the rose window in the south transept is given to Belgium by the British Army and the Royal Air Force. This memorial gift was subscribed for in the year 1935 by all ranks active and retired the women's services and the dominion forces whilst special assistance was given by the 5th Royal Inniskilling Dragoon Guards, the League of Remembrance (1914-1919) the British Legion and the Ypres League. We the subscribers are most happy to have this opportunity to express our high esteem and appreciation of King Albert's noble service in the Great War. The subject of the window is the glory of God as testified in the Te Deum. The crests are those of Belgium, His Majesty's Army, the Royal Air Force and the 5th Royal Inniskilling Dragoon Guards

(Badge of the 5th RIDG)

'My sword I give to him that shall succeed me in my pilgrimage. My courage and skill to him that can get it. My marks and scars I carry with me to be a witness for me that have fought his battles who will now be my rewarder'... so he passed over and all the trumpets sounded for him on the other side

A contribution by Alf Jenkins

It is felt that the second world war could appropriately be described as 'the greatest of all wars' but the many years of peace which many expected to follow from it did not, in fact, materialise. For several years before the cessation of hostilities, Hitler's Germany had been in battle on two fronts - to the east fighting the Russians, to the west fighting the Allied forces. As the war was nearing the end, however, the Russians made rapid advances on their front which culminated in the capture of Berlin together with extensive areas of the European continent to the west of the German capital. At the Armistice the Allied forces in the west - US, France and Great Britain - had therefore to be content in sharing with the Russians responsibility for the control of Berlin. Although 'East' and 'West', by fighting the common enemy, had become allies, nevertheless, Russia as a superpower had successfully achieved a most dominating role. A state of tension developed between them as there was marked distrust and hostility towards each other, fortunately though without actual fighting. This became known as the 'Cold War' and it lasted for upwards of half a century - for many people for most of their lives!

And between the two former allies a huge wall was built - which became known as the 'Iron Curtain' - not only separating the people of Berlin from each other but also as a constant reminder of the two ideologies, Communism (ruled by the State) and Democracy (the free world).

In any war there has to be many 'ifs'! Despite having overwhelming forces available for an attack on Berlin, Gen Eisenhower, as Supreme Allied Commander in the West, decided that a strong US force should advance towards the Alpine area of Western Austria and Southern Bavaria known as the National Redoubt. He thought that the Germans were planning a monstrous stronghold in the region and there he hoped to find Hitler and his leading Nazis. In the event Hitler and his entourage remained in Berlin, so the US thrust to the National Redoubt was of little military importance at such a critical time. If Montgomery and Churchill had been responsible for deciding issues of such significance, a thrust to Berlin would undoubtedly have come first. The capture of the German capital before the Russians was of paramount importance politically and militarily. Berlin was the big prize for the Allied forces enduring nearly six years of a hard fought war. Those of us who were in the Allied Army in Germany in the last few days of the war were, to say the least, bewildered by what happened 'at the top' as the end drew near. The loss of the vital political objective at the most crucial of all times was there for all to see and was most unfortunate as the events of the Cold War, as previously mentioned, clearly showed.

The author, Howard Hollingshead 11 October 1946.

Epilogue

'Many of the tours that Howard Hollingshead has been on have been concerned with the two World Wars. If it is true to say that up until 1815 our main rivals were the French, the 20th Century has been dominated by the Germans. Twice this century they have set about dominating Europe by conquest and twice mercifully they have failed. But the German psyche believes in domination whether through military, political, industrial or economic means.

I believe it is for this reason that Europe is right to 'tie' the Germans within the European Community. This is so that from within their midst there is no chance of another Hitler emerging for a third attempt at being the military masters of Europe.'

Lt Col Mike Martin
Chairman, Holts Tours

A warning for battlefield visitors

If you find, as you walk the battlefields,
a shell or grenade in the mud,
don't dig it out,
or chuck it about,
'cos it might just not be a 'dud".

For although it's so old, often covered with mould,
and the rusty metal's corroded,
many lives have been lost,
as they found to their cost,
when the innocent 'dud' has exploded!

Alan J Colley
'At the Bugle's Call'

5th Royal Inniskilling Dragoon Guards Regimental Association

(now The Royal Dragoon Guards)

Shortly after touring with Holts' Battlefield Tours I joined my Regimental Association since when I have had the pleasure of travelling on several tours with Old Comrades and attending many convivial gatherings. Capt CJ (Jim) Boardman, as Regimental Secretary, had arranged the tours over many years until his retirement when, together with his successor, Maj JE Etherington, they have continued to do so. Capt Jim Boardman is the author of a book, *Tracks in Europe*, containing extensive coverage of a variety of Regimental activities and numerous contributions by many who served in the Regiment during the second world war. Home Headquarters and a Museum are in York and there are several Regimental Association Branches throughout the UK, one covering London and the South East of which I am the Branch Secretary.

On the second Sunday in March at the Military Chapel in Chelsea Barracks an Annual Commemoration Service is held for Capt Lawrence Edward Grace Oates which includes the regimental Collect:

*O God, our house of defence and our castle, whose Blessed Son hath taught us that no man having put his hand to the plough and looking back is fit for Thy kingdom, strengthen we pray Thee the *5th Royal Inniskilling Dragoon Guards that they may never, for any hardness of His Word, go back and walk no more with Him but, like His faithful apostles, may choose rather to follow Him to death, Who hath the words of eternal life, the same Thy Son, Jesus Christ our Lord.*

Amen

*now the Royal Dragoon Guards

Maj and Mrs Holts' Battlefield Tours

My first tour in 1984 - a 40th anniversary of the Normandy Landings - followed an article in a well-known daily newspaper. From the detailed brochure which I received from them I expected the tour to be most informative and nostalgic and in neither respect was I disappointed. Additionally what I do remember most of all was the friendship and patience shown to me as a newcomer by both Tonie and Valmai and this has always been so whenever on tour. It was a delightful feeling to be in a party as 'one of us', so sincerely. When their retirement came from the company, Col Mike Martin and his wife, Pat, took the helm, indeed they had joined Tonie and Valmai at the same time that I became a traveller, thus our friendship and experience is well shared.

Although in view of my forces service my main military interest is WW2, nevertheless I have enjoyed a variety of WW1 tours and others throughout the years. A 'one-off' tour to South Africa in the autumn of 1990 for the Boer and Zulu Wars will always head my list of 60-plus very memorable tours.

As authors, Tonie and Valmai have written 15 books including an extensive Visitor's Guide - Normandy Landing Beaches - a WW2 book well worth having on everyone's bookshelf.

The Western Front Association - WFA

As a member of the WFA I attend the monthly meetings of my Branch, Surrey, also, those of the London Branch together with regular national meetings which are held at the National Army Museum, Chelsea. The WFA remembers the WW1 period 1914-1918 with its principal objective to perpetuate the memory, courage and comradeship of those who served in the war. The Patron, John Terraine, is an author who has written many military books one of which *The Right of the Line* has for reference purposes been most helpful to me.

'After the Battle'

The series of *After the Battle* magazines covers a wide range of subjects - battles, personalities and weapons in all theatres of war, 1939-45. There is no better way to find a WW2 story. A contents list is a 'must' for anyone with the slightest interest in the second world war and its many aspects.

A brief history of The 5th Royal Inniskilling Dragoon Guards

1685 5th Dragoon Guards - first known as Shrewsbury's Horse, was raised in Chester, Bridgnorth, Lichfield, and Kingston-upon-Thames.

1689 6th Inniskilling Dragoons - raised in Enniskillen and known as Conyngham's Dragoons.

1922 The two Regiments amalgamated and the title chosen was 5th/6th Dragoons.

1927 5th Inniskilling Dragoon Guards became the new title.

1935 5th Royal Inniskilling Dragoon Guards - distinction by King George V as a 'Royal Regiment'.

1937 King George VI approved mechanisation of the Regiment.

1992 5th Royal Inniskilling Dragoon Guards amalgamated with 4th/7th Royal Dragoon Guards with a new title: The Royal Dragoon Guards.

Distinguished 'Skins'

Most Regiments in their history have noteworthy persons, the following having served in years past - Lt Col Robert Baden-Powell, founder of the Boy Scout movement; Field Marshal the Viscount Allenby in the 1914-18 war; and Capt Lawrence Edward Grace Oates who died at the South Pole on 17 March 1912. The Regimental history records:

It was not only in the realms of soldiering and sport that the Regiment gained in reputation. In February 1913, came the news of the gallant sacrifice of Capt LEG Oates.

Oates, already conspicuous as an officer whose early promise in South Africa was being amply fulfilled, had been seconded from the Regiment in 1910 so as to enable him to accompany an expedition to the South Pole under the leadership of Capt Scott. Owing to a series of misfortunes which were entirely unpreventible, Scott and all his men were lost, but the relief expedition were able to recover a diary and papers which revealed an epic story of unflinching bravery and steadfast endurance.

In that epic, Lawrence Oates's selfless courage is set forth in simple words. It seems that in helping a sailor, Edgar Evans, who was injured by a fall, Oates sacrificed his own safety and dangerously exposed himself to the searing, bitter cold. Struck by the most dreadful frostbite and almost completely crippled, he struggled on, his one thought not to hold back his fellows. As soon as he saw that he was hindering the march, he asked his fellow comrades to leave him where he was, in his sleeping-bag. They refused, and for one more march he staggered gamely on; then Capt Scott wrote: 'He slept through the night hoping not to wake, but he awoke in the morning. It was blowing a blizzard. Oates said: 'I am just going outside, and I may be some time.' He went out into the blizzard and we have not seen him since. We knew that Oates was walking to his death, but though we tried to dissuade him, we knew it was the act of a brave man and an English gentleman.'

Scott himself, when a little later he lay dying, the pencil almost dropping from his frozen fingers wrote: 'How much better has this all been than lounging in too great comfort at home'.

It was on St Patrick's Day, 1912 his birthday, that Lawrence Oates walked out into the snow. Since then each year 'Oates Sunday' has been observed, first in the Inniskillings and afterwards in the 5th Royal Inniskilling Dragoon Guards, in proud memory of the sacrifice to comradeship made by a fine officer and 'an English gentleman.'

Abbreviations

ADC	Aide-de-camp.
APT	Army Physical Training.
BEF	British Expeditionary Force.
CWGC	Commonwealth War Graves Commission.
DCM	Distinguished Conduct Medal.
D-Day	The D simply meant an unnamed day which was to be the opening of the Allied invasion of Europe. It has come to mean any critical day of action.
KRRs	King's Royal Rifles.
MM	Military Medal.
NAAFI	Navy, Army and Air Force Institutes.
NCO	Non-commissioned officer.
POW	Prisoner of War.
PTW	Primary Training Wing.
RAC	Royal Armoured Corps.
RBL	The Royal British Legion.
RFC/RAF	Royal Flying Corps/Royal Air Force.
RSM	Regimental Sergeant Major.
UJ	Union Jack.
UK	United Kingdom.
VC	Victoria Cross.
WFA	The Western Front Association (Remembering World War One).
WWI	World War One - 1914-1918.
WWII	World War Two - 1939-1945.
'252'	Army form giving personal details and the offence charged with.

Chronological list of 50th Anniversaries

3 September 1989	Declaration of WW2
2 June 1990	BEF Evacuation Dunkirk, France
15 September 1990	Battle of Britian
19 August 1992	Canadian Raid of Dieppe, France
23 October 1992	Battle of El Alamein, North Africa
24 May 1993	Battle of the Atlantic
18 February 1994	Allied Air Raid, Amiens Prison, France
6 June 1994	Battle of Normandy, France
29 July 1994	Normany and Northern France
17 September 1994	Battle of Arnhem, Holland
30 September 1994	Frontline Britain - Dover
27 October 1994	Battle of s'Hertogenbosch, Holland
13 January 1995	Battle of Roer Triangle, Holland
24 March 1995	Crossing the Rhine, Germany
8 May 1995	Victory in Europe
15 August 1995	Victory in Japan

Commonwealth War Graves Commission

The Commonwealth War Graves Commission was established by Royal Charter of 21 May 1917, the provisions of which were amended and extended by a Supplemental Charter of 8 June 1964.

Its duties are to mark and maintain the graves of the members of the forces of the Commonwealth who died in the two world wars, to build and maintain memorials to the dead whose graves are unknown, and to keep

records and registers. The cost is shared by the partner governments - those of Australia, Britain, Canada, India, New Zealand and South Africa - in proportions based on the numbers of their graves.

Tyne Cot Cemetery, Passchendaele, Belgium

Almost all the war cemeteries and memorials are maintained by the Commission's own staff, although in a number of countries, mainly within the Commonwealth, special arrangements exist whereby the governments of those countries carry out care and maintenance on the Commission's behalf, usually free of charge. The care of the war graves in civil cemeteries and churchyards is mostly entrusted to local and church authorities which maintain them by agreement with the Commission.

The work is founded upon principles which have remained unaltered since they were first articulated: that each of the dead should be commemorated individually by name either on the headstone on the grave or by an inscription on a memorial; that the headstones and memorials should be permanent; that the headstones should be uniform and that no distinction should be made on account of military or civil rank, race or creed.

The headstones are two feet eight inches in height; at the top of each is engraved the national emblem or the service or regimental badge, followed by the rank, name, unit, date of death, age and, usually, a religious emblem. And at the foot, in many cases, is an inscription chosen by relatives. In some cemeteries, notably on the Gallipoli Peninsula in Macedonia and in the Far East and the Pacific, where there is a risk of earth movement, stone or bronze plaques on low pedestals are used instead of headstones.

Dieppe Canadian War Cemetery, France

Climate permitting, the headstones stand in narrow borders, where floribunda roses and small perennials grow, in a setting of lawn trees and shrubs. Two monuments are common to the cemeteries: the Cross of Sacrifice, set usually upon an octagonal base and bearing a bronze sword upon its shaft; and, in the larger cemeteries, the Stone of Remembrance, upon which are carved the words from the Book of Ecclesiasticus: *Their name liveth for evermore.*

The men and women whose graves are unknown, or whose remains were cremated, are commemorated on memorials ranging from small tablets bearing a few names to great monuments bearing many thousands, such as the Menin Gate.

In many of the foreign countries in which the Commission operates, its work is protected by a series of international agreements which recognise the Commission as the authority responsible for the care of the graves and memorials. The governments of these and many other countries have acquired the land occupied by the cemeteries and have generously granted its perpetual use to the Commission.

For further information of the Commonwealth War Graves Commission including details on its registers, maps, videos and information sheets please call 01628 634221 or write to: Commonwealth War Graves Commission, 2 Marlow Road, Maidenhead, Berks SL6 7DX.